McGRAW-HILL
SPELLING

AUTHORS

Dr. Gillian E. Cook

Dr. Marisa Farnum

Terry R. Gabrielson

Dr. Charles Temple

CONSULTANT

Dr. Judy Wallis

McGraw-Hill
School Division

New York   Farmington

McGraw-Hill School Division

A Division of The McGraw·Hill Companies

Copyright © 1998 McGraw-Hill School Division, a Division of the Educational and Professional Publishing Group of The McGraw-Hill Companies, Inc.

Alphabet font used with permission of Zaner-Bloser.

McGraw-Hill School Division
1221 Avenue of the Americas
New York, New York 10020

Printed in the United States of America
ISBN 0-02-2442316 / 6

6 7 8 9 VHJ 02 01 00 99

To the Student,

Spelling is part of everything you do in school. It helps you in your writing, in your reading, and in your other subjects. Spelling is also important outside of school. Knowing how to spell helps you share information with friends, family, and other people you need to communicate with.

This book will help you learn to spell the words in each lesson. It will also give you important tools, hints, and tips that you can use with any words at any time.

 Spelling words that are pointed out have unusual spellings of a sound. Pay special attention to these words so that you will remember how to spell them.

In the back of the book, you will find resources to help you as a speller and a writer. Take a look at the contents on page 158 to see what's there.

You can help yourself by creating your own **Spelling Journal**. All you need is a lined notebook. Start by making different sections. Here are some ideas.

■ **A Personal Dictionary** Label each right-hand page with a letter of the alphabet. If you fill the page, use the back of the page. Add words throughout the year that are important for you to remember how to spell and to use in your writing.

■ **Difficult Words** Keep track of words that give you trouble. Write the word and circle the part that is hard for you. Refer to this section regularly as you write.

■ **Related Words** List words that are related in meaning and spelling. For example, the long vowel sound you hear in *please* can help you to remember how to spell *pleasure*. Add to this section whenever you come across words that will help you to spell other words.

■ **Memory Helpers** Collect sayings that you make up that help you remember certain words. A saying such as *You are a youth* can help you remember that the word *youth* contains *y-o-u*.

Remember, this is your journal! You may want to add a section all your own.

Contents

Word Study Steps

1. **Look** at the word and **say** it carefully.

2. **Picture** the word in your mind.

3. **Study** each letter in the word.

4. **Write** the word carefully.

5. **Check** the spelling.

Did you spell the word correctly? If you made a mistake, repeat each step.

WORDS WITH Short Vowels

PHONICS PATTERNS

1. rapidly
2. dodge
3. exact
4. envy
5. won
6. strictly
7. publish
8. attempt
9. limit
10. prison
11. establish
12. similar
13. punishment
14. closet
15. presence
16. hesitate
17. method
18. profit
19. bottom
20. vanish

Learn Spelling Patterns

LOOK & SAY Listen for the sounds in each word.

PICTURE Close your eyes. See each word in your mind.

STUDY These spelling words have short vowels. The symbols for short vowel sounds are /a/, /e/, /i/, /o/, and /u/.

WRITE Sort the words. Which words have the short vowel sounds below in the accented syllable?

/a/ (1) (2) (3) (4)
/e/ (5) (6) (7) (8) (9)
/i/ (10) (11) (12) (13)
/o/ (14) (15) (16) (17)
/u/ (18) (19) (20)

CHECK Did you spell each word correctly? Circle the letter that stands for the short vowel sound in the accented syllable.

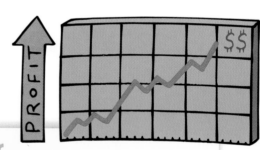

Pattern Power

How can the short vowel sounds be spelled with one letter?

(21) or (22) or (23) or (24) or (25)

Other Words

Write words you would like to add to this week's list.

_____ _____ _____ _____ _____

Practice Word Meanings

Synonyms and Antonyms

A **synonym** is a word that means the same or nearly the same as another word. An **antonym** is a word that is opposite or nearly opposite in meaning from another word. Write each word. Then write the spelling word that is a synonym or antonym for each word. Then write *synonym* or *antonym* after the word.

1. loss *profit* *antonym*
2. reward ____ ____
3. jealousy ____ ____
4. slowly ____ ____
5. lost ____ ____
6. disappear ____ ____
7. cupboard ____ ____
8. avoid ____ ____
9. top ____ ____
10. jail ____ ____

Challenge Words • Math

Write the challenge word that best completes each sentence. Use the **Spelling Dictionary** on page 214 to help you. Circle the spelling of the short vowel sound in each accented syllable.

11. You can write cents as a ____.
12. Use ____ to find equal parts of a number.
13. One fourth is a ____ of a whole.
14. The equator traces the ____ of the earth.
15. The study of angles is part of ____.

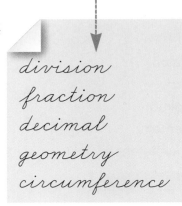

division
fraction
decimal
geometry
circumference

ⓢpelling Tip

Sound out long words one syllable at a time. Remember, each syllable must have a vowel sound.

✦ There are three syllables in *hesitate.*

✦ Say each syllable. Listen for the vowel sound.

✦ Write the word one syllable at a time.   **hes+ i + tate**

3

List Words

rapidly

dodge

exact

envy

won

strictly

publish

attempt

limit

prison

establish

similar

punishment

closet

presence

hesitate

method

profit

bottom

vanish

Challenge Words

division

fraction

decimal

geometry

circumference

Review Words

expect

gigantic

shocking

ugly

insect

Build Vocabulary

Related Words

■ How are these words similar in spelling and meaning?

regular   regularity

Say each word and listen to the sound of the letter *a*. How does the pronunciation of the *a* in *regularity* help you to spell the schwa sound in the last syllable of *regular*?

■ Write the spelling word that you see in each word. Write each word. Then circle the letter in the longer word that helps you spell the schwa sound in the last syllable of the list word. Use the **Spelling Dictionary** on page 214 to help you.

1. methodical ____   3. presentable ____

2. similarity ____

■ Use the spelling words you wrote to complete these sentences.

4. Jamal had a ____ for organizing his science notes.

5. Juan's loud laugh announced his ____ in the class.

Review Words

Write the review words that have a short vowel sound spelled with the letters in the accented syllable.

a 6. ____   o 9. ____

e 7. ____   u 10. ____

i 8. ____

expect
gigantic
shocking
ugly
insect

T A K E   H O M E

Write your spelling words in alphabetical order. Circle the letters that spell the short vowel sound in the accented syllable of each word. Use your lists to practice at home.

4

Apply Spelling Skills

Using the Thesaurus

In your **Spelling Thesaurus** beginning on page 182, look up the entry for the word *exact*. Use the information in the entry to answer the questions below.

1. What synonyms are given for the word *exact*?

   _____   _____   _____

2. What part of speech is each synonym used as? _____

3. What is the example sentence for the second synonym? _____

4. Use one of the synonyms in a sentence of your own. _____

Proofreading

Proofread the paragraph. Check for spelling, capital letters, and punctuation. Then rewrite the paragraph. There are six mistakes.

> Lets establish a math contest strickly for students. We will publisch the question next monday. Any student may attemp to solve it. There will be no limet to the number of entries.

Writing • *About Math*

PREWRITE: List some ideas for an article in a math magazine.
DRAFT: Choose one idea. Write an entertaining opening paragraph.
REVISE: Does your paragraph introduce your main idea? Use the **Spelling Thesaurus** on page 182 as you revise.
EDIT/PROOFREAD: Use editing marks. Then rewrite your paragraph.
PUBLISH: Contribute your paragraph to a class math magazine.

EDITING MARKS

◯ check spelling
≡ capital letter
╱ lowercase letter
⊙ add a period
∧ add
✗ take out
¶ indent the paragraph
↻ move

For more help, see page 171.

WORDS WITH /ā/ and /ē/

PHONICS PATTERNS

1. braid
2. keen
3. gain
4. favorite
5. bead
6. neat
7. blame
8. niece
9. bathe
10. beef
11. tame
12. pave
13. ache
14. heap
15. cheat
16. maid
17. locate
18. steep
19. trail
20. grief

Learn Spelling Patterns

LOOK & SAY   Listen for the sounds in each word.

PICTURE   Close your eyes. See each word in your mind.

STUDY   These spelling words have /ā/ and /ē/.

WRITE   Sort the words. Which words have /ā/ spelled with the letters below?

a   (1)
ai   (2)   (3)   (4)   (5)
a-e   (6)   (7)   (8)
    (9)   (10)   (11)

Which words have /ē/ spelled with the letters below?

ea   (12)   (13)   (14)   (15)
ee   (16)   (17)   (18)
ie   (19)   (20)

CHECK   Did you spell each word correctly? Circle the letters that spell /ā/ or /ē/.

Pattern Power

How can /ā/ be spelled? (21) or (22) or (23) How can /ē/ be spelled? (24) or (25) or (26)

Other Words

Write words you would like to add to this week's list.

_____ _____ _____ _____ _____

Practice Word Meanings

Analogies

An **analogy** is a comparison between two things.

Smile is to *happy* as *frown* is to *sad*.

The relationship between *smile* and *happy* is the same as the relationship between *frown* and *sad*. Write the spelling word that completes each analogy.

1. *Nephew* is to *boy* as _____ is to *girl*.

2. *Joy* is to *happiness* as _____ is to *sadness*.

3. *Street* is to *city* as _____ is to *forest*.

4. *Praise* is to *good* as _____ is to *bad*.

5. *Knot* is to *rope* as _____ is to *hair*.

6. *Add* is to *subtract* as _____ is to *lose*.

7. *Stack* is to *order* as _____ is to *disorder*.

8. *Swim* is to *ocean* as _____ is to *bathtub*.

Challenge Words • *Science*

Write the challenge word that matches each word group. Use the **Spelling Dictionary** to help you. Circle the spelling of /ā/ or /ē/.

9. hilly, mountainous, flat, rocky _____

10. summer, autumn, winter, spring _____

11. bear, winter, sleep, hide _____

12. genus, biology, classification _____

13. plants, trees, flowers, grass _____

seasonal
species
vegetation
terrain
hibernate

Spelling Tip

Use words you know how to spell to help you spell new words. For example, if you want to spell the word *cheat:*

✦ Listen to the sound at the beginning of *cheat*. Do you know how to spell a word that begins with /ch/?

✦ Listen to the sounds at the end of *cheat*. What other word has the same sounds?

✦ Put the letters that stand for the sounds together.

/ch/ **ch**in   /ēt/ rep**eat**   **ch** + **eat** = **cheat**

7

List Words

braid
keen
gain
favorite
bead
neat
blame
niece
bathe
beef
tame
pave
ache
heap
cheat
maid
locate
steep
trail
grief

Challenge Words

seasonal
species
vegetation
terrain
hibernate

Review Words

delay
sweep
paste
leader
decorate

Build Vocabulary

Suffixes

■ The suffix *-ly* means "in a particular manner."

rapid + ly = rapidly

Add *-ly* to these list words.

1. keen _____   **3.** tame _____

2. neat _____   **4.** steep _____

■ The suffix *-est* is used in comparing more than two things and means "most."

warm + est = warmest

Add *-est* to these list words. You may have to drop a final *e* before adding the ending.

5. keen _____   **7.** tame _____

6. neat _____   **8.** steep _____

■ Use words you made to complete these sentences.

9. He _____ hung up his clothes in the closet.

10. The parakeet is one of the _____ birds in our store.

Review Words

Write the review words with /ā/ spelled with these letters. Circle the letters.

a-e 11. _____   **ay 13.** _____

  12. _____

Write the review words with /ē/ spelled with these letters. Circle the letters.

ea 14. _____   **ee 15.** _____

delay
sweep
paste
leader
decorate

T A K E   H O M E

Write your spelling words in two lists: words with the /ā/ sound, and words with the /ē/ sound. Circle the spelling of /ā/ or /ē/ in each word. Use your lists to practice at home.

8

Apply Spelling Skills

Dictionary Skills

In a dictionary entry, parts of speech are abbreviated. Look up each of these spelling words in the **Spelling Dictionary** on page 214. Write the abbreviation for the part of speech for the entry. Then write the definition. If there are several, write the first.

1. ache _____ _____

2. beef _____ _____

3. pave _____ _____

4. maid _____ _____

5. cheat _____ _____

6. bead _____ _____

Proofreading

Proofread the paragraph. Check for spelling, capital letters, and punctuation. Then rewrite the paragraph. There are six mistakes.

> Birds are carla's faverit hobby. She likes to locait many kinds of birds. Her family puts out beaf fat and seeds to attract birds She is fighting a plan to paive a wooded area nearby.

Writing • About Science

PREWRITE: List some facts about the animal you admire the most.

DRAFT: Write a paragraph about why you admire this animal.

REVISE: Did you include supporting details? Use the **Spelling Thesaurus** on page 182 as you revise.

EDIT/PROOFREAD: Use editing marks. Then rewrite your paragraph.

PUBLISH: Read your paragraph and show an illustration during a class reading hour.

EDITING MARKS

⬯ check spelling

☰ capital letter

／ lowercase letter

⊙ add a period

⌃ add

✁ take out

¶ indent the paragraph

↻ move

For more help, see page 171.

9

WORDS WITH /ī/ and /ō/

PHONICS PATTERNS

1. dine
2. midnight
3. fellow
4. roam
5. hoe
6. froze
7. hero
8. mighty
9. deny
10. invite
11. colt
12. pride
13. tying
14. arrive
15. omit
16. sorrow
17. boast
18. devote
19. poet
20. vine

Learn Spelling Patterns

LOOK & SAY   Listen for the sounds in each word.

PICTURE   Close your eyes. See each word in your mind.

STUDY   These spelling words have /ī/ and /ō/.

WRITE   Sort the words. Which words have /ī/ spelled with the letters below?

igh   (1)   (2)

y   (3)   (4)

i-e   (5)   (6)   (7)   (8)   (9)

Which words have /ō/ spelled with the letters below?

ow   (10)   (11)

oe   (12)

o-e   (13)   (14)

oa   (15)   (16)

o   (17)   (18)   (19)   (20)

CHECK   Did you spell each word correctly? Circle the letters that spell /ī/ or /ō/.

Pattern Power

How can /ī/ be spelled?

(21) or (22) or (23)

How can /ō/ be spelled?

(24) or (25) or (26) or (27) or (28)

Other Words

Write words you would like to add to this week's list.

_____ _____ _____ _____ _____

Practice Word Meanings

Definitions

Write the spelling word whose definition matches each clue below.

1. champion _____
2. sadness _____
3. to eat _____
4. wander _____
5. to brag _____
6. powerful _____

7. a boy or man _____
8. writer of verse _____
9. creeping plant _____
10. young horse _____
11. to leave out _____

Challenge Words • *Social Studies*

Write the challenge word that best completes each sentence. Use the **Spelling Dictionary** on page 214 to help you. Circle the spelling of /ī/ or /ō/ in each word.

12. They let the land lie _____ for several years to improve the soil.

13. In the Southwest, people sometimes use _____ bricks to build houses.

14. The people feared the cruel _____ who ruled the country.

15. The potato crop was severely damaged by a _____.

16. Mount St. Helens is an active _____ that erupted in 1980.

tyrant
volcano
adobe
blight
fallow

Spelling Tip

Words that are related in meaning are often related in spelling, even if they have different sounds. For example:

+ *Poem, poet, poetry,* and *poetic* are related in meaning.
+ *Poem* has the long vowel sound followed by a *schwa* sound.
+ *Poet* has the long vowel sound followed by a short *i* sound.
+ *Poetry* has the long vowel sound followed by a short *i* sound.
+ *Poetic* has the long vowel sound followed by a short *e* sound.

Remembering the short *e* sound in *poetic* can help you spell the other words with hard-to-hear vowels.

List Words

dine

midnight

fellow

roam

hoe

froze

hero

mighty

deny

invite

colt

pride

tying

arrive

omit

sorrow

boast

devote

poet

vine

Challenge Words

tyrant

volcano

adobe

blight

fallow

Review Words

excite

obey

climate

follow

identify

Build Vocabulary

Word Building

■ New words can be formed by adding endings like -*s*, -*ed*, and -*ing*. Prefixes and suffixes can also be added to build words. If the base word ends in *e*, the *e* is dropped when -*ed* is added.

place + **ed** = placed   **re** + placed = replaced

Build new words from each list word below.

1. hoe   +   ed   =   ____

2. froze   +   en   =   ____

3. pride   +   ed   =   ____

4. un   +   tying   =   ____

5. re   +   froze   =   ____

■ Use words you made to complete these sentences.

6. Alma ____ herself on her good study habits.

7. The new blast of cold air ____ the lake.

Review Words

Write the review words that have /ī/ or /ō/ spelled with the letters below. Circle the letters.

i-e   **8.** ____   **o**   **11.** ____

i   **9.** ____   **ow**   **12.** ____

i and **y**   **10.** ____

excite

obey

climate

follow

identify

TAKE HOME

Write your spelling words in alphabetical order. Then circle the words that follow the pattern i-consonant-e or o-consonant-e. Use your lists to practice at home.

Apply Spelling Skills

Dictionary Skills

Write the spelling words that match the **respellings** below.
Use your **Spelling Dictionary** on page 214 for help.

1. mid′nīt′   _____
2. ə rīv′   _____
3. di nī′   _____
4. di vōt′   _____
5. in vīt′   _____

Pattern Power

Look at the words you just wrote.

• Circle the letters that spell /ī/ or /ō/.

Proofreading

Proofread the paragraph. Check for spelling, capital letters, and punctuation.
Then rewrite the paragraph. There are six mistakes.

> One night during a great storm, a scared colte bolted through the open barn door. jeremy was a heroe, dashing out into the rain and tieing him up again. What a brave fello my brother is

Writing • About Social Studies

PREWRITE: What region of the country would you like to visit? List some places that interest you.

DRAFT: Choose one place to write about. Write a paragraph describing what you would expect to see in the place that you visit.

REVISE: Did you include details? Use the **Spelling Thesaurus** on page 182 as you revise.

EDIT/PROOFREAD: Use editing marks. Then rewrite your paragraph.

PUBLISH: Include your paragraph in a class travel brochure folder.

EDITING MARKS

⬭ check spelling
≡ capital letter
／ lowercase letter
⊙ add a period
∧ add
⚊ take out
¶ indent the paragraph
↻ move

For more help, see page 171.

WORDS WITH /ü/ and /ū/

PHONICS PATTERNS

1. hoop
2. perfume
3. proof
4. excuse
5. coupon
6. value
7. rude
8. youth
9. tool
10. approve
11. cruise
12. shampoo
13. student
14. bugle
15. lunar
16. grapefruit
17. issue
18. troop
19. view
20. vacuum

Learn Spelling Patterns

LOOK & SAY   Listen for the sounds in each word.

PICTURE   Close your eyes. See each word in your mind.

STUDY   These spelling words have /ü/ and /ū/.

WRITE   Sort the words. Which words have /ü/ spelled with the letters below?

u-e   (1)
o-e   (2)
ou   (3)   (4)
ue   (5)
ui   (6)   (7)
u   (8)   (9)
oo   (10)   (11)   (12)   (13)   (14)

Which words have /ū/ spelled with the letters below?

u-e   (15)   (16)
ue   (17)
u   (18)
iew   (19)
uu   (20)

CHECK   Did you spell each word correctly? Circle the letters that spell /ü/ or /ū/.

Pattern Power

How can /ü/ be spelled with two vowels? (21) or (22) or (23) or (24) or (25) or (26) How can /ū/ be spelled with two vowels? (27) or (28) or (29)

Other Words

Write words you would like to add to this week's list.

_____ _____ _____ _____ _____

14

Practice Word Meanings

Word Context

Write the spelling word that matches the meaning of each underlined word below.

1. Did you happen to see the <u>moon</u> eclipse last night? *lunar*

2. The soldier played <u>a small trumpet</u> at six A.M. _____

3. One <u>young person</u> raised his hand. _____

4. Mother used the <u>sweeper</u> to clean the rug. _____

5. There is no <u>evidence</u> that life exists on Mars. _____

6. Frank was <u>impolite</u> to his brother. _____

7 Her <u>scent</u> reminded me of flowers. _____

8. How do astronauts <u>wash</u> their hair? _____

Challenge Words • *Science* -----------------

Write the challenge word that answers each riddle. Use the **Spelling Dictionary** on page 214 to help you. Circle the spelling of /ü/ or /ū/ in each word.

9. What is a hard casing for an insect? _____

10. What happens when metals melt together? _____

11. What kind of weather brings stormy seas? _____

12. What is at the heart of the matter? _____

13. What kind of animal is a type of deer? _____

nucleus
typhoon
fusion
caribou
cocoon

ⓢpelling Tip

Say the words *cruise* and *crews*. They are homophones: they sound alike and have some of the same letters, but they are spelled differently and have different meanings.

✦ For words that sound alike, decide which word is right in your sentence.

✦ Use a dictionary if necessary to check which word is right.

✦ When you check something you have written, look especially for homophones. Use the context of the sentence to decide which spelling is correct.

hoop
perfume
proof
excuse
coupon
value
rude
youth
tool
approve
cruise
shampoo
student
bugle
lunar
grapefruit
issue
troop
view
vacuum

nucleus
typhoon
fusion
caribou
cocoon

useful
lose
spoon
suitcase
reunion

Build Vocabulary

Word Endings

■ A **base word** is the simplest form of a word. You can form new words by adding endings to base words. Remember to drop the final *e* before adding *-ed*.

use + **ed** = used

Add *-ed* to the list words.

1. approve _____
2. view _____
3. troop _____
4. cruise _____
5. shampoo _____
6. excuse _____
7. issue _____
8. value _____
9. vacuum _____

■ Use words you made to complete these sentences.

10. The post office _____ new stamps for Valentine's Day.

11. We _____ the paintings at the art museum.

Review Words

Write the review words in which /ü/ or /ū/ is spelled with the letters below.

oo 12. _____   **u-e** 15. _____

o-e 13. _____   **u** 16. _____

ui 14. _____

useful
lose
spoon
suitcase
reunion

TAKE HOME

Write your spelling words in alphabetical order. Circle the spelling of /ü/ or /ū/ in each word. Use your lists to practice at home.

Apply Spelling Skills

Dictionary Skills

A dictionary entry may include an **example sentence** that shows how the word is used. Look up the list words below in the **Spelling Dictionary** on page 214. Write the example sentence for each word.

1. coupon _____

2. troop _____

Proofreading

Proofread the paragraph. Check for spelling, capital letters, and punctuation. Then rewrite the paragraph. There are six mistakes.

> After a year as a studint at the luner station, could I get used to earth's stronger gravity Would I be able to eat a grapefrute or throw a basketball through a houp?

EDITING MARKS

⬭ check spelling

≡ capital letter

/ lowercase letter

⊙ add a period

∧ add

ℛ take out

¶ indent the paragraph

↻ move

For more help, see page 171.

Writing • *About Science*

PREWRITE: List some reasons why you would or wouldn't want to go to the moon.

DRAFT: Write a paragraph that explains why you made your choice.

REVISE: Did you explain your opinion? Use the **Spelling Thesaurus** on page 182 as you revise.

EDIT/PROOFREAD: Use editing marks. Then rewrite your paragraph.

PUBLISH: Read your paragraph in a debate about whether it would be interesting to go to the moon.

5

Long and Short Vowel Sounds

PHONICS PATTERNS

1. census
2. pronoun
3. dismiss
4. costume
5. suffix
6. cable
7. frustrate
8. identity
9. decent
10. odor
11. separate
12. silent
13. concrete
14. pilot
15. classic
16. disgrace
17. enclose
18. desire
19. resign
20. accent

Learn Spelling Patterns

LOOK & SAY Listen for the sounds in each word.

PICTURE Close your eyes. See each word in your mind.

STUDY These spelling words have long and short vowel sounds in the accented syllable.

WRITE Sort the words. Which words have the short vowel sound in the accented syllable spelled with the letters below?

a	(1) (2)	o	(7) (8)
e	(3) (4) (5)	u	(9) (10)
i	(6)		

Which words have the long vowel sound in the accented syllable spelled with the letters below?

a   (11)
a-e   (12)
e   (13)
i   (14) (15) (16)
i-e   (17)
o   (18) (19)
o-e   (20)

CHECK Did you spell each word correctly? Circle the letters that spell the long and short vowel sounds.

Pattern Power

What kind of vowel sound is usually found in an accented syllable that ends with a consonant? (21) What kind of vowel sound is usually found in an accented syllable that ends with a vowel? (22)

Other Words

Write words you would like to add to this week's list.

_____ _____ _____ _____ _____

Practice Word Meanings

Related Meanings

Write a spelling word to complete each of these word groups.

1. verb   conjunction   _pronoun_

2. language   dialect   _____

3. wire   rope   _____

4. adobe   mortar   _____

5. mask   outfit   _____

6. driver   captain   _____

7. personality   individual   _____

8. kind   nice   _____

9. count   population   _____

10. refined   traditional   _____

Challenge Words • Science

Write the challenge word that best completes each sentence. Use the **Spelling Dictionary** on page 214 to help you. Circle the spelling of the long or short vowel in the accented syllable of each word.

11. A _____, like a neutron, is part of an atom.

12. A _____ attracts metal filings.

13. Blood _____ carries red and white blood cells.

14. When objects _____ they create sound.

15. A _____ is a tiny living thing that can cause disease.

magnet
plasma
proton
vibrate
microbe

ⓢpelling Tip

Words that are related in meaning are often related in spelling.

✦ *Grace* and *disgrace* are related in meaning.

✦ Remembering how to spell *grace* can help you spell *disgrace*.

Can you think of a word that will help you remember the silent *g* in *resign*?

census

pronoun

dismiss

costume

suffix

cable

frustrate

identity

decent

odor

separate

silent

concrete

pilot

classic

disgrace

enclose

desire

resign

accent

Challenge Words

magnet

plasma

proton

vibrate

microbe

Review Words

bubble

prefix

channel

triumph

basic

Build Vocabulary

Word Endings

■ If a base word ends in *e*, the *e* is dropped when the ending *-ing* is added. You can form new words by adding *-ing* to base words.

excuse + **ing** = excusing

Add *-ing* to these list words.

1. dismiss _____

2. frustrate _____

3. separate _____

4. disgrace _____

5. enclose _____

6. desire _____

7. resign _____

■ Use words you made to complete these sentences.

8. Sometimes Claire has trouble _____ the egg yolk from the white.

9. It is _____ when you know the answer but you can't remember it.

Review Words

Write the review words that have the sounds below in their accented syllable.

/a/   10. _____

/ā/   11. _____

/ē/   12. _____

/ī/   13. _____

/u/   14. _____

bubble
prefix
channel
triumph
basic

TAKE HOME

Write your spelling words in two lists: words with short vowel sounds in the accented syllable and words with long vowel sounds in the accented syllable. Use your lists to practice at home.

Apply Spelling Skills

Dictionary Skills

Guide words appear at the top of each dictionary page. The first guide word is the first entry word on that page. The second guide word is the last entry word on the page. Write the spelling word that you would find on a page with each set of guide words below. Choose from the words in the box.

| census   odor   silent   suffix   enclose   pronoun |

1. drama/exit _enclose_
2. sight/silver _____
3. cat/cute _____
4. student/swat _____
5. nest/open _____
6. promise/prove _____

Proofreading

Proofread the paragraph. Check for spelling, capital letters, and punctuation. Then rewrite the paragraph. There are six mistakes.

> Working in the silint lab, we mixed together the contents of two seperate bottles A white color and a strange oder appeared. what was the identitie of this new matter?

Writing • About Science

PREWRITE: List some scientific discoveries that you know about.

DRAFT: Choose one discovery. Write a paragraph that tells why you think the discovery was important.

REVISE: Did you support your opinion with details? Use the **Spelling Thesaurus** on page 182 as you revise.

EDIT/PROOFREAD: Use editing marks. Then rewrite your paragraph.

PUBLISH: Contribute your paragraph to a class Scientific Discoveries bulletin board.

Pattern Power

Look at the list words you just wrote.

- Circle the letters that spell the long or short vowel sound in the accented syllable.

EDITING MARKS

- ⬯ check spelling
- ≡ capital letter
- / lowercase letter
- ⊙ add a period
- ∧ add
- ⤲ take out
- ¶ indent the paragraph
- ⟳ move

For more help, see page 171.

21

6 REVIEW Spelling Patterns

Sort the words in each list. Write each word. Circle the spelling pattern.

rapidly
dodge
envy
won
limit
closet
presence
method
profit
vanish
	Lesson 1
	**Words in which the accented syllable
	has the short vowel sound.**
	
	/a/ 1. _____ /i/ 6. _____
	       2. _____ /o/ 7. _____
	/e/ 3. _____ 8. _____
	       4. _____ 9. _____
	       5. _____ /u/ 10. _____

keen
gain
favorite
bead
niece
tame
pave
heap
trail
grief
	Lesson 2
	
	Words with /ā/ spelled **Words with /ē/ spelled**
	
	   a 11. _____ ea 16. _____
	  ai 12. _____ 17. _____
	      13. _____ ee 18. _____
	a-e 14. _____ ie 19. _____
	      15. _____ 20. _____

midnight
fellow
hoe
froze
deny
colt
arrive
sorrow
boast
devote
	Lesson 3
	
	Words with /ī/ spelled **Words with /ō/ spelled**
	
	igh 21. _____ o 24. _____
	i-e 22. _____ ow 25. _____
	  y 23. _____ 26. _____
	                  oe 27. _____
	               o-e 28. _____
	                    29. _____
	               oa 30. _____

proof	

Lesson 4

proof	**Words with /ü/ spelled**	**Words with /ū/ spelled**
excuse		
value	o-e 31. _____	iew 39. _____
youth	ou 32. _____	uu 40. _____
approve	ui 33. _____	
cruise	u 34. _____	
student	35. _____	
lunar	oo 36. _____	
view	u-e 37. _____	
vacuum	ue 38. _____	

dismiss	
costume	
frustrate	
decent	
odor	
separate	
silent	
classic	
disgrace	
desire	

Lesson 5

Words in which the accented syllables have the short or long vowel sounds

/a/ 41. _____		/ā/ 46. _____	
/e/ 42. _____		/ē/ 47. _____	
/i/ 43. _____		/ī/ 48. _____	
/o/ 44. _____		49. _____	
/u/ 45. _____		/ō/ 50. _____	

Spelling Tip

How can you figure out the spelling of a long word? Long words are easier to spell when you sound them out one syllable at a time. Each syllable must have a vowel sound.

✦ Listen for the first syllable in *rapidly*. What vowel sound do you hear?

✦ Listen for the next syllable. What vowel sound do you hear?

✦ Listen for the last syllable. What vowel sound do you hear?

Write the word one syllable at a time.

rap + id + ly

Try sounding out these other spelling words and writing them one syllable at a time.

1. favorite _____   2. frustrate _____

favorite
frustrate

Word Meaning Mixed Lesson Review

sorrow
vanish
disgrace
keen
separate
silent

Synonyms and Antonyms

Write the spelling word that is a synonym or antonym for each word below. Then write *synonym* or *antonym* after each word pair.

1. loud   _____   _____
2. join   _____   _____
3. unhappiness   _____   _____
4. appear   _____   _____
5. shame   _____   _____
6. dull   _____   _____

odor
froze
student
cruise
envy
niece

Analogies

Write a spelling word to complete each analogy below.

7. *Flight* is to *airplane* as _____ is to *ship*.
8. *Athlete* is to *coach* as _____ is to *teacher*.
9. *Nephew* is to *male* as _____ is to *female*.
10. *Sound* is to *hear* as _____ is to *smell*.
11. *Admiration* is to *respect* as _____ is to *jealousy*.
12. *Heat* is to *baked* as _____ is to *froze*.

grief
colt
closet
dodge
fellow
frustrate
favorite
vacuum

Definitions

Write a spelling word to match each clue below.

13. a place to hang clothes   _____
14. deep sorrow   _____
15. a young horse   _____
16. a machine to sweep with   _____
17. person or thing liked best   _____
18. a man or boy   _____
19. disappoint or defeat   _____
20. keep away or avoid   _____

Vocabulary Mixed Lesson Review

Word Endings

Add *-ing* and *-ed* to each of these list words to make a new word. You may need to drop a final *e* before adding the ending.

	-ing	-ed
1. profit	_____	_____
2. excuse	_____	_____
3. arrive	_____	_____
4. dismiss	_____	_____
5. desire	_____	_____
6. gain	_____	_____
7. limit	_____	_____
8. boast	_____	_____
9. approve	_____	_____
10. view	_____	_____

profit

excuse

arrive

dismiss

desire

gain

limit

boast

approve

view

Dictionary Skills

Read this part of a dictionary entry and complete the items below.

tame (tām) *adj.,* **tam•er, tam•est. 1.** taken by humans from a state of native wildness and domesticated: *a tame elephant.* **2.** not ferocious, fearful, or shy; gentle: *The deer was tame enough to let us photograph it.*

1. How many definitions does the entry word list? _____
2. What part of speech is the entry word? _____
3. What is the synonym for the second definition of the entry word? _____
4. Write your own example sentence for the first definiton of *tame.* _____

Spelling and Writing

A business letter can be a form of descriptive writing. The writer gives reasons for the reader to buy his or her product.

INCLUDE PROPER HEADING AND CLOSING

25 Horatio Street
Wilmington, DE 25609
September 31, 1997

Wyans Household Helpers, Inc.
668 South Ave.
Chicago, IL 60604

USE CONVINCING DETAILS

Dear Sir or Madam:

   I would like to offer your company the opportunity to manufacture my recent invention, the Sonic Sweeper.

   My new vacuum cleaner is almost silent. Its unique feature is that it uses positive and negative ions to attract dust and dirt to the nozzle. A fan then sucks the dirt into a dust bag, just as in a classic machine. The Sonic Sweeper will be welcomed by people who suffer from dust allergies.

   Please contact me at the above address if you would like me to ship you a Sonic Sweeper for your inspection.

Sincerely yours,
Julia Melville

WRITING TIPS!!

Descriptive Writing

- Use vivid words to help the reader see, hear, and feel the subject.
- Introduce your subject in a clear and interesting way.
- Use convincing details about the item you are describing.
- Clearly express a feeling about the subject.
- Include the proper heading and closing for a business letter.

Now write your own business letter. Try to use some of the spelling words in your paragraph.

PREWRITE: What kind of product do you think you could sell? List different things you think might interest people.

DRAFT: Write a business letter about the item you choose to sell. Begin with a topic sentence that names the item. Then write sentences that describe it.

REVISE: Share your business letter with a classmate. Use your classmate's comments and the Writing Tips as you revise.

EDIT/PROOFREAD: Use editing marks to correct your capitalization, spelling, and punctuation.

PUBLISH: Illustrate your business letter with a drawing of the product you are offering. Post your business letter on the bulletin board.

SPELLING FUN
CUMULATIVE REVIEW

REFRIGERATOR MAGNETS

- Choose some words from Lessons 1–5 that could be used together in a silly sentence.
- Write your words on an index card or cards, and then cut out each word to make your refrigerator magnets.

- Draw a refrigerator, or cut out a picture from a magazine. Glue your cut-out words on the picture in the order that they appear in your sentence.
- Below your picture, add other words you need to write a complete sentence.

CATEGORIES

- Play Categories in teams of four.
- Choose one word from any list in Lessons 1–5. Decide on a category in which your word could be included. Tell your teammates the category and the number of letters in your word.
- Your teammates make a blank for each letter of your word on a piece of paper. They then take turns asking questions

about your word. You can only answer *yes* or *no* to every question.

- Make a tally mark for each question you are asked until your word is guessed. After each team member has had a turn choosing a word, see which word took the most questions to guess. No team is allowed to ask more than a total of twenty questions.

SPELLING BEE

- Two teams write words from Lessons 1–5 on cards. Each team then gets half the cards and places them face down in a stack.
- The first player on Team A turns over a card and asks the first player on Team B to spell the word.

- If the word is spelled correctly, the card is removed from the pile. If not, the card is returned to the pile.
- Then, the next player on Team B calls out a word for the next player on Team A to spell.
- The first team to finish the other team's pile wins the spelling bee.

7

WORDS WITH /ôr/ and /ô/

PHONICS PATTERNS

1. nor
2. ore
3. therefore
4. ignore
5. laundry
6. pork
7. install
8. dawn
9. tall
10. loss
11. faucet
12. walrus
13. fortune
14. afford
15. mourn
16. audience
17. thoughtless
18. flaw
19. waltz
20. horrible

Learn Spelling Patterns

LOOK & SAY Listen for the sounds in each word.

PICTURE Close your eyes. See each word in your mind.

STUDY These spelling words have /ôr/ or /ô/.

WRITE Sort the words. Which words have /ôr/ spelled with the following letters?

orr	(1)		
ore	(2)	(3)	(4)
our	(5)		
or	(6) (7) (8) (9)		

Which words have /ô/ spelled with the following letters?

ough	(10)		
aw	(11) (12)		
au	(13) (14) (15)		
o	(16)		
a	(17) (18) (19) (20)		

CHECK Did you spell each word correctly? Circle the letters that spell /ôr/ and /ô/.

Pattern Power

Which vowel do the spellings of /ôr/ usually begin with? __(21)__ Which vowels may begin a spelling of /ô/ or spell /ô/ by themselves? __(22)__ or __(23)__

Other Words

Write words you would like to add to this week's list.

_____ _____ _____ _____ _____

Practice Word Meanings

Context Sentences

Write the spelling word that best completes each sentence.

1. The Tigers' _____ to the Bears was a big disappointment.

2. The plumber will be here on Monday to _____ the new pipe.

3. Paul Bunyan was so _____ that he could see his loggers' camp seven miles away.

4. She woke at _____ to watch the sun come up.

Synonyms and Antonyms

Write a spelling word that is a **synonym (S)** or **antonym (A)** for each word below.

5. thoughtful (A) _____

6. wonderful (A) _____

7. error (S) _____

8. wash (S) _____

9. grieve (S) _____

Challenge Words • *Science* ----------------------------

Write the challenge word that best answers each question. Use the **Spelling Dictionary** on page 214 to help you. Circle the spelling of /ôr/ or /ô/ in each word.

10. What is a creature very similar to a shrimp? _____

11. What is an animal that eats only meat? _____

12. What is a playful mammal similar to a dolphin? _____

13. What is a substance that makes plants green? _____

14. What is a word that means "animal life"? _____

chlorophyll
porpoise
carnivore
fauna
prawn

pelling Tip

Sometimes knowing the Latin root of a word will help you spell it correctly.

✦ The root of the word *audience* comes from the Latin word *audire*, which means "to hear."

✦ The word *audible* means "capable of being heard."

What other words do you know that contain the Latin root *aud*?

List Words

nor

ore

therefore

ignore

laundry

pork

install

dawn

tall

loss

faucet

walrus

fortune

afford

mourn

audience

thoughtless

flaw

waltz

horrible

Challenge Words

chlorophyll

porpoise

carnivore

fauna

prawn

Review Words

border

explore

saucer

crawl

astronaut

Build Vocabulary

Plural Nouns

■ A **singular noun** names one person, place, thing, or idea. A **plural noun** names more than one. You can form most plural nouns by adding -s to the base word.

flaw   flaw**s**

Nouns are made plural in different ways. Singular nouns that end in *s, ss, z, sh, ch,* and *x* are usually made plural by adding -es to the base word.

dress   dress**es**   bench   bench**es**

Write the plural form of these spelling words by adding -s or -es.

1. audience _____   4. fortune _____

2. waltz _____   5. loss _____

3. walrus _____   6. faucet _____

■ Use words you made to complete these sentences.

7. We danced two _____ and a tango.

8. They moved to the big city to seek their _____.

9. _____ always love that musical.

Review Words

Write the review words that have /ôr/ spelled with the letters below.

ore 10. _____   **or** 11. _____

Write the review words that have /ô/ spelled with the letters below.

au 12. _____   **aw** 14. _____

    13. _____

border

explore

saucer

crawl

astronaut

T A K E   H O M E

Write your spelling words in three lists: one-syllable, two-syllable, and three-syllable words. Circle the spelling of /ôr/ or /ô/ in each word. Use your lists to practice at home.

Apply Spelling Skills

Dictionary Skills

Which pair of guide words below would appear on the page where the word *fortune* could be found?

faucet/fawn   forsake/foster   fell/foam

1. _____

Write the spelling words below that could be found on a dictionary page that had these guide words:

order/post   2. _____

3. _____

test/throw   4. _____

5. _____

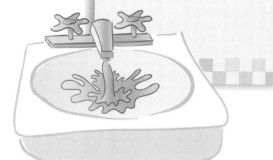

Pattern Power

Look at the spelling words you wrote.
• Circle the letters that spell /ôr/ or /ô/ in each word.

Proofreading

Proofread the paragraph. Check spelling, capital letters, and punctuation. Then rewrite the paragraph. There are six mistakes.

the scientist talked about the horribel loss of many kinds of animals in the world. "We cannot aford to ignor the problem any longer, nore can we leave it to others," she said

Writing • *About Science*

PREWRITE: List some topics related to the people, animals, and weather of the arctic.

DRAFT: Choose details to use in an ad for an arctic vacation.

REVISE: Did you include interesting details? Use the **Spelling Thesaurus** on page 182 as you revise.

EDIT/PROOFREAD: Use editing marks. Then rewrite your paragraph.

PUBLISH: Post your ad on the bulletin board.

EDITING MARKS

◯ **check spelling**

= **capital letter**

/ **lowercase letter**

⊙ **add a period**

∧ **add**

⁊ **take out**

⁋ **indent the paragraph**

◯ **move**

For more help, see page 171.

WORDS WITH /îr/ and /ûr/

PHONICS PATTERNS

1. urgent
2. workout
3. pearl
4. burnt
5. worthy
6. mere
7. interfere
8. nourish
9. curb
10. nerve
11. squirt
12. rehearse
13. furnace
14. courtesy
15. journal
16. hurdle
17. pioneer
18. permit
19. pierce
20. twirl

Learn Spelling Patterns

LOOK & SAY Listen for the sounds in each word.

PICTURE Close your eyes. See each word in your mind.

STUDY These spelling words have /îr/ or /ûr/.

WRITE Sort the words. Which words have /îr/ spelled with the letters below?

ere   (1)   (2)
ier   (3)
eer   (4)

Which words have /ûr/ spelled with the letters below?

ur   (5)   (6)   (7)   (8)   (9)
our   (10) (11) (12)
er   (13) (14)
ir   (15) (16)
or   (17) (18)
ear   (19) (20)

CHECK Did you spell each word correctly? Circle the letters that spell /îr/ and /ûr/.

Pattern Power

With what letters is /îr/ usually spelled? (21) or (22) or (23)

How can /ûr/ be spelled with two letters? (24) or (25) or (26) or (27)

Other Words

Write words you would like to add to this week's list.

_____ _____ _____ _____ _____

Practice Word Meanings

Context Sentences

Write the spelling word that best completes each sentence.

1. The building is heated by a _____.

2. We needed a _____ to enter the factory.

3. King Arthur said Sir Lancelot was _____ of many honors.

4. It is a _____ to send a thank-you card.

5. The _____ built a cabin on her land.

6. Please _____ some mustard on the hot dogs.

7. The police answered an _____ call for help.

8. The diver found a _____ inside the oyster.

9. The overcooked meat was too _____ to eat.

10. We stood on the _____ and watched the parade.

Challenge Words • *The Arts*

Write the challenge word that best completes each sentence. Use the **Spelling Dictionary** on page 214 to help you. Circle the spelling of /îr/ or /ûr/ in each word.

11. The ballerina did a _____ across the stage.

12. The actor gave her _____ of the famous speech.

13. Once we've mastered the basics, we'll add a _____ to our dance routine.

14. The dancers _____ the star performer.

15. He played the chord in a different _____.

interpretation
pirouette
encircle
flourish
inversion

Spelling Tip

When deciding if a word is spelled with *ei* or *ie*, remember this rule:

✦ Use *i* before *e* except after *c*, or when the letters spell /ā/, as in *weigh*.

Which spelling word follows this rule?

List Words

urgent

workout

pearl

burnt

worthy

mere

interfere

nourish

curb

nerve

squirt

rehearse

furnace

courtesy

journal

hurdle

pioneer

permit

pierce

twirl

Challenge Words

interpretation

pirouette

encircle

flourish

inversion

Review Words

deserve

return

severe

frontier

journey

Build Vocabulary

Word Endings

■ You can form new words by adding -er and -ing to base words. If you add -er or -ing to a word that ends in e, remember to drop the e before adding the ending.

mine + **er** = miner   mine + **ing** = mining

Add -er or -ing to the following words.

1. twirl   +   er   =   _____

2. hurdle   +   er   =   _____

3. interfere   +   ing   =   _____

4. nourish   +   ing   =   _____

5. pierce   +   ing   =   _____

■ Use words you made to complete these sentences.

6. Milk is a _____ drink.

7. The _____ threw the baton high in the air.

8. Please stop _____ in our baseball game!

9. The _____ lost the race when he tripped and fell.

10. The needle is _____ the cloth easily.

Review Words

Write the review words that have /îr/ spelled with the letters below.

ere 11. _____   **ier** 12. _____

Write the review words that have /ûr/ spelled with the letters below.

er 13. _____   **our** 15. _____

ur 14. _____

deserve
return
severe
frontier
journey

T A K E   H O M E

Write your spelling words in two lists: words with /îr/ or /ûr/ spelled with two letters, and words with /îr/ or /ûr/ spelled with three letters. Circle the spelling of /îr/ or /ûr/ in each word. Use your lists to practice at home.

Apply Spelling Skills

Dictionary Skills

Many of the words in the English language have come from other languages. Often, the spelling of a word has changed over time. Sometimes, its meaning has also changed. Many dictionaries give a short history, or **etymology,** of certain entry words. Look at the etymology for *mere*.

> From the Latin *merus*, meaning "clear, pure, or unmixed."

Use the **Spelling Dictionary** on page 214 to complete this etymology.

The word *pioneer* comes from the 1. _____ word,

2. _____, meaning 3. _____, from the 4. _____ word

5. _____, meaning 6. _____.

Proofreading

Check spelling, capital letters, and punctuation. Then rewrite the paragraph. There are six mistakes.

> Jenna watched the dance group rehearce. After the werkout, she finally had the nerv to try out. That night jenna wrote in her journal, "In a meer matter of days, I'll know if I made it.

Writing • *About the Arts*

PREWRITE: Make a list of performances—such as plays, dances, or concerts—that you have attended.

DRAFT: Choose one performance. Write a short review telling your classmates what you liked or didn't like about it.

REVISE: Ask a classmate to check your use of descriptive words.

EDIT/PROOFREAD: Use editing marks. Then rewrite your review.

PUBLISH: Compile all the reviews into a class book.

EDITING MARKS

- ⬭ check spelling
- ≡ capital letter
- / lowercase letter
- ⊙ add a period
- ∧ add
- ⌔ take out
- ⌗ indent the paragraph
- ↻ move

For more help, see page 171.

WORDS WITH /är/ and /âr/

PHONICS PATTERNS

1. careless
2. armchair
3. farewell
4. barely
5. charm
6. nowhere
7. scarlet
8. artist
9. tar
10. vary
11. flare
12. mare
13. garlic
14. regard
15. despair
16. barbecue
17. aware
18. bargain
19. guard
20. sergeant

Learn Spelling Patterns

LOOK & SAY Listen for the sounds in each word.

PICTURE Close your eyes. See each word in your mind.

STUDY These spelling words have /är/ or /âr/.

WRITE Sort the words. Which words have /är/ spelled with the letters below?

ar
(1) (2) (3) (4) (5)
(6) (7) (8) (9)
(10)

er
(11)

Which words have /âr/ spelled with the letters below?

are
(12) (13) (14)
(15) (16) (17)

air
(18) (19)

ere
(20)

ar
(21)

CHECK Did you spell each word correctly? Circle the letters that spell /är/ and /âr/.

Pattern Power

With what letters is /är/ almost always spelled? (22)

With what letters may /âr/ be spelled?

(23) or (24) or (25) or (26)

Other Words

Write words you would like to add to this week's list.

_____ _____ _____ _____ _____

36

Practice Word Meanings

Riddles

Write the spelling word that best matches each clue.

1. I am a thick, sticky liquid used to pave roads. ＿＿＿

2. My baby is called a foal. People can ride on my back. ＿＿＿

3. I am a comfortable seat with sides. ＿＿＿

4. I am a feeling of grief or hopelessness. ＿＿＿

5. I am a "good-bye" from one friend to another. ＿＿＿

6. I am a picnic where people eat grilled food. ＿＿＿

7. I use my imagination to create things. ＿＿＿

8. I am a good deal at a store or a market. ＿＿＿

Challenge Words • *Health*

Write the challenge word that best completes each sentence. Use the **Spelling Dictionary** on page 214 to help you. Circle the spelling of /är/ or /âr/ in each word.

9. Is that little fish an anchovy or a ＿＿＿?

10. The ＿＿＿ pie was tart, juicy, and full of fiber!

11. Starch is not a protein, but a ＿＿＿.

12. Do you want butter or ＿＿＿ on your toast?

13. It's hard to eat a balanced diet when there's a ＿＿＿ of fresh fruits and vegetables.

margarine
rhubarb
sardine
scarcity
carbohydrate

Spelling Tip

Some words are hard to spell. It helps to figure out which part or parts give you trouble.

✦ Look at the word *sergeant*. Both syllables are spelled with unusual letter combinations.

✦ In the first syllable, /är/ is spelled *er*.

✦ In the second syllable, the /ə/ sound is spelled *ea*.

When you are learning to spell difficult words, use your Word Study Steps. Pay special attention to the letters that are hardest for you.

List Words

- careless
- armchair
- farewell
- barely
- charm
- nowhere
- scarlet
- artist
- tar
- vary
- flare
- mare
- garlic
- regard
- despair
- barbecue
- aware
- bargain
- guard
- sergeant

Challenge Words

- margarine
- rhubarb
- sardine
- scarcity
- carbohydrate

Review Words

- remark
- wherever
- prepare
- carve
- affair

Build Vocabulary

Adjectives

■ You can change the form of a verb by adding the ending -ing. Often the -ing form can be used as an adjective. Add -ing to these verbs.

1. flare _____   4. vary _____

2. care _____   5. despair _____

3. charm _____

■ The suffix -less means "without." You can form an adjective by adding -less to a noun. Add -less to the nouns below.

6. regard _____   9. power _____

7. worth _____   10. care _____

8. hope _____

■ Use words you made to complete these sentences.

11. Everyone loves him for his _____ personality.

12. We will have fun at the picnic _____ of the weather.

13. The _____ student was sure she would fail the test.

Review Words

Write the review words that have /är/ spelled with the letters below.

ar 14. _____   15. _____

Write the review words that have /âr/ spelled with the letters below.

air 16. _____   er 18. _____

are 17. _____

remark
wherever
prepare
carve
affair

TAKE HOME

Write your spelling words in three lists: one-, two-, and three-syllable words. Circle the spelling of /är/ and/or /âr/ in each word. Use your lists to practice at home.

Apply Spelling Skills

Dictionary Skills

Dictionaries use sound symbols to show how words are pronounced. The **pronunciation key** at the front of every dictionary lists each sound symbol and shows what sound the symbol stands for. Using the pronunciation key in your **Spelling Dictionary** on page 217, write the word from each pair below that has the sound symbol shown.

1. /är/ careless, artist   _artist_

2. /är/ scarlet, flare   _____

3. /âr/ charm, aware   _____

4. /är/ sergeant, vary   _____

5. /âr/ guard, nowhere   _____

6. /är/ barely, garlic   _____

Pattern Power

Look at the list words you just wrote.
- Circle the letters in each word that spell /är/ or /âr/.
- Which word has /är/ spelled unusually?

Proofreading

Check spelling, capital letters, and punctuation. Then rewrite the paragraph. There are six mistakes.

> With Sally's Sauce, say fairwell to fat and salt. You will bareley know our sauce is there, but your food will taste great. What a bargin it is, too So gaurd your health with Sallys.

EDITING MARKS

◯	check spelling
≡	capital letter
/	lowercase letter
⊙	add a period
∧	add
℘	take out
⌗	indent the paragraph
◯～	move

For more help, see page 171.

Writing • *About Health*

PREWRITE: List some ways to have a healthier body.

DRAFT: Choose one way. Make a rough draft of a poster about it.

REVISING: Is your poster eye-catching? Did you use precise words?

EDIT/PROOFREAD: Use editing marks. Make a final copy of your poster.

PUBLISH: Hang your poster in the cafeteria or gym.

WORDS WITH /əl/ and /shəl/

1. material
2. tickle
3. natural
4. idle
5. signal
6. panel
7. official
8. cradle
9. pencil
10. fertile
11. article
12. icicle
13. nostril
14. fatal
15. cycle
16. social
17. local
18. practical
19. sample
20. funnel

Learn Spelling Patterns

LOOK & SAY Listen for the sounds in each word.

PICTURE Close your eyes. See each word in your mind.

STUDY These spelling words have /əl/ or /shəl/.

WRITE Sort the words. Which words have /əl/ spelled with the following letters?

ile   (1)

il   (2)   (3)

le   (4)   (5)   (6)   (7)
       (8)   (9)   (10)

el   (11) (12)

al   (13) (14) (15)
       (16) (17) (18)

Which words have /shəl/ spelled with the following letters?

cial   (19) (20)

CHECK Did you spell each word correctly? Circle the letters that spell /əl/ or /shəl/.

Pattern Power

How can /əl/ be spelled with two letters? (21) or (22) or (23) or (24) With what letters is /shəl/ spelled in many words? (25)

Other Words

Write words you would like to add to this week's list.

_____ _____ _____ _____ _____

Practice Word Meanings

Analogies

Write the spelling word that completes each analogy below.

1. *Lip* is to *mouth* as _____ is to *nose*.

2. *Pen* is to *ink* as _____ is to *lead*.

3. *Chair* is to *sit* as _____ is to *sleep*.

4. *Chapter* is to *book* as _____ is to *magazine*.

5. *Steam* is to *hot* as _____ is to *cold*.

Word Categories

Read each group of words below. Write the word that does not belong with the rest.

6. fertile, barren, empty _____

7. sensible, idle, practical _____

8. natural, imitation, artificial _____

9. example, social, sample _____

10. local, global, international _____

Challenge Words • *Math* --------------------------------

Write the challenge word that best completes each sentence. Use the **Spelling Dictionary** on page 214 to help you. Circle the spelling of /əl/ in each word.

11. The opposite of *horizontal* is _____.

12. Four is a _____ of two.

13. The new software is _____ with my computer.

14. A _____ line made two triangles out of a square.

15. *First, second,* and *third* are _____ numbers.

multiple
ordinal
vertical
compatible
diagonal

Spelling Tip

The letter *c* can be pronounced in different ways.

✦ The letter *c* usually is pronounced /s/ when it comes before *i, e,* or *y* (examples: *pencil, celery,* and *cycle*).

✦ It is usually pronounced /k/ before *a* or *o* (as in *local* or *coupon*).

✦ It may be pronounced /sh/ in word endings such as *-cial* (as in *social*), *-cian* (as in *magician*), or *-cious* (as in *delicious*).

List Words

material
tickle
natural
idle
signal
panel
official
cradle
pencil
fertile
article
icicle
nostril
fatal
cycle
social
local
practical
sample
funnel

Challenge Words

multiple
ordinal
vertical
compatible
diagonal

Review Words

puzzle
special
tunnel
council
syllable

Build Vocabulary

Related Words

■ How are these words similar in spelling and meaning?

totality   total

Say each word and listen to the sound of the letter *a*. How does the pronunciation of the *a* in *totality* help you spell the /ə/ in *total*?

Write the word ending in /əl/ that you see in each word below. Then circle the letter in the longer word that helps you spell the /ə/ sound in the word you wrote. Use the **Spelling Dictionary** on page 214 to help you.

1. locality   _____   3. practicality   _____

2. fatality   _____   4. generality   _____

Review Words

Write the review words that have /əl/ spelled with the letters below.

el 5. _____   **le** 7. _____

il 6. _____   8. _____

Write the review word that has /shəl/ spelled with the letters below.

cial 9. _____

Look at each list word below. Write the review word or words that have the same spelling of /əl/ or /shəl/.

10. funnel   _____   12. nostril   _____

11. social   _____

puzzle
special
tunnel
council
syllable

TAKE HOME

Write your spelling words in three lists: two-, three-, and four-syllable words. Circle the spelling of /əl/ or /shəl/ in each word. Use your lists to practice at home.

Apply Spelling Skills

Dictionary Skills

When dividing a word at the end of a line of writing, you should divide it between two syllables. The dictionary can show you how. Dots in the entry words—like those below—show where the word is divided into syllables.

sig • nal   ter • ri • ble

Write each word below with spaces between the syllables. Use the **Spelling Dictionary** on page 214 to check your work.

1. material _____
2. cycle _____
3. funnel _____
4. sample _____

5. tickle _____
6. official _____
7. signal _____
8. panel _____

Pattern Power

Look at the list words you just wrote.

- Circle the letters in each word that spell /əl/ or /shəl/.

Proofreading

Check spelling, capital letters, and punctuation. Then rewrite the paragraph. There are six mistakes.

> Math has many practicle uses It is the nacheral way to spot a good buy, check your change, share a pie, or understand a science artical. usually you do not even need a pencel.

Writing • About Math

PREWRITE: Think of the last time you used math in your everyday life. Jot down a few details about how and why.

DRAFT: Write a paragraph about your experience.

REVISE: Did you include details? Is your paragraph entertaining? Use the **Spelling Thesaurus** on page 182 as you revise.

EDIT/PROOFREAD: Use editing marks. Then rewrite your paragraph.

PUBLISH: Publish your paragraph by sending it to a friend in a letter.

EDITING MARKS

⬯ **check spelling**
= **capital letter**
/ **lowercase letter**
⊙ **add a period**
∧ **add**
⋏ **take out**
⁋ **indent the paragraph**
↻ **move**

For more help, see page 171.

11

WORDS WITH /ən/ and /ər/

PHONICS PATTERNS

1. shorten
2. eraser
3. melon
4. urban
5. rotten
6. actor
7. chapter
8. bother
9. bitter
10. thunder
11. mistaken
12. pedestrian
13. given
14. major
15. carbon
16. linen
17. hangar
18. officer
19. cedar
20. dungeon

Learn Spelling Patterns

LOOK & SAY Listen for the sounds in each word.

PICTURE Close your eyes. See each word in your mind.

STUDY These spelling words have /ən/ or /ər/.

WRITE Sort the words. Which words have /ən/ spelled with the letters below?

en (1)___ (2)___ (3)___ (4)___ (5)___
an (6)___ (7)___
on (8)___ (9)___ (10)___

Which words have /ər/ spelled with the letters below?

ar (11)___ (12)___
or (13)___ (14)___
er (15)___ (16)___ (17)___
   (18)___ (19)___ (20)___

CHECK Did you spell each word correctly? Circle the letters that spell /ən/ or /ər/.

Pattern Power

How can /ən/ be spelled?

(21)___ or (22)___ or (23)___

How is /ər/ spelled in most words? (24)___ or (25)___ or (26)___

Other Words

Write words you would like to add to this week's list.

_____ _____ _____ _____ _____

Practice Word Meanings

Context Sentences

Write the spelling word that best completes each sentence below.

1. The _____ under the castle was dark and cold.

2. We were _____ ten minutes to finish our project.

3. I read the third _____ of my library book last night.

4. My grandmother brought us a _____ tablecloth from Ireland.

5. When I heard the _____, I grabbed my umbrella from the closet.

6. That plum can't be ripe since it tastes so _____.

7. I tried to _____ the dog's leash by knotting it.

8. The bird made a nest in the trunk of an old _____.

9. We planted three different kinds of _____.

Challenge Words • Social Studies

Write the challenge word that best answers each question. Use the **Spelling Dictionary** on page 214 to help you. Circle the spelling of /ən/ or /ər/ in each word.

10. What is a way to defy authority? _____

11. What is a form of energy? _____

12. What is a severe decline in the economy? _____

13. What is a ruler who has absolute power? _____

14. What is a government run by an absolute ruler? _____

depression
dictator
rebellion
nuclear
totalitarian

Spelling Tip

Some beginning sounds can be spelled more than one way. Knowing the different spellings can help you use the dictionary to find out how to spell a word. For example, /s/ at the beginning of a word can be spelled *s* or *c*.

Here's a hint to help you decide between *cedar* or *sedar*:

✦ Look up a word that starts with /s/ under *s*.

✦ If you don't find it, try *c*.

shorten

eraser

melon

urban

rotten

actor

chapter

bother

bitter

thunder

mistaken

pedestrian

given

major

carbon

linen

hangar

officer

cedar

dungeon

Challenge Words

depression

dictator

rebellion

nuclear

totalitarian

Review Words

pardon

foreign

discover

beggar

flavor

Build Vocabulary

Base Words

■ Each word below was formed by adding the suffix *-er*, *-ar*, *-or*, or *-en* to a base word. Write the base word for each word. Some words with suffixes may have doubled a consonant or dropped the final *e*.

1. actor _____

2. eraser _____

3. mistaken _____

4. officer _____

5. shorten _____

6. rotten _____

■ Use a word with a suffix from above and its base word to complete each sentence.

7. Use the pink _____ to _____ your mistakes.

8. That _____ taught many students how to _____.

Review Words

Write the review words that have /ən/ spelled with the letters below.

on 9. _____ **eign** 10. _____

Write the review words that have /ər/ spelled with these letters.

ar 11. _____ **er** 13. _____

or 12. _____

pardon
foreign
discover
beggar
flavor

T A K E H O M E

Write your spelling words in three lists: nouns, verbs, and adjectives. Some words may appear on more than one list. Circle the spelling of /ən/ or /ər/ in each word. Use your lists to practice at home.

Apply Spelling Skills

Thesaurus Skills

When you write, a **thesaurus** can help you avoid using the same words over and over. Use your **Spelling Thesaurus** to find a synonym for each spelling word below. Then write a sentence using the synonym you found.

1. major   _____

2. bother   _____

3. pedestrian   _____

4. mistaken   _____

Proofreading

Check spelling, capital letters, and punctuation. Then rewrite the paragraph. There are six mistakes.

> In a majer urbin area, dont bother to take a taxi during rush hour. You'll get there faster as a pidestrian Of course, you may suffer carban monoxide poisoning on the way!

EDITING MARKS

  ◯ check spelling

  = capital letter

  / lowercase letter

  ⊙ add a period

  ∧ add

  ⌿ take out

  ⌗ indent the paragraph

  ↺ move

For more help, see page 171.

Writing • *About Social Studies*

PREWRITE: Write down some advantages and disadvantages of living in a city.

DRAFT: Write a paragraph describing one really great—or really bad—thing about city life.

REVISE: Did you illustrate your ideas with specific examples? Use the **Spelling Thesaurus** on page 182 as you revise.

EDIT/PROOFREAD: Use editing marks. Then rewrite your paragraph.

PUBLISH: Set up a class debate for and against city living, and read your paragraph.

12 REVIEW Spelling Patterns

Sort the words in each list. Write each word. Circle the spelling pattern.

nor	**Lesson 7**		
ignore	**Words with /ô/ spelled**		**Words with /ôr/ spelled**
laundry	au	1. _____	our	6. _____
install		2. _____	or	7. _____
dawn	aw	3. _____		8. _____
faucet	a	4. _____	ore	9. _____
afford	ough	5. _____	orr	10. _____
mourn				
thoughtless				
horrible				

(Lesson 7 word list: nor, ignore, laundry, install, dawn, faucet, afford, mourn, thoughtless, horrible)

urgent	**Lesson 8**		
workout	**Words with /ûr/ spelled**		**Words with /îr/ spelled**
mere	ear	11. _____	ere	18. _____
nourish	er	12. _____	ier	19. _____
nerve		13. _____	eer	20. _____
rehearse	ur	14. _____		
journal	or	15. _____		
pioneer	our	16. _____		
permit		17. _____		
pierce				

(Lesson 8 word list: urgent, workout, mere, nourish, nerve, rehearse, journal, pioneer, permit, pierce)

careless	**Lesson 9**		
farewell	**Words with /är/ spelled**		**Words with /âr/ spelled**
charm	uar	21. _____	are	26. _____
nowhere	ar	22. _____		27. _____
artist		23. _____		28. _____
regard		24. _____	ere	29. _____
despair	er	25. _____	air	30. _____
aware				
guard				
sergeant				

(Lesson 9 word list: careless, farewell, charm, nowhere, artist, regard, despair, aware, guard, sergeant)

natural
panel
official
pencil
fertile
article
nostril
practical
sample
funnel

Lesson 10

Words with /əl/ spelled

ile 31. _____

le   32. _____

33. _____

al   34. _____

35. _____

il   36. _____

37. _____

el   38. _____

39. _____

Words with /shəl/ spelled

cial 40. _____

melon
urban
actor
chapter
thunder
mistaken
pedestrian
given
hangar
dungeon

Lesson 11

Words with /ən/ spelled

on 41. _____

42. _____

an 43. _____

44. _____

en 45. _____

46. _____

Words with /ər/ spelled

er 47. _____

48. _____

or 49. _____

ar 50. _____

dungeon
guard
rehearse
fertile

pelling Tip

Sometimes sounds are spelled with unusual letter combinations. You can use your Word Study Steps to help you memorize hard-to-spell words like *dungeon*, *guard*, *rehearse*, and *fertile*.

✦ Repeat the Word Study Steps for these words until you have spelled each one successfully.

✦ Work with a partner. Quiz each other on hard-to-spell words.

Word Meaning Mixed Lesson Review

dawn
faucet
workout
actor
fertile

Analogies
Write spelling words to complete the analogies below.

1. *Dusk* is to *evening* as ____ is to *morning*.

2. *Ripe* is to *apple* as ____ is to *soil*.

3. *Dancer* is to *ballet* as ____ is to *movie*.

4. *Shelf* is to *carpenter* as ____ is to *plumber*.

5. *Dinner* is to *restaurant* as ____ is to *gym*.

mourn
permit
nowhere
farewell
guard
urban
dungeon

Synonyms and Antonyms
Write the spelling word that is a synonym (S) or an antonym (A) for each word below.

6. everywhere   (A)   ____

7. license   (S)   ____

8. protect   (S)   ____

9. rejoice   (A)   ____

10. prison   (S)   ____

11. good-bye   (S)   ____

12. rural   (A)   ____

install
afford
rehearse
pierce
sergeant
funnel
hangar

Context Sentences
Write a spelling word to complete each sentence below.

13. The actors got together to ____ the play.

14. My cousin is a ____ in the army.

15. Do you have enough money to ____ that sweater?

16. Tomorrow, the workers will ____ the new cabinets.

17. The pilot returned the airplane to the ____.

18. ____ the meat with a fork to see whether it is done.

19. Use a ____ to pour the water into the jar.

Vocabulary Mixed Lesson Review

Word Endings

■ Add *-er* or *-ing* to the words below. You may have to drop the final *e* before adding the ending.

er	ing
1. sample ____	3. thunder ____
2. charm ____	4. ignore ____

■ Add *-ly* to each adjective below to form an adverb.

5. mistaken ____

6. practical ____

7. natural ____

■ Each word below was formed by adding the suffix *-less* or *-ist* to a base word. Write the base word for each.

8. thoughtless ____

9. artist ____

10. careless ____

Dictionary Skills

■ Write the spelling word that would appear on a dictionary page having each pair of guide words listed below.

1. neon/nice ____	3. mend/met ____
2. meet/melt ____	4. notice/now ____

■ Write the spelling word that matches the given sound symbol. Use the pronunciation key in the **Spelling Dictionary** on p. 214 to help you.

5. /ôr/ laundry, nor ____

6. /âr/ regard, despair ____

7. /shəl/ official, nostril ____

mere

nourish

nerve

melon

Spelling and Writing

When writing a campaign speech, a candidate might use comparison and contrast to explain why he or she is a better choice than the other candidates.

SUBJECT OF COMPARISON

As you are probably aware, the class election is a mere two days away. I hope you won't vote carelessly. Let me explain why the natural choice for class president is Lisa! José and Lisa are both good students. And José does some really cool things, like writing great articles for the school paper. But Lisa has the leadership experience that José lacks. Last year, she was secretary of our fifth grade class. And she is now the president of the Artists' Club. José has never held an office. If you want a president who *really* knows what she's doing, vote for Lisa!

DETAILS SHOW SIMILARITIES OR DIFFERENCES

WRITING TIPS!!

Comparison and Contrast

- Name subjects to be compared and contrasted.
- Use details about each subject.
- Present details about one and then the other. Or present a topic and then a related detail from each subject.
- Include reasons to persuade your reader or listener why one is better than the other.

Now write your own campaign speech, comparing and contrasting two candidates (real or made up) for class president.

PREWRITE: List the ways the candidates are alike and the ways they are different.

DRAFT: Write a short speech explaining why your candidate is the better choice. Use the items you listed to support your point of view.

REVISE: Did you use persuasive language? Did you use logical arguments?

PROOFREAD: Use editing marks to correct your capitalization, spelling, and punctuation. Rewrite your speech neatly.

PUBLISH: Give your speech during a class speech day.

SPELLING FUN
CUMULATIVE REVIEW

- Choose at least three or four words from Lessons 1–5 that start with the same letter.
- Write a tongue twister that includes the spelling words you chose.
- Illustrate and publish your tongue twister.
- Do as many as you like. Start a class collection.

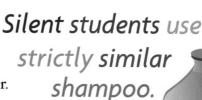

Silent students use strictly similar shampoo.

PLAY BEETLE

- Choose a long word (at least seven letters) from any list in Lessons 7–11.
- To begin, draw a circle. This is your beetle's body. Write the spelling pattern for your word in the center of the circle.
- Next to the beetle make one blank for each letter of your word.

- Your partner names a letter. If it is in your word, fill in the correct blank. If not, add a leg or antenna to the beetle. Your partner tries to complete the word before you complete the beetle's six legs and two antennae.
- When you're done, switch roles.

SPELLING BEE

- Two teams share the job of writing 40 words from Lessons 1–11 on cards. Each team gets half the cards.
- The first player on Team A calls out a word.
- The first player on Team B writes the word on the chalkboard or on a piece of paper.

- If the word is spelled correctly, the card is taken out of the pile. If not, the card is returned to the pile.
- The next Team B player then calls out the next word for the next Team A player. Continue on.
- The first team to finish the other team's pile of cards wins.

13

WORDS WITH /ou/ and /oi/

PHONICS PATTERNS

1. decoy
2. bound
3. oyster
4. account
5. counter
6. boycott
7. towel
8. moisture
9. coward
10. void
11. background
12. corduroy
13. employer
14. poise
15. vowel
16. blouse
17. browse
18. loiter
19. pouch
20. rowdy

Learn Spelling Patterns

LOOK & SAY Listen for the sounds in each word.

PICTURE Close your eyes. See each word in your mind.

STUDY These spelling words have /ou/ and /oi/.

WRITE Sort the words. Which words have /ou/ spelled with the letters below?

ou (1)___ (2)___ (3)___
(4)___ (5)___ (6)___

ow (7)___ (8)___ (9)___
(10)___ (11)___

Which words have /oi/ spelled with the letters below?

oy (12)___ (13)___ (14)___
(15)___ (16)___

oi (17)___ (18)___ (19)___ (20)___

CHECK Did you spell each word correctly? Circle the letters that stand for /ou/ or /oi/.

Pattern Power

How is /oi/ usually spelled in the middle of a word or syllable? (21)___ How is /oi/ usually spelled at the end of a word or syllable? (22)___ How can /ou/ be spelled? (23)___ or (24)___

Other Words

Write words you would like to add to this week's list.

___ ___ ___ ___ ___

Practice Word Meanings

Words in Context

Write the spelling word that best completes each sentence.

1. Dorothy called the lion a _____ because he was always afraid.

2. A _____ can be worn under a vest or a sweater.

3. James used a _____ to wipe up the spill.

Synonyms and Antonyms

Write the spelling word that is a synonym or an antonym for each word below. Then write *synonym* or *antonym* after the word.

4. empty _____ _____

5. bag _____ _____

6. dryness _____ _____

7. awkwardness _____ _____

8. lure _____ _____

Challenge Words • *Math*

Write the challenge word that fits each definition. Use the **Spelling Dictionary** on page 214 to help you. Circle the spelling of /ou/ or /oi/.

9. the money that is taken off the regular price _____

10. the amount of something that is produced _____

11. a four-sided figure that has two parallel sides _____

12. a list of items and their prices _____

13. the number after 999th _____

invoice
discount
trapezoid
thousandth
output

Spelling Tip

A small word can help you build larger words that are related in spelling and meaning.

✦ These words are related to the small word *count:*

en	+	count	+	er	=	encounter
dis	+	count	=			discount
re	+	count	+	ed	=	recounted

What spelling words can you find that contain the word *count?*

decoy
bound
oyster
account
counter
boycott
towel
moisture
coward
void
background
corduroy
employer
poise
vowel
blouse
browse
loiter
pouch
rowdy

Challenge Words

invoice
discount
trapezoid
thousandth
output

Review Words

couch
enjoyable
hoist
howl
announce

Build Vocabulary

Suffixes

■ The suffix -*er* sometimes means "one who does something."

drive + **er** = driver

Write the list words that have the suffix -*er.*

1. _____   2. _____

Add -*er* to the words below. You may have to drop the final *e.*

3. boycott _____   5. loiter _____

4. browse _____

■ Use words you made to complete these sentences.

6. He was a _____ who enjoyed spending hours in bookstores.

7. The _____ was always hanging around in front of the store.

Review Words

Write the review words that have /ou/ spelled with the letters below.

ou   8. _____   **ow**   10. _____

9. _____

Write the review words that have /oi/ spelled with the letters below.

oi   11. _____   **oy**   12. _____

Write the review word that rhymes with each list word below.

13. pouch _____

14. vowel _____

couch
enjoyable
hoist
howl
announce

TAKE HOME

Write your words in three lists: words with one, two, and three syllables. Circle the spelling of /ou/ or /oi/ in each word. Use your lists to practice at home.

56

Apply Spelling Skills

Dictionary Skills

The syllable division of an entry word shows how to divide a word at the end of a line. When you divide a word, use a **hyphen (-)** to show that the rest of the word will follow on the next line. Look up each word in the **Spelling Dictionary** on page 214. Write the words with hyphens to show where the words could be divided.

1. corduroy ____
2. background ____
3. vowel ____
4. account ____
5. moisture ____

6. bound ____
7. rowdy ____
8. void ____
9. oyster ____
10. counter ____

Pattern Power

Look at the words you just wrote.

- Circle the letters that spell /ou/ or /oi/ in each word.

Proofreading

Proofread the paragraph. Use editing marks. Check spelling, capital letters, and punctuation. Then rewrite the paragraph. There are six mistakes.

> My new emploir has a backgrownd in math and is very successful in his accounting business. he encourages me to brouse through his library. I admire his poize with customers

Writing • About Math

PREWRITE: List some businesses that require a knowledge of math.

DRAFT: Choose one business. Write a Help Wanted ad that explains what skills you need to work in that business.

REVISE: Did you explain the skills in a clear, concise way? Did you relate the skill to the business? Use the **Spelling Thesaurus** on page 182 as you revise.

EDIT/PROOFREAD: Use editing marks. Then rewrite your ad.

PUBLISH: Contribute your ad to a class Help Wanted section.

EDITING MARKS

⬭ check spelling
≡ capital letter
／ lowercase letter
⊙ add a period
∧ add
⌔ take out
⌗ indent the paragraph
↷ move

For more help, see page 171.

14

Consonant Sounds; Silent *gh*

PHONICS PATTERNS

1. character
2. frighten
3. chemical
4. moonlight
5. quietly
6. symphony
7. request
8. quality
9. chorus
10. autograph
11. banquet
12. quarrel
13. drought
14. phrase
15. chord
16. require
17. orchestra
18. chrome
19. photo
20. doughnut

Learn Spelling Patterns

LOOK & SAY Listen for the sounds in each word.

PICTURE Close your eyes. See each word in your mind.

STUDY These spelling words have /k/ spelled *ch*, /kw/ spelled *qu*, /f/ spelled *ph*, or silent *gh*.

WRITE Sort the words. Which words have these sounds?

/k/ (1) (2) (3)
    (4) (5) (6)

/kw/ (7) (8) (9)
     (10) (11) (12)

/f/ (13) (14)
    (15) (16)

Which words have the silent letters *gh*?

(17) (18) (19) (20)

CHECK Did you spell each word correctly? Circle /k/ spelled *ch*, /kw/ spelled *qu*, /f/ spelled *ph*, or the silent letters *gh*.

Pattern Power

Which two consonants can spell /k/? (21)

How can /kw/ be spelled? (22) Which two consonants can spell /f/? (23)

Other Words

Write words you would like to add to this week's list.

_____ _____ _____ _____ _____

Practice Word Meanings

Greek Roots

The root word *graph* comes from the Greek *graphos*, which means "written or writing." *Graph* also means "a machine that writes or records." Write the list word that contains *graph*.

1. _____

Add the root *graph* to these words. *Photo*, from the Greek *photos*, means "light," and *phon*, from the Greek *phonos* means "sound." You may have to drop a final *e* and add an *o*.

2. photo _____   3. phone _____

Analogies

Write the spelling words that complete the analogies below.

4. *Sunshine* is to *day* as _____ is to *night*.

5. *Monsoon* is to *wet* as _____ is to *dry.*

6. *Limb* is to *tree* as _____ is to *sentence*.

7. *Trim* is to a *shirt* as _____ is to a *car*.

Challenge Words • Art

Write the challenge word that best completes each sentence below. Use the **Spelling Dictionary** on page 214 to help you. Circle the spelling of /k/, /kw/, or /f/ or the silent letters *gh*.

8. The four musicians perform together as a _____.

9. The _____ sang at the New Year's celebration.

10. The _____ to the novel is as good as the first book.

11. The photographer's _____ casts shadows.

12. She will _____ a ballet for the grand opening.

sequel
quartet
choreograph
choir
lighting

Spelling Tip

The history of the parts of a word can help you remember how to spell the word.

✦ The word *autograph* is made up of two Greek roots.
✦ The root *auto* means "self."
✦ The root *graph* means "writing."
✦ The word *autograph* means "a person's own writing."

Knowing Greek and Latin roots will help you spell and understand many words.

character
frighten
chemical
moonlight
quietly
symphony
request
quality
chorus
autograph
banquet
quarrel
drought
phrase
chord
require
orchestra
chrome
photo
doughnut

sequel
quartet
choreograph
choir
lighting

equipment
trophy
gopher
brighten
bough

Build Vocabulary

Suffixes

■ The suffix *-ic* means "of, relating to, or like."
■ The suffix *-al* means "of, relating to, or characterized by."
■ The suffix *-some* means "characterized by" or "tending to be."

athlete + **ic** = athletic

music + **al** = musical

trouble + **some** = troublesome

Add the given suffix to each base word below. You may have to make some base-word spelling changes.

Base Word		Suffix	New Word
1. artist	+	ic	_____
2. bother	+	some	_____
3. orchestra	+	al	_____
4. symphony	+	ic	_____
5. quarrel	+	some	_____
6. chorus	+	al	_____

■ Use words you made to complete these sentences.

7. Her drawings showed her _____ talent.

8. The long test had made him tired and _____.

Review Words

Write the review words that have /kw/ or /f/ spelled with the letters below.

qu 9. _____

ph 10. _____ 11. _____

Write the review words that have the silent letters *gh*.

12. _____ 13. _____

equipment
trophy
gopher
brighten
bough

Write your spelling words in alphabetical order. Circle the spelling of /k/, /kw/, or /f/ or the silent letters *gh* in each word. Use your lists to practice at home.

Apply Spelling Skills

Using the Thesaurus

Like a dictionary, a thesaurus is arranged alphabetically and uses guide words to help you locate a particular word quickly. You can use a thesaurus to expand your vocabulary. Write the spelling word or words you would find on a thesaurus page with the following guide words.

1. request/resign   ____   ____
2. central/cherish   ____   ____
3. fresh/fringe   ____
4. double/down   ____

Proofreading

Check for spelling, capital letters, and punctuation. Then rewrite the paragraph. There are six mistakes.

> The orchestra played well from the opening cord of the symphony. The Music began quitely and grew slowly to a stormy kwality. the performance was a bancquet for the ears.

Writing • *About the Arts*

PREWRITE: List some concerts, dances, photographs, or films that you have enjoyed.

DRAFT: Choose one event and write a newspaper review of it. Describe what you saw, and tell why you liked it.

REVISE: Read your review aloud to a partner. Then allow your partner to read the paragraph silently and write comments for you in a note. Use the **Spelling Thesaurus** on page 182 as you revise.

EDIT/PROOFREAD: Use editing marks. Then rewrite your work.

PUBLISH: Contribute your review to a class art review anthology.

EDITING MARKS

⬭ **check spelling**
≡ **capital letter**
／ **lowercase letter**
⊙ **add a period**
∧ **add**
ℛ **take out**
¶ **indent the paragraph**
↻ **move**

For more help, see page 171.

WORDS WITH /m/ and /n/

1. manner
2. calm
3. shown
4. lemonade
5. promise
6. drawn
7. tuna
8. knack
9. plumber
10. design
11. innocent
12. knowledge
13. annual
14. absent
15. seldom
16. become
17. numb
18. immigrant
19. condemn
20. beneath

Learn Spelling Patterns

LOOK & SAY   Listen for the sounds in each word.

PICTURE   Close your eyes. See each word in your mind.

STUDY   These spelling words have /m/ and /n/. Some of the spellings have silent consonants.

WRITE   Sort the words. Which words have /m/ or /n/ spelled with the letters below?

m	(1) (2) (3)		
	(4) (5)		
mm	(6)		
lm	(7)		
mn	(8)		
mb	(9) (10)		
nn	(11) (12) (13)		
n	(14) (15) (16)		
	(17) (18) (19) (20)		
	(21) (22) (23)		
kn	(24) (25)		
gn	(26)		

CHECK   Did you spell each word correctly? Circle the letters that stand for /m/ and /n/.

Pattern Power

How can /m/ be spelled? (27), (28), (29), (30), (31) How can /n/ be spelled? (32), (33), (34), (35)

Other Words

Write words you would like to add to this week's list.

_____ _____ _____ _____ _____

Practice Word Meanings

Words in Context

Write the spelling word that best completes each sentence.

1. The chef added _____ to her salad because her guests liked fish.
2. We couldn't play the game until we were _____ how by my brother.
3. My mother was an _____ to this country from Italy.

Analogies

Write the spelling words that complete these analogies.

4. *Sandwich* is to *eat* as _____ is to *drink*.
5. *Mechanic* is to *cars* as _____ is to *water pipes*.
6. *Frequent* is to *often* as _____ is to *rarely*.
7. *Daily* is to *day* as _____ is to *year*.
8. *Yen* is to *desire* as _____ is to *ability*.

Challenge Words • *Social Studies*

Write the challenge word that is an antonym for each word or phrase below. Use the **Spelling Dictionary** on page 214 to help you. Circle all spellings of /m/ and /n/.

9. joyful _____
10. not in line _____
11. majority _____
12. gentleman _____
13. harm _____

minority
benefit
knave
align
solemn

Spelling Tip

Some beginning sounds can be spelled more than one way. Knowing the different spellings can help you.

For example, here's a hint to help you find a word starting with /n/ in the dictionary.

✦ Look up a word that starts with /n/ under *n*.
✦ If you don't find it, look for other spellings of /n/ in the Common Spelling Patterns list.

List Words
manner
calm
shown
lemonade
promise
drawn
tuna
knack
plumber
design
innocent
knowledge
annual
absent
seldom
become
numb
immigrant
condemn
beneath

Challenge Words

minority
benefit
knave
align
solemn

Review Words

plum
banner
palm
known
column

Build Vocabulary

Suffixes

■ The suffix *-ly* can change an adjective to an adverb.
It means "in a particular way."

quiet	quiet**ly**

Add *-ly* to the list words below.

1. numb   _____

2. calm   _____

3. innocent _____

4. absent   _____

5. annual   _____

■ Choose the best word to complete each sentence.

6. The guilty cat meowed _____, but there were canary
feathers between his teeth.

7. The girl spoke _____ despite the danger.

Review Words

Write the review words that have
/m/ or /n/ spelled with the letters below.

m   8. _____

mn 9. _____

lm 10. _____

nn 11. _____

kn 12. _____

Write the review word that is
related to the list word below.

13. knowledge   _____

plum
banner
palm
known
column

T A K E   H O M E

Write your words in three lists: words with /m/, words with /n/,
and words with both /m/ and /n/. Circle all spellings of /m/
and /n/. Use your lists to practice at home.

Apply Spelling Skills

Dictionary Skills

Look at the dictionary entry below.

an•nu•al (an′ū əl) *adj.* **1.** relating to or measured by the year.

The **respelling** of an entry word shows how the word is pronounced. The respelling is written in syllables with the sound symbols used in the pronunciation key. The **accent mark (′)** shows that the syllable before the accent is stressed.

Write the list words for the respellings below. Use the **Spelling Dictionary** on page 214 to help you.

1. nol′ij   _____
2. kən dem′   _____
3. man′ər   _____
4. di zīn′   _____

Pattern Power

Look at the words you just wrote.

- Circle the letters that spell /m/ and /n/.

Proofreading

Check spelling, capital letters, and punctuation. Then rewrite the paragraph. There are six mistakes.

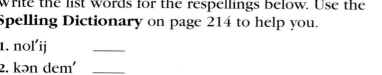

> For three centuries, people have been draun to America, the land of promis. Millions have sailed to New york and passed beneeth the Statue of liberty, hoping to bacome Americans.

Writing • *About Social Studies*

PREWRITE: List some ways in which immigration has affected the ways Americans eat, dress, speak, work, or play.

DRAFT: Write a short report about the ways in which immigration has shaped American life.

REVISE: Did you present your ideas logically?

EDIT/PROOFREAD: Use editing marks. Then rewrite your work.

PUBLISH: Include your writing in an American Way display.

EDITING MARKS

◯ check spelling

≡ capital letter

／ lowercase letter

⊙ add a period

∧ add

✄ take out

indent the paragraph

◌ move

For more help, see page 171.

16

/sh/, /ch/, and /chər/

PHONICS PATTERNS

1. chestnut
2. shade
3. furnish
4. sheet
5. foolish
6. shallow
7. starch
8. partial
9. venture
10. lecture
11. parachute
12. chandelier
13. shelter
14. impatient
15. creature
16. approach
17. marshal
18. charity
19. chef
20. feature

Learn Spelling Patterns

LOOK & SAY Listen for the sounds in each word.

PICTURE Close your eyes. See each word in your mind.

STUDY These spelling words have /sh/, /ch/, and /chər/.

WRITE Sort the words. Which words have /sh/ spelled with the letters below?

sh (1) (2) (3)
(4) (5) (6) (7)

ti (8) (9)

ch (10) (11) (12)

Which words have /ch/, or /chər/ spelled as below?

ch (13) (14) (15) (16)
ture (17) (18) (19) (20)

CHECK Did you spell each word correctly? Circle the letters that stand for /sh/, /ch/, and /chər/.

Pattern Power

How can /sh/ be spelled? (21) or (22) or (23) How is /ch/ usually spelled? (24) How can /chər/ be spelled? (25)

Other Words

Write words you would like to add to this week's list.

_____ _____ _____ _____ _____

Practice Word Meanings

Riddles

Write the spelling words that solve these riddles.

1. I hang from a ceiling, and have many lights. ____
2. I am given to people who are in need. ____
3. I am an officer who works for a city or town. ____
4. I am what you do when you come near. ____
5. I am a cloth to cover your mattress. ____
6. I float people down gently from airplanes. ____
7. I am a little silly. ____
8. I am an expert on cooking. ____
9. I am used to make clothing stiff. ____
10. I am what you do when you buy furniture. ____

Challenge Words • Health

Write the challenge word that can be included in each group of words below. Use the **Spelling Dictionary** on page 214 to help you. Circle the spelling of /sh/, /ch/, and /chər/.

11. manicure, shampoo, grooming ____
12. twitch, quiver, shake ____
13. blend, mix, compound ____
14. renew, refill, refresh ____
15. degrees, Celsius, thermometer ____

mixture
facial
replenish
temperature
shiver

pelling Tip

Sometimes a word has a spelling that you do not expect because it comes from another language. Usually /sh/ at the beginning of a word is spelled *sh*.

✦ The word *chandelier* comes from the French language.
✦ In many English words that come from French, /sh/ is spelled with *ch* at the beginning of the word.

Some other words from French that follow this spelling pattern are *chauffeur* and *chaperone*.

Build Vocabulary

Related Words

■ You have learned that related words are similar in spelling and meaning. Knowing how to pronounce one of the words can help you spell the other word. In the list word *lecture*, the letters *ture* are pronounced /chər/. In the related word *lectern*, the letter *t* is pronounced /t/.

lecture   **lect**ern

Write the list word that is related to each word below. Circle the letter in the shorter word that helps you spell /ch/ or /sh/ in the list word.

1. part   _____

2. feat   _____

3. create   _____

■ Use words you wrote to complete these sentences.

4. Air bags are a _____ of many new cars.

5. The moon is not completely covered by the sun's shadow in a _____ eclipse.

Review Words

Write the review words that have the sounds below.

/sh/   6. _____

7. _____

/ch/   8. _____

9. _____

/chər/ 10. _____

Write the review word you see in the list word below.

11. impatient   _____

manufacture
stitch
patient
shine
orchard

TAKE HOME

Write your spelling words in three lists: words with /sh/, words with /ch/, and words with /chər/. Circle the spelling of /sh/, /ch/, or /chər/ in each word. Use your lists to practice at home.

Apply Spelling Skills

Dictionary Skills

Write the spelling word for each respelling below.

1. shād ____
2. im pā′shənt ____
3. par′ə shüt′ ____
4. lek′chər ____
5. fē′chər ____
6. shel′tər ____
7. ches′nut ____
8. shal′ō ____

Pattern Power

Look at the words you just wrote.

- Circle the letters that spell /sh/, /ch/, or /chər/ in each word.

Proofreading

Check spelling, capital letters, and punctuation. Then rewrite the paragraph. There are six mistakes.

> My sister's fever began to approche 103 degrees. she took sheleter under a sheat and a pile of blankets. We brought her juice and soup Finally she was able to venchure out.

EDITING MARKS

⬭	check spelling
≡	capital letter
/	lowercase letter
⊙	add a period
∧	add
✗	take out
¶	indent the paragraph
⟳	move

For more help, see page 171.

Writing • *About Health*

PREWRITE: Make notes about steps people can take to prevent illness.

DRAFT: Create an informative and persuasive poster that convinces your schoolmates to follow your instructions for preventing illnesses.

REVISE: Did you offer specific suggestions? Illustrate your poster with drawings and magazine cutouts.

EDIT/PROOFREAD: Double-check spelling and punctuation.

PUBLISH: Hang your poster in the school lunchroom.

Consonant Clusters

PHONICS PATTERNS

1. mist
2. instrument
3. skyscraper
4. risk
5. stomach
6. steam
7. crept
8. scatter
9. fled
10. crust
11. skillful
12. modest
13. tramp
14. sparrow
15. scholar
16. tremble
17. trial
18. scald
19. threat
20. stress

Learn Spelling Patterns

LOOK & SAY Listen for the sounds in each word.

PICTURE Close your eyes. See each word in your mind.

STUDY These spelling words contain consonant clusters. Some have /sk/ spelled *sch, sc,* or *sk*; others contain *st, tr, cr, str, fl, sp, thr,* or *scr.*

WRITE Sort the words. Which words begin or end with /sk/ spelled with the letters below?

sch   (1)

sc   (2) (3)

sk   (4) (5) (6)

Which words have the consonant clusters below anywhere in the word?

st   (7) (8) (9) (10) (11)

tr   (12) (13) (14)

cr   (15) (16)

str   (17) (18)

fl   (19)

sp   (20)

thr   (21)

scr   (22)

CHECK Did you spell each word correctly? Circle the consonant clusters.

Pattern Power

How can /sk/ be spelled? (23)

or (24) or (25) A consonant cluster can be

made up of how many letters? (26)

Other Words

Write words you would like to add to this week's list.

_____ _____ _____ _____ _____

Practice Word Meanings

Context Words

Write the spelling word that best completes
each sentence below.

1. The scout _____ silently through the dark forest.

2. A _____ carpenter made that fine cabinet.

3. Don't _____ your hand on the boiling water.

4. The _____ is the tallest building downtown.

5. The thief _____ from the scene of the crime.

6. Deadlines and high expectations can cause _____.

7. Twelve people were on the jury for the _____.

Challenge Words • *Science*

Write the challenge word that fits each definition below.
Use the **Spelling Dictionary** on page 214 to help you.
Circle the spelling of /sk/ or the consonant cluster *tr, fl, sp,*
or *thr* in each word.

8. a young bird _____

9. the valve that regulates the flow of fuel to an engine

_____

10. relating to the structural part of the body _____

11. dealing with electricity _____

12. having a strong, rugged appearance _____

skeletal
fledgling
muscular
electrical
throttle

Spelling Tip

Usually /sk/ at the beginning of a word is spelled *sc* or *sk*. In
such words as *school* or *scholar*, /sk/ is spelled *sch*. Here are two
ways to help you remember the spelling of these.

✦ The beginning of **ch**ild can be found in s**ch**ool.

✦ The words *school* and *scholar* have the same beginning spelling
of /sk/.

List Words

mist
instrument
skyscraper
risk
stomach
steam
crept
scatter
fled
crust
skillful
modest
tramp
sparrow
scholar
tremble
trial
scald
threat
stress

Challenge Words

skeletal
fledgling
muscular
electrical
throttle

Review Words

treatment
flight
strength
scheme
sprang

Build Vocabulary

Suffixes

■ The suffix -*y* can change a noun to an adjective. It means "full of," "like," or "inclined to."

shade + **y** = shady

Add -*y* to the list words below.

1. mist ____

2. risk ____

3. crust ____

4. steam ____

5. dust ____

■ Use words you made to complete these sentences.

6. The chef decided that her new recipe made the bread too ____.

7. Crossing a busy street can be ____.

Review Words

Write the review word that contains each consonant cluster below.

sch **8.** ____

tr **9.** ____

str **10.** ____

fl **11.** ____

spr **12.** ____

treatment
flight
strength
scheme
sprang

TAKE HOME

Write your words in alphabetical order. Circle the spelling of /sk/ or the consonant cluster *st, tr, cr, str, fl, sp, thr,* or *scr* in each word. Use your lists to practice at home.

Apply Spelling Skills

Dictionary Skills

Look up the entry for *skillful* in your **Spelling Dictionary**. At the end of the entry, you will notice a dash followed by the word *skillfully*. This is called a **run-on entry**. It shows you another form of the entry word. The run-on entry has a label to show its part of speech. Use the **Spelling Dictionary** to find the run-on entries for these words. Write the first run-on entry and its part of speech.

1. modest ____ ____
2. tremble ____ ____
3. scatter ____ ____
4. tramp ____ ____

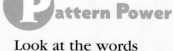

Pattern Power

Look at the words you just wrote.
- Circle the spelling of /sk/.
- Circle the consonant clusters *st* and *tr*.

Proofreading

Check spelling, capital letters, and punctuation. Then rewrite the paragraph. There are six mistakes.

A science scolar spoke about the sparow. This small brown bird fills its stumick with seeds and insects. hawks are a thret to it. Its song is unmatched by any musical insterment.

EDITING MARKS

⬯ check spelling
= capital letter
/ lowercase letter
⊙ add a period
∧ add
✀ take out
¶ indent the paragraph
↻ move

For more help, see page 171.

Writing • *About Science*

PREWRITE: Some animals have features that people don't. What animal features would you like to have? Write your ideas.

DRAFT: Write a descriptive paragraph that tells what you would like and why. Add a sketch of your ideal person.

REVISE: Did you present your ideas in a logical order?

EDIT/PROOFREAD: Use editing marks. Then rewrite your paragraph.

PUBLISH: Present your paragraph and sketch to the class.

18 REVIEW Spelling Patterns

Sort the words in each list. Write each word. Circle the spelling pattern.

decoy	**Lesson 13**
account	**Words with /ou/ spelled** **Words with /oi/ spelled**
counter	
towel	ou 1. _____ oy 7. _____
void	2. _____ 8. _____
background	3. _____ oi 9. _____
corduroy	4. _____ 10. _____
poise	ow 5. _____
vowel	6. _____
pouch	

character	**Lesson 14**
moonlight	**Words with /kw/ spelled** **Words with /f/ spelled**
quietly	qu 11. _____ ph 17. _____
symphony	12. _____ 18. _____
quality	13. _____ **Words with the silent letters**
quarrel	14. _____
drought	**Words with /k/ spelled** gh 19. _____
chord	ch 15. _____ 20. _____
require	16. _____
photo	

manner	**Lesson 15**
calm	**Write the words in alphabetical order. Circle all spellings of /m/ and /n/.**
drawn	
plumber	21. _____ 26. _____
design	22. _____ 27. _____
innocent	23. _____ 28. _____
knowledge	24. _____ 29. _____
immigrant	25. _____ 30. _____
condemn	
beneath	

chestnut	**Lesson 16**
shade	**Words with /ch/ spelled**
foolish	ch 31. _____
partial	32. _____
venture	
parachute	**Words with /chər/ spelled**
chandelier	ture 33. _____
impatient	34. _____
approach	
feature	

Words with /sh/ spelled

ch 35. _____

36. _____

ti 37. _____

38. _____

sh 39. _____

40. _____

mist	**Lesson 17**
instrument	**Words with /sk/ spelled**
skyscraper	
risk	sch 41. _____
fled	sc 42. _____
sparrow	sk 43. _____
scholar	44. _____
trial	
scald	
threat	

Words with these clusters

st 45. _____

tr 46. _____

str 47. _____

fl 48. _____

sp 49. _____

thr 50. _____

Spelling Tip

A familiar small word can help you build larger words that are related in spelling and meaning.

Write the spelling word that contains each smaller word below.

1. sign _____

2. know _____

3. scrape _____

4. part _____

5. ground _____

partial
knowledge
design
background
skyscraper

Word Meaning Mixed Lesson Review

immigrant
quietly
poise
venture
fled
condemn
threat
instrument
void
quarrel

Synonyms and Antonyms

Write the spelling word that is a synonym or an antonym for each word below. Then write *synonym* or *antonym* after each word pair.

1. escaped _____ _____
2. loudly _____ _____
3. tool _____ _____
4. praise _____ _____
5. experiment _____ _____
6. argue _____ _____
7. menace _____ _____
8. native _____ _____
9. emptiness _____ _____
10. awkwardness _____ _____

beneath
drought
chord
towel
plumber

Analogies

Write the spelling word that completes each analogy below.

11. *Soap* is to *wash* as _____ is to *dry.*
12. *Flood* is to *wet* as _____ is to *dry.*
13. *Electrician* is to *wires* as _____ is to *pipes.*
14. *Above* is to *sky* as _____ is to *ground.*
15. *Sentence* is to *language* as _____ is to *music.*

pouch
decoy
chestnut
chandelier
character

Riddles

Write the spelling word that matches each definition below.

16. I may lead you into a trap. _____
17. Without me, you'd be a different person. _____
18. I grow on a tree and I am edible. _____
19. I'll carry your books for you. _____
20. I hang from the ceiling and shed light. _____

Vocabulary Mixed Lesson Review

Add the suffix *-ly* to change these adjectives to adverbs.

1. partial   _____
2. calm   _____
3. innocent   _____
4. foolish   _____
5. impatient   _____

Add the suffix *-y* to change these nouns to adjectives.

6. mist   _____
7. risk   _____
8. shade   _____

partial

calm

innocent

foolish

impatient

mist

risk

shade

Dictionary Skills

Read the dictionary entry and complete the items below.

fea•ture (fē′chər) *n.* **1.** an important or distinctive part or characteristic of something: *Great speed is a feature of this car.* **2.** the main attraction, as a film or a newspaper column. **fea•tured, fea•tur•ing** — *v.* to give an important place to.

1. What part of speech is the entry word? _____
2. Write the example sentence for the first definition. _____ _____
3. Write the verb forms for *feature*. _____ _____
4. Write an example sentence of your own for the second definition of *feature*. _____
5. Write an example sentence of your own for a verb form of *feature.*

_____

Spelling and Writing

A news release is a form of explanatory writing. The writer gives information about a subject in the news.

From: The Inventors' Association
For Immediate Release:

EXPRESS MAIN IDEA

Today **Alison Potts** announced that she received a patent for her **new musical instrument**, the Soloband. Her unique design allows one person to play the keyboard, guitar, drums, and cymbals all at once. She created her masterpiece **at her university**. Asked why she created the Soloband, Ms. Potts replied that her invention permits a solo musician **to do many things at once with poise**. The musical members of the Inventors Association have tested her device and declared it to be a treat. Impatient customers have already called the Inventors Association, and we are making the Soloband available on a trial basis by direct mail. That means that instead of waiting months to acquire this amazing invention, musicians can own the Soloband right now. News media are invited to a demonstration on **Wednesday afternoon at 3 p.m.** to meet the inventor, take photos, and experience the quality of the Soloband for themselves.

GIVE ESSENTIAL INFORMATION

WRITING TIPS!!

Explanatory Writing

- Start by expressing your purpose.
- Tell the reader essential information.
- Present the details in a good order.
- Reread! Pretend you know nothing about the subject. Is it clear?

Now write your own explanatory news release. Try to use some of the spelling words in your paragraph.

PREWRITE: What real or imagined invention would you like to write about? List the important information about the invention.

DRAFT: Write a news release about the invention. Begin your paragraph by telling the purpose of the invention. Include information and details that explain the invention.

REVISE: Exchange paragraphs with a classmate. Use your classmate's comments and the Writing Tips as you revise.

EDIT/PROOFREAD: Use editing marks to correct your capitalization, spelling, and punctuation. Rewrite your paragraph neatly.

PUBLISH: Contribute your news release to a class Inventors' Journal.

SPELLING FUN
CUMULATIVE REVIEW

POSTER WORDS

- Choose a word from Lessons 1–11 that could be the subject of an advertising poster.
- Write the word.
- Illustrate your poster with drawings and graphics.
- Include your poster in a class advertising exhibit.

MEMORY CHALLENGE

- With a partner, choose pairs of words from Lessons 13–17 that begin with the same letter or consonant sound. Choose ten pairs of words.
- Write each word on an index card, mix up the cards, and place them face down in a 5 x 4 array.
- Take turns. Turn over two cards at a time. Try to turn over pairs of cards that begin with the same letter or consonant sound.
- When you turn over a pair, give the cards to your partner who will ask you to spell the words. If you spell them both correctly, keep the cards. If not, return them to the array, face down.
- The player who has the most cards when all the cards are gone from the array wins. If you have a tie, play again!

SPELLING BEE

- Two teams share the job of writing thirty words from Lessons 1–17 on cards. Each team gets half of the cards.
- The first player on Team A calls out a word.
- The first player on Team B spells it aloud.
- If the word is spelled correctly, the card is taken out of the pile. If not, correct the word and return the card to the pile.
- Then the next Team B player calls out the word for the next Team A player to spell. Continue until all the words have been used.
- The first team to finish the other team's pile wins!

WORDS WITH Suffixes

1. experience
2. servant
3. different
4. importance
5. distance
6. sentence
7. silence
8. instance
9. disturbance
10. fragrant
11. dependent
12. annoyance
13. descendant
14. attendant
15. excellent
16. ambulance
17. influence
18. ignorant
19. vacant
20. frequent

Learn Spelling Patterns

LOOK & SAY Listen for the sounds in each word.

PICTURE Close your eyes. See each word in your mind.

STUDY These spelling words end with suffixes. The suffixes -*ant* and -*ent* may mean "a person or thing that does" or "doing or being." The suffixes -*ance* and -*ence* may mean "the action or state of" or "the state of being."

WRITE Sort the words. Which words end with these suffixes?

ant (1) (2) (3)
     (4) (5) (6)

ent (7) (8) (9) (10)

ance (11) (12) (13)
      (14) (15) (16)

ence (17) (18) (19) (20)

CHECK Did you spell each word correctly? Circle the endings.

Pattern Power

Which suffixes often mean "a person or thing that does"? (21) and (22)

Which suffixes often mean "the action of or state of"? (23) and (24)

Other Words

Write words you would like to add to this week's list.

_____ _____ _____ _____ _____

Practice Word Meanings

Antonyms

Write the spelling word that is an antonym for each word below.

1. noise _____
2. educated _____
3. seldom _____

4. similar _____
5. occupied _____

Context Sentences

Write the spelling word that best completes each sentence below.

6. Be sure to begin each _____ with a capital letter.

7. With binoculars, you can see things at a _____.

8. They called an _____ to take me to the hospital.

9. I can't think of a single _____ when they were late.

10. The crying baby caused a _____ in the library.

Challenge Words • *Health*

Write the challenge word that best completes each sentence. Use the **Spelling Dictionary** on page 214 to help you. Circle the suffix at the end of each word.

11. A water _____ made our whole town ill.

12. Eating well increases your _____ to disease.

13. A high test score shows _____.

14. During your teenage years you are an _____.

15. Health _____ helps with medical costs.

resistance
adolescent
pollutant
insurance
intelligence

Spelling Tip

Sometimes smaller words within a long word can help you to spell the longer word.

✦ Listen to the word *disturbance*. Can you hear the small word *disturb*?

✦ Add the suffix *-ance* to the small word.

disturb + ance = disturbance

Can you find other small words in the words on your spelling list? Use them to help you remember how to spell the words.

List Words

experience
servant
different
importance
distance
sentence
silence
instance
disturbance
fragrant
dependent
annoyance
descendant
attendant
excellent
ambulance
influence
ignorant
vacant
frequent

Challenge Words

resistance
adolescent
pollutant
insurance
intelligence

Review Words

allowance
prevent
performance
invent
entrance

Build Vocabulary

Suffixes

■ Look at these words and their suffixes:

ignor<u>ant</u>—adjective   **excell<u>ent</u>**—adjective

ignor<u>ance</u>—noun   **excell<u>ence</u>**—noun

If the adjective form is spelled *-ant*, the noun will be spelled *-ance*. If the adjective form is spelled *-ent*, the noun form will be spelled *-ence*.

Change the adjectives below to nouns by adding the right ending.

1. distant ____   **3.** silent ____

2. important ____   **4.** fragrant ____

■ The suffixes *-ent* and *-ant* can mean "one who." For example, an *entrant* is "one who enters."

Write the spelling word that matches each meaning below.

5. one who serves someone ____

6. one who depends on another ____

7. one who attends, or helps, someone ____

8. one who descends from ancestors ____

Review Words

Write the review words that end with these letters.

ance **9.** ____   **11.** ____

        10. ____

ent **12.** ____   **13.** ____

allowance
prevent
performance
invent
entrance

TAKE HOME

Write your spelling words in three lists: two-, three-, and four-syllable words. Circle the suffix at the end of each word. Use your lists to practice at home.

Apply Spelling Skills

Dictionary Skills

■ The *-ed* and *-ing* forms of verbs are called **inflected forms**. For example, *approved* and *approving* are inflected forms of *approve*. Inflected forms usually appear right after the part of speech label in a dictionary entry.

Look in the **Spelling Dictionary** beginning on page 214 to find the inflected forms of *approve*. Then find the inflected forms of these words.

1. influence _____ _____

2. experience _____ _____

■ Run-on entries are found at the end of a dictionary entry. Write the run-on entry for each of these words.

3. excellent _____   4. dependent _____

Pattern Power

Look at the spelling words listed at the left.

• Circle the suffix in each word.

Proofreading

Proofread the paragraph. Use editing marks. Check spelling, capital letters, and punctuation. Then rewrite the paragraph. There are six mistakes.

> Some people think that working out is an annoyence, but i am the descendent of an active family. my doctor says that frequint exercise is excelent for my health. I say it's fun!

EDITING MARKS

⬭ check spelling

≡ capital letter

／ lowercase letter

⊙ add a period

⌃ add

✐ take out

indent the paragraph

↻ move

For more help, see page 171.

Writing • *About Health*

PREWRITE: List times you have seen doctors, dentists, or nurses.

DRAFT: Choose one experience with a medical person. Was it funny? Dramatic? Write a paragraph about your experience.

REVISE: Ask a classmate to comment on your paragraph. Use the **Spelling Thesaurus** on page 182 as you revise.

EDIT/PROOFREAD: Use editing marks. Rewrite your paragraph.

PUBLISH: Read your paragraph aloud to a group of classmates.

20

WORDS WITH Suffixes

1. motion
2. union
3. section
4. location
5. notion
6. permission
7. conservation
8. description
9. companion
10. vision
11. conversation
12. connection
13. reservation
14. abbreviation
15. fashion
16. provision
17. champion
18. opinion
19. profession
20. mention

Learn Spelling Patterns

LOOK & SAY Listen for the sounds in each word.

PICTURE Close your eyes. See each word in your mind.

STUDY These spelling words end with the suffixes *-ation, -tion, -sion,* and *-ion.* These suffixes usually mean "the act of."

WRITE Sort the words. Which words end with the following letters?

ation (1)　(2)　(3)
(4)　(5)

tion (6)　(7)　(8)
(9)　(10)　(11)

sion (12)　(13)　(14)　(15)

ion (16)　(17)　(18)　(19)　(20)

CHECK Did you spell each word correctly? Circle the endings.

Pattern Power

Which suffixes often mean "the act of "?

(21)　, (22)　, (23)　, and (24)

Other Words

Write words you would like to add to this week's list.

_____ _____ _____ _____ _____

Practice Word Meanings

Context Clues

Write the spelling word that matches each clue below.

1. a person's point of view ____
2. a game or contest winner ____
3. a joining together of two or more things ____
4. giving or supplying ____
5. protecting natural resources ____
6. movement or action ____
7. a talk between people ____
8. to refer to or talk about briefly ____
9. a style or trend ____
10. consent or approval ____

Challenge Words • *Social Studies*

Write the challenge word that best completes each sentence. Use the **Spelling Dictionary** on page 214 to help you. Circle *-ation, -tion, -sion,* or *-ion* at the end of each word.

11. Flying the flag is an Independence Day ____.

12. The civil rights movement led to school ____.

13. Unfair ____ was one cause of the American Revolution.

14. A special ____ tackled the littering problem.

15. The union workers are happy with the ____ of their contracts.

integration
tradition
taxation
negotiation
commission

Spelling Tip

Sometimes knowing a root word can help you remember a group of words related in spelling and meaning.

✦ The Latin root *loc* means "place" or "put."
✦ It is the root word in *local,* meaning "having to do with a particular place" and *locate,* meaning "to find the place."

Which spelling word has the root *loc*? How is it related in meaning to *local* and *locate*?

motion
union
section
location
notion
permission
conservation
description
companion
vision
conversation
connection
reservation
abbreviation
fashion
provision
champion
opinion
profession
mention

Challenge Words

integration
tradition
taxation
negotiation
commission

Review Words

position
imagination
education
correction
conviction

Build Vocabulary

Related Words

■ The suffixes *-ation, -tion,* and *-sion* end with the sound /shən/ or /zhən/. These sounds may be hard to spell, but knowing related words can help you. How do the underlined letters in the base words in the left column help you spell the words with suffixes in the right column?

ac<u>t</u>   a<u>ct</u>ion

confe<u>ss</u>   confe<u>ss</u>ion

Write the spelling word that is related to each base word below. Circle the letter or letters in the base word that help you spell the suffix in the spelling word.

1. locate _____   4. abbreviate _____

2. note _____   5. profess _____

3. connect _____

Review Words

Use review words to complete these sentences.

6. I made a _____ when I rewrote my poem.

7. Use your _____ to write a story.

8. If I sit in this _____, my legs will fall asleep.

9. The _____ was appealed to a higher court.

10. This school will give me a good _____.

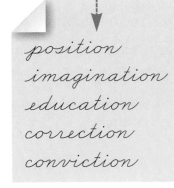

position
imagination
education
correction
conviction

Write your spelling words in alphabetical order. Circle the suffix at the end of each word. Use your lists to practice at home.

Apply Spelling Skills

Dictionary Skills

Some suffixes are listed as entries in the dictionary because they add common meanings to base words. Find the suffixes below in the **Spelling Dictionary** on page 214. Write the first definition given for each suffix.

1. *ion* _____

2. *ation* _____

3. *ance* _____

4. *ence* _____

Proofreading

Proofread the paragraph. Use editing marks. Check for spelling, capital letters, and punctuation. Then rewrite the paragraph. There are six mistakes.

> My grandmother travels with a companon. They make a resirvation in a quiet section of the train. grandmother's visen is not good, so she asks for a descripshon of the view,

EDITING MARKS

⬭ check spelling

≡ capital letter

/ lowercase letter

⊙ add a period

∧ add

⤲ take out

⌇ indent the paragraph

↻ move

For more help, see page 171.

Writing • *About Social Studies*

PREWRITE: Think about a trip you once took. List what you liked about the place you visited.

DRAFT: Write a paragraph telling your classmates about it.

REVISE: Did you include all the important details? Use the **Spelling Thesaurus** on page 182 as you revise.

EDIT/PROOFREAD: Use editing marks. Then rewrite your paragraph.

PUBLISH: Collect the paragraphs in a class newsletter.

Words with Suffixes

1. electricity
2. probably
3. safely
4. happily
5. finally
6. delivery
7. likely
8. simply
9. lonely
10. lately
11. recently
12. daily
13. quantity
14. activity
15. easily
16. gravity
17. liberty
18. busily
19. immediately
20. variety

Learn Spelling Patterns

LOOK & SAY Listen for the sounds in each word.

PICTURE Close your eyes. See each word in your mind.

STUDY These words end with suffixes. The suffixes *-ity* and *-ty* often mean "the state or quality of being." The suffix *-ly* usually means "in a particular manner." The suffix *-y* may mean "the act of."

WRITE Sort the words. Which words have these suffixes?

ly   (1)   (2)   (3)   (4)
     (5)   (6)   (7)
     (8)   (9)   (10)
     (11)   (12)   (13)

ity   (14)   (15)   (16)   (17)

ty   (18)   (19)

y   (20)

CHECK Did you spell each word correctly? Circle the suffixes.

Pattern Power

Which suffixes often mean

"the state or quality of being"? (21) and (22)

Which suffix means "in a particular manner"? (23)

Other Words

Write words you would like to add to this week's list.

_____ _____ _____ _____ _____

Practice Word Meanings

Synonyms

Write the spelling word that is a synonym of each word below.

1. freedom _____
2. likely _____
3. energy _____
4. plainly _____
5. amount _____

6. lonesome _____
7. seriousness _____
8. shipment _____
9. joyfully _____
10. lastly _____

Challenge Words • *Science*

Write the challenge word that best completes each sentence. Use the **Spelling Dictionary** on page 214 to help you. Circle the suffix at the end of each word.

11. The color of your eyes is determined by _____.

12. It has been _____ proven that vegetables are good for you.

13. Another word for *speed* is _____.

14. To be _____ fit, you must exercise regularly.

15. Albert Einstein is known for his theory of _____.

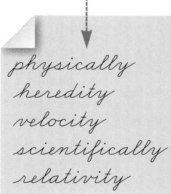

physically
heredity
velocity
scientifically
relativity

$\mathcal{S}$pelling Tip

Here's a tip to help you figure out the spelling of a word with a suffix. Sometimes there is a familiar small word inside a longer word.

✦ Listen to the word *activity*. You can hear the small word *active*.

✦ Drop the final *e* and add the suffix *-ity* to the small word.

active + ity = activity

Look for other small words within the longer words on your spelling list. Use them to help you remember how to spell the words.

List Words

electricity

probably

safely

happily

finally

delivery

likely

simply

lonely

lately

recently

daily

quantity

activity

easily

gravity

liberty

busily

immediately

variety

Challenge Words

physically

heredity

velocity

scientifically

relativity

Review Words

loyalty

truly

especially

naughty

carefully

Build Vocabulary

Suffixes

When the suffix *-ly* is added to a word that ends in *y*, change the *y* to *i* before adding *-ly*.

merry + **ly** = merrily

■ Add the suffix *-ly* to the base words below.

1. final _____

6. late _____

2. immediate _____

7. happy _____

3. busy _____

8. recent _____

4. safe _____

9. like _____

5. easy _____

10. day _____

■ Use words you wrote to complete these sentences.

11. At the signal we all started working _____.

12. I finished my math problems _____, but my science project was a bit more difficult.

13. When you hear the fire alarm, leave the building _____.

14. Gina is a good runner and will most _____ win the race.

Review Words ----------

Write the review words that end with these suffixes.

ty 15. _____

ly 16. _____

17. _____

18. _____

y 19. _____

loyalty

truly

especially

naughty

carefully

▲TAKE HOME◢

Write your spelling words in three lists: nouns, adverbs, and adjectives. Circle the suffix at the end of each word. Use your lists to practice at home.

Apply Spelling Skills

Dictionary Skills

The partial entry below shows that *courtesy* is a noun and that *courtesies* is the plural form of the entry word. Use the **Spelling Dictionary** on page 214 to help you write the plural form of each word below. Then complete the sentence.

cour•te•sy (kûr′ tə sē) *n., pl.* **cour•te•sies**

1. **variety** (və rī′i tē) *n., pl.* _____
2. **activity** (ak tiv′i tē) *n., pl.* _____
3. **delivery** (di liv′ə rē) *n., pl.* _____
4. **quantity** (kwon′ti tē) *n., pl.* _____
5. If a noun ends in consonant + _____, the plural form usually ends in _____.

Proofreading

Check spelling, capital letters, and punctuation. Then rewrite the paragraph. There are six mistakes.

> After working busyly for several days, I finaly finished my science Project. It shows how electrisity is changed to light. I chose my topic easaly because I like to watch lightning

EDITING MARKS

⬭ check spelling
≡ capital letter
/ lowercase letter
⊙ add a period
⋀ add
↫ take out
⌗ indent the paragraph
↻ move

For more help, see page 171.

Writing • *About Science*

PREWRITE: List some important discoveries made by people observing nature.

DRAFT: Choose one. Write a paragraph about it.

REVISE: Does your paragraph have a strong topic sentence? Use the **Spelling Thesaurus** on page 182 as you revise.

EDIT/PROOFREAD: Use editing marks. Then rewrite your paragraph.

PUBLISH: Make a display about discoveries in the school lunchroom.

22

WORDS WITH Prefixes

1. misunderstand
2. international
3. improve
4. disagree
5. misspell
6. incorrect
7. disobey
8. intersection
9. interstate
10. improper
11. import
12. interview
13. impolite
14. indirect
15. misfortune
16. invisible
17. independence
18. inactive
19. dispose
20. impractical

Learn Spelling Patterns

LOOK & SAY   Listen for the sounds in each word.

PICTURE   Close your eyes. See each word in your mind.

STUDY   These words start with prefixes. The prefix *dis-* usually means "not"; the prefixes *im-* and *in-* may mean "not" or "in"; *mis-* means "bad" or "wrongly"; *inter-* means "between" or "among."

WRITE   Sort the words. Which words start with these prefixes?

im   (1) (2) (3) (4) (5)
in   (6) (7) (8) (9) (10)
dis   (11) (12) (13)
mis   (14) (15) (16)
inter   (17) (18) (19) (20)

CHECK   Did you spell each word correctly? Circle the prefixes.

Pattern Power

Which prefixes may mean "not"? (21) or (22) or (23) Which prefix means "bad" or "wrongly"? (24) Which prefix means "between" or "among"? (25)

Other Words

Write words you would like to add to this week's list.

_____ _____ _____ _____ _____

Practice Word Meanings

Opposites

Look at the word pairs.

approve/disapprove   movable/immovable
secure/insecure

The prefixes *dis-*, *im-*, and *in-* may mean "not." A word that has one of these prefixes often means the opposite of the base word. Write the spelling word that means the opposite of each word below.

1. agree _____
2. proper _____
3. spell _____
4. practical _____
5. visible _____

6. active _____
7. polite _____
8. direct _____
9. dependence _____
10. obey _____

Challenge Words • Math

Write the challenge word that best answers each question. Use the **Spelling Dictionary** on page 214 to help you. Circle the prefix at the beginning of each word.

11. What word describes something that is extremely large?

_____

12. What word means "to figure incorrectly"? _____
13. What is a word for the time or space between two things? _____
14. What word describes something limitless? _____
15. What word relates to a rule of multiplication? _____

miscalculate
infinite
interval
distributive
immense

Spelling Tip

How can you figure out the spelling of a word with a prefix? There is usually a small word inside of the longer word. If possible, use the small word to help you spell the longer word.

✦ Listen to the word *indirect*. You can hear the small word *direct*.

✦ Add the prefix -*in* to the small word.

in + direct = indirect

Look for other small words within the longer words on your spelling list. Use them to help you remember how to spell the words.

List Words

misunderstand
international
improve
disagree
misspell
incorrect
disobey
intersection
interstate
improper
import
interview
impolite
indirect
misfortune
invisible
independence
inactive
dispose
impractical

Challenge Words

miscalculate
infinite
interval
distributive
immense

Review Words

impossible
informal
disapprove
mistake
information

Build Vocabulary

Prefixes

■ Choose the prefixes from the box below that mean the same as the words in quotations. Add them to the given base words to make spelling words.

mis- inter- in- im- dis-

1. "not"   +   polite   =   *impolite*
2. "between"   +   national   =   ____
3. "bad"   +   fortune   =   ____
4. "between"   +   section   =   ____
5. "wrongly"   +   understand =   ____
6. "between"   +   state   =   ____
7. "between"   +   view   =   ____

■ Use words you made above to complete these sentences.

8. We drove from Illinois to Michigan on an ____ highway.

9. While out for a walk, I had the ____ to lose my house keys.

Review Words

Write the review words that begin with these prefixes.

dis 10. ____   **in**   12. ____
im   11. ____   13. ____
                     mis 14. ____

Look at the list word below. Write the review words that have the same prefix.

indirect 15. ____   16. ____

impossible
informal
disapprove
mistake
information

Write your spelling words in three lists: nouns, verbs, and adjectives. Some words could go on more than one list. Circle the prefix at the beginning of each word. Use your lists to practice at home.

Apply Spelling Skills

Using the Thesaurus

Good writers avoid overusing words. Use the **Spelling Thesaurus** on page 182 to find a replacement for each underlined word below.

1. Jim valued his independence and learning to drive a car gave him more <u>independence</u>. ____

2. He apologized for his impolite behavior and promised not to be so <u>impolite</u> again. ____

3. The hot weather made everyone inactive and the <u>inactive</u> children did not feel like playing outside. ____

Pattern Power

Look at the underlined words in the sentences at the left.

- Circle the prefix in each underlined word.

Proofreading

Check spelling, capital letters, and punctuation. Then rewrite the paragraph. There are six mistakes.

> To impruv your math skills, do not
> disspose of homework with incorect
> answers. it is of great inport that you
> figure out what you did wrong Then you
> can get it right the next time!

EDITING MARKS

◯ check spelling
≡ capital letter
／ lowercase letter
⊙ add a period
∧ add
⤲ take out
⌗ indent the paragraph
◯⤳ move

For more help, see page 171.

Writing • *About Math*

PREWRITE: List a few tips for improving your math skills.

DRAFT: Choose one tip. Write a paragraph explaining it.

REVISE: Did you give clear instructions for making use of your math tip? Use the **Spelling Thesaurus** on page 182 as you revise.

EDIT/PROOFREAD: Use editing marks. Then rewrite your paragraph.

PUBLISH: Post your paragraph in a Math Corner to share with others.

23

WORDS WITH Prefixes

1. continue
2. consider
3. complete
4. complain
5. compound
6. company
7. condition
8. control
9. contain
10. collapse
11. concern
12. contract
13. compose
14. coexist
15. confuse
16. consist
17. collide
18. cooperate
19. compete
20. consonant

Learn Spelling Patterns

LOOK & SAY Listen for the sounds in each word.

PICTURE Close your eyes. See each word in your mind.

STUDY These words start with prefixes. The prefixes *col-*, *com-*, *con-*, and *co-* usually mean "with" or "together."

WRITE Sort the words. Which words start with these prefixes?

col   (1)   (2)

com   (3)   (4)   (5)
      (6)   (7)   (8)

co   (9)   (10)

con   (11) (12) (13)
      (14) (15) (16)
      (17) (18) (19) (20)

CHECK Did you spell each word correctly? Circle the prefixes.

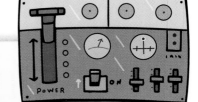

Pattern Power

What prefixes can mean "with" or "together"?

(21) or (22) or (23) or (24)

Other Words

Write words you would like to add to this week's list.

_____ _____ _____ _____ _____

Practice Word Meanings

Prefixes

Words with the prefixes *com-*, *con-*, *col-*, and *co-* often have meanings related to being together or being with something. Write the spelling word that has the same meaning as each underlined phrase in the sentences below. Circle the prefix in each spelling word.

1. The new book will <u>hold together</u> all the works of William Shakespeare. _____

2. We were grateful for the <u>people gathered together</u> at our holiday meal. _____

3. This cot will <u>fold together</u> for easy storage. _____

4. Animals and birds <u>live together</u> in the forest. _____

5. This Mother's Day, I will <u>put together</u> a poem for my mom. _____

6. The top two teams will <u>play together</u> for the championship. _____

Challenge Words • The Arts

Write the challenge word that best completes each sentence. Use the **Spelling Dictionary** on page 214 to help you. Circle the prefix at the beginning of each word.

7. When the _____ enters, the audience applauds.

8. That singer took first place in the talent _____.

9. For my last piano recital, I learned a difficult _____.

10. The song is an original _____ by a new song writer.

11. The two writers composed the song in _____.

competition
concerto
composition
conductor
collaboration

Spelling Tip

Knowing prefixes and suffixes can help you figure out the spelling of some long words.

✦ First, listen for a familiar prefix. Think about how to spell it.

✦ Next, think about the other syllables in the word. Are any of the remaining syllables familiar suffixes?

✦ Put the syllables together. **con + di + tion = condition**

List Words

continue
consider
complete
complain
compound
company
condition
control
contain
collapse
concern
contract
compose
coexist
confuse
consist
collide
cooperate
compete
consonant

Challenge Words

competition
concerto
composition
conductor
collaboration

Review Words

committee
concentration
command
collection
compare

Build Vocabulary

Suffixes

■ The suffixes *-ation, -tion, -sion,* and *-ion* are added to verbs to make nouns. Write the words that are formed by adding the given suffixes to these spelling words. For some words, you may have to make changes in the base word before adding the suffix.

1. continue + ation = _____

2. contract + ion = _____

3. complete + ion = _____

4. consider + ation = _____

5. confuse + ion = _____

6. collide + sion = _____

7. cooperate + ion = _____

8. compete + tion = _____

9. compose + tion = _____

■ Use words you made to complete these sentences.

10. The unclear directions left us in a state of _____.

11. Please show some _____ for your neighbors by lowering the volume on your stereo.

Review Words

Write the review words that begin with these prefixes.

col 12. _____   **con** 16. _____

com 13. _____

14. _____

15. _____

committee
concentration
command
collection
compare

T A K E   H O M E

Write your spelling words in three lists: two-, three-, and four-syllable words. Circle the prefix at the beginning of each word. Use your lists to practice at home.

Apply Spelling Skills

Dictionary Skills

Look at the entry for *conduct* in the **Spelling Dictionary** on page 214. When *conduct* is used as a noun, the first syllable is stressed. But when *conduct* is used as a verb, the second syllable is stressed. Look up *compound* in the **Spelling Dictionary**.

1. What part of speech is *compound* when it has this respelling: kəm pound′? _____
2. Write the adjective *compound* in syllables and underline the stressed syllable. _____
3. Write a sentence using *compound* as a noun, verb, or adjective. _____

Proofreading

Check spelling, capital letters, and punctuation. Then rewrite the paragraph. There are six mistakes.

My spelling class went to see an odd play. I didn't know what it would consest of. I couldn't controll my excitement. I wouldnt conplain, but it was about a vowel's concern for her lost consonent.

Writing • *About the Arts*

PREWRITE: Choose a performance you enjoyed. List a few things you liked about it.

DRAFT: Write a paragraph explaining your choice.

REVISE: Did you state your opinion? Did you include supporting details? Use the **Spelling Thesaurus** on page 182 as you revise.

EDIT/PROOFREAD: Use editing marks. Then rewrite your paragraph.

PUBLISH: Contribute your paragraph to a class entertainment magazine.

EDITING MARKS

- ◯ check spelling
- ≡ capital letter
- / lowercase letter
- ⊙ add a period
- ∧ add
- ℒ take out
- ℉ indent the paragraph
- ◯↝ move

For more help, see page 171.

24 REVIEW Spelling Patterns

Sort the words in each list. Write each word next to the correct suffix or prefix. Then circle the suffix or prefix.

experience	**Lesson 19**	
servant		
different	**Words with these suffixes**	
importance		
distance	ance 1. _____	ent 6. _____
descendant	2. _____	7. _____
excellent	ant 3. _____	8. _____
influence	4. _____	ence 9. _____
ignorant	5. _____	10. _____
frequent		

union	**Lesson 20**	
location		
permission	**Words with these suffixes**	
description		
companion	ation 11. _____	tion 16. _____
conversation	12. _____	ion 17. _____
reservation	13. _____	18. _____
provision	sion 14. _____	19. _____
champion	15. _____	20. _____
opinion		

electricity	**Lesson 21**	
probably		
happily	**Words with these suffixes**	
delivery		
simply	ly 21. _____	ity 26. _____
daily	22. _____	27. _____
quantity	23. _____	ty 28. _____
liberty	24. _____	29. _____
variety	25. _____	y 30. _____
immediately		

misunderstand	**Lesson 22**
improve	**Words with these prefixes**
disagree	
misspell	
disobey	
interview	
impolite	
inactive	
indirect	
dispose	

Lesson 22

Words with these prefixes

inter 31. _____   dis 36. _____

mis   32. _____   37. _____

      33. _____   38. _____

im   34. _____   in   39. _____

      35. _____   40. _____

continue	**Lesson 23**
complain	**Words with these prefixes**
company	
control	
collapse	
compose	
coexist	
collide	
cooperate	
compete	

Lesson 23

Words with these prefixes

com 41. _____   col 47. _____

     42. _____   48. _____

     43. _____   co   49. _____

     44. _____   50. _____

con 45. _____

     46. _____

Spelling Tip

Learn the spellings and meanings of different suffixes and prefixes. Look them up in the **Spelling Dictionary** starting on page 214. Knowing these prefixes and suffixes will help you spell words that contain them. It will also give you clues to the meanings of the words.

Write the words that have these meanings.

1. the act of conversing   _____

2. the state of being important   _____

3. not agree   _____

-ance

dis-

-ation

Word Meaning Mixed Lesson Review

champion
complain
compose
descendant
description
distance
experience
ignorant
quantity

Context Sentences

Write spelling words to complete these sentences.

1. You have to run a long ____ to complete a marathon.
2. Riding in a hot-air balloon is a thrilling ____.
3. The prince is a ____ of a famous king.
4. Leslie beat all the other players and was declared the ____.
5. My sister is trying to ____ a letter of application for college.
6. You shouldn't ____ about having too much to do.
7. We order a large ____ of caps for the team.
8. Being ____ of the law is no excuse.
9. The poem began with a ____ of the poet's garden.

companion
improve
inactive
misspell
permission
location
union

Synonyms and Antonyms

Write the spelling word that is a synonym or antonym for each underlined word or word group below. Then write **S** or **A**.

10. Our teacher gave her <u>consent</u> for us to eat lunch outdoors. ____ ____

11. Lena worked hard to <u>worsen</u> her basketball skills. ____ ____

12. If you <u>correctly spell</u> a review word, you must study it again. ____ ____

13. The workers formed an <u>association</u> to fight for their rights. ____ ____

14. Most bears are <u>energetic</u> during the winter months. ____ ____

15. The new <u>site</u> for the school will be in Dixville. ____ ____

16. Ike is my <u>friend</u> on most outings. ____ ____

Vocabulary Mixed Lesson Review

Prefixes and Suffixes

Add suffixes to these spelling words to make new words. You may have to change the spelling of the base word before adding the suffix.

1. day + ly = _____
2. happy + ly = _____
3. simple + ly = _____
4. dispose + ition = _____
5. electric + ity = _____
6. indirect + ly = _____
7. continue + ation = _____
8. provide + sion = _____

Write the spelling words that are formed by adding prefixes (P) or suffixes (S) to these base words.

9. understand (P) _____
10. excel (S) _____
11. serve (S) _____
12. polite (P) _____
13. differ (S) _____
14. reserve (S) _____
15. exist (P) _____
16. immediate (S) _____

Dictionary Skills

Look in the **Spelling Dictionary** starting on page 214 to find the plural form of each word below. Write the plural.

1. variety _____
2. company _____
3. delivery _____
4. liberty _____

Find the underlined words in the **Spelling Dictionary.** Then answer the following questions by writing the correct run-on entry.

5. What word means "a person who <u>interviews</u>"? _____
6. What is the adverb form of <u>frequent</u>? _____
7. What is an adjective form of <u>control</u>? _____

Spelling and Writing

HISTORICAL FIGURES

You might choose to write a nonfiction story about a historical figure whose life or work interests you.

FACTS IN ORDER

Sacajawea belonged to a Native American nation called the Shoshone, who lived in the Rocky Mountains. As a young girl, she was **captured** and brought east. **Then, in 1804, when Sacajawea was about 16**, **Meriwether Lewis and William Clark** hired her as a guide. They needed her to help them explore the area between the Mississippi River and the Rocky Mountains. Sacajawea had some **exciting adventures** on the journey west. But the most exciting part, for her, was a **joyful reunion** with the Shoshone people when she reached the Rocky Mountains.

VIVID WORDS

WRITING TIPS!!

Narrative Writing

- Make an outline as you gather information about your historical figure.
- Will the actions and events of the story be interesting to the reader?
- When you write your story, refer to your outline and include everything you can in chronological order.
- Use vivid words to make the story come to life.

Now write your own story about a historical character. Your character can be someone famous, or someone not-so-famous, such as an ancestor, or a founder of your town.

PREWRITE: Choose a historical figure. List some interesting facts about him or her.

DRAFT: Write a story about an event in the life of your character.

REVISE: Did you use transition words to show story order? Use the Writing Tips as you revise.

PROOFREAD: Use editing marks to correct your capitalization, spelling, and punctuation. Rewrite your paragraph neatly.

PUBLISH: Include your story in a class anthology of biographies.

SPELLING FUN
CUMULATIVE REVIEW

TELL ALL ABOUT IT

- Choose a noun from Lessons 1–17. Write it down the middle of a sheet of paper.
- Write some words that tell about your noun. Each word should include a different letter of the noun.
- Keep going until you've come up with a word for each letter of your noun.
- Do as many as you like. Display your work for the class.

twisting
rocky
woodland
climbing
long

PLAY CONCENTRATION

- With a partner, choose some prefixes and suffixes from Lessons 19–23.
- On index cards, write pairs of words containing the prefixes and suffixes you chose. Write one word per card. Underline the prefix or suffix of each word.
- Lay the cards face down in a square in random order.

- Take turns choosing pairs of cards. If the prefixes or suffixes match, keep the pair. If not, return the pair face down to the array.
- The player who gets the most pairs wins.

confuse

control

SPELLING BEE

- Two teams share the job of writing words from Lessons 1–23 on cards. Each team gets half the cards.
- The first player on Team A calls out a word.
- The first player on Team B writes the word on the board.
- If the word is spelled correctly, Team B gets one point and the card is taken

out of the pile. If not, the card is returned to the pile.
- Then, the next Team B player calls out the word for the next Team A player. Continue on until all the cards are used.
- The team with the most points wins.

WORDS WITH Prefixes

1. unnecessary
2. research
3. exchange
4. uneven
5. decrease
6. unlike
7. describe
8. export
9. remind
10. unpopular
11. uncertain
12. recite
13. refreshment
14. respect
15. unusual
16. explode
17. detail
18. experiment
19. determine
20. express

Learn Spelling Patterns

LOOK & SAY   Listen for the sounds in each word.

PICTURE   Close your eyes. See each word in your mind.

STUDY   The words below contain prefixes. The prefix *un-* means "not"; *de-* may mean "do the opposite of" or "down"; *re-* means "again" or "back"; *ex-* usually means "out."

WRITE   Sort the words. Which words begin with the prefixes below?

un   (1)   (2)   (3)
     (4)   (5)   (6)

de   (7)   (8)   (9)   (10)

re   (11)   (12)   (13)   (14)   (15)

ex   (16)   (17)   (18)   (19)   (20)

CHECK   Did you spell each word correctly? Circle the prefixes.

Pattern Power

Which prefix may mean "not"? (21)

Which may mean "do the opposite of"? (22)

Which means "again" or "back"? (23) Which may mean "out"? (24)

Other Words

Write words you would like to add to this week's list.

_____ _____ _____ _____ _____

Practice Word Meanings

Context Sentences

Write the spelling word that best completes each sentence below. Circle the prefix in each word.

1. We went to the library to _____ our topics.

2. We could hear the fireworks _____ in the distance.

3. It is _____ a punctual person like Maya to be late.

4. We need CO_2 for our science _____.

5. You _____ me of your older brother.

6. You can see strange and _____ things when you go scuba diving.

7. After the game, Jimmy needed rest and _____.

8. He used a stopwatch to _____ how long it took us.

9. That movie was _____ and closed after a week.

Challenge Words • *Social Studies*

Write the challenge word that matches each definition below. Use the **Spelling Dictionary** on page 214 to help you. Circle the spelling of the prefix in each word.

10. journey for a specific purpose _____

11. build again _____

12. the act of leaving _____

13. not run by the people _____

14. a person who speaks for others _____

departure
undemocratic
representative
expedition
reconstruct

ⓈPelling Tip

To spell long words, sound them out one syllable at a time.

✦ Listen for the first syllable in *experiment*. What sound do you hear? Remember, each syllable must have a vowel sound.

✦ Say the other syllables and listen closely.

✦ Write the word one syllable at a time.

ex + per + i + ment = experiment

List Words

unnecessary

research

exchange

uneven

decrease

unlike

describe

export

remind

unpopular

uncertain

recite

refreshment

respect

unusual

explode

detail

experiment

determine

express

Challenge Words

departure

undemocratic

representative

expedition

reconstruct

Review Words

despite

repay

explosion

review

recall

Build Vocabulary

Latin Roots

■ Many English words come from Latin, the language of the Romans. Often, these words combine a prefix or a suffix with a **Latin root**. For example, *port* is a Latin root meaning "carry."

> ***re + port*** = back + carry = "to carry back"

Combine the prefix and the Latin root to form a word. Use the meanings of the prefix and the root to write the meaning of the word.

Prefix	Latin Root	New Word	Meaning
1. ex +	port (carry)	= _____	_____
2. de +	crease (grow)	= _____	_____
3. re +	flect (bend)	= _____	_____
4. de +	scribe (write)	= _____	_____
5. ex +	clude (shut)	= _____	_____
6. re +	cite (call)	= _____	_____

■ Use words you made to complete these sentences.

7. They will _____ the toys to other countries.

8. Can you _____ the whole poem from memory?

Review Words

Write the review words that have the prefixes below.

de   9. _____   **ex**   13. _____

re   10. _____

11. _____

12. _____

Write the review words that have the same prefixes as the list words below.

14. exchange _____

15. describe _____

despite

repay

explosion

review

recall

T A K E   H O M E

Write your spelling words in alphabetical order. Circle the prefix *un-*, *de-*, *re-*, or *ex-* in each word. Use your list to practice spelling the words at home.

Apply Spelling Skills

Thesaurus Skills

Use your **Spelling Thesaurus** beginning on page 182 to look up synonyms and antonyms of your spelling words. A thesaurus can help you find exactly the right word for your report or story.

Write one synonym and one antonym for each spelling word below.

1. unnecessary _____
2. uneven _____
3. uncertain _____
4. respect _____
5. decrease _____

Proofreading

Check spelling, capital letters, and punctuation. Then rewrite the paragraph. There are six mistakes.

> I can deskribe my dream vacation in great detal. We would take an expres train to niagara Falls Then we would exchang our coats for raincoats and walk under the huge waterfall.

EDITING MARKS

◯	check spelling
⹀	capital letter
/	lowercase letter
⊙	add a period
∧	add
⤶	take out
⌗	indent the paragraph
◯↝	move

For more help, see page 171.

Writing • *About Social Studies*

PREWRITE: List some sights you might see on a dream vacation.

DRAFT: Write a two or three paragraph story about your trip.

REVISE: Did you include interesting details? Do the events happen in a logical order?

EDIT/PROOFREAD: Use editing marks. Then rewrite your story.

PUBLISH: Read your story to a group of classmates.

26

WORDS FROM Foreign Languages

1. chocolate
2. bazaar
3. boomerang
4. bamboo
5. chipmunk
6. banjo
7. plaid
8. tulip
9. pizza
10. sympathy
11. cocoa
12. coyote
13. umbrella
14. guitar
15. patio
16. jaguar
17. myth
18. prairie
19. plateau
20. igloo

Learn Spelling Patterns

LOOK & SAY Listen for the sounds in each word.

PICTURE Close your eyes. See each word in your mind.

STUDY These words come from languages other than the English language. Use your **Spelling Dictionary** on page 214 to find the origin of each word.

WRITE Sort the words. Which words come from each of the languages listed below?

French	(1)	(2)	
Spanish	(3)	(4)	
Aztec	(5)	(6)	(7)
Greek	(8)	(9)	
Gaelic	(10)		
Italian	(11)	(12)	
Inuit	(13)		
Turkish	(14)		
Malay	(15)		
Tupi	(16)		
Australian	(17)		
Bantu	(18)		
Persian	(19)		
Algonquin	(20)		

CHECK Did you spell each word correctly?

Pattern Power

From what languages do we get the names of three animals? (21) , (22) , and (23) The names of two musical instruments? (24) and (25)

Other Words

Write words you would like to add to this week's list.

_____ _____ _____ _____ _____

Practice Word Meanings

Categories

Write the spelling words that fit into each category below.

foods   **1.** _____   **2.** _____   **3.** _____

animals   **4.** _____   **5.** _____   **6.** _____

musical instruments   **7.** _____   **8.** _____

plants   **9.** _____   **10.** _____

geography   **11.** _____   **12.** _____

Context Sentences

Write the spelling word that best completes
each sentence below.

13. Our school raised money by selling items at a _____.

14. I threw the _____ and waited for it to come back.

15. We read a Greek _____ about the stars.

16. Bring your _____ in case it rains.

Challenge Words • *Math* ----------------------

Write the challenge word that fits each definition below.
Use the **Spelling Dictionary** on page 214 to help you.

17. a branch of mathematics _____

18. the number below the line in a fraction _____

19. a unit of storage capacity in a computer _____

20. a square-based figure with triangular sides _____

21. to figure out by using math _____

> *pyramid*
> *algebra*
> *megabyte*
> *calculate*
> *denominator*

Spelling Tip

Sometimes a word has a spelling that you do not expect because
it comes from another language. Usually /ō/ at the end of a word
is spelled *o, ow,* or *oe.*

✦ The word *plateau* comes from the French language.

✦ In many English words that come from French, /ō/ is spelled with
eau at the end of a word.

Some other words from French that follow this spelling pattern
are *chateau* and *bureau.*

chocolate
bazaar
boomerang
bamboo
chipmunk
banjo
plaid
tulip
pizza
sympathy
cocoa
coyote
umbrella
guitar
patio
jaguar
myth
prairie
plateau
igloo

pyramid
algebra
megabyte
calculate
denominator

wharf
carton
turquoise
script
sketch

Build Vocabulary

Plural Nouns

■ Add -s or -es to each list word below to form a **plural noun.** You may have to change the final *y* to *i* before adding -es. Use the **Spelling Dictionary** on page 214 to help you.

1. umbrella _____
2. igloo _____
3. prairie _____
4. patio _____
5. boomerang _____
6. sympathy _____
7. myth _____
8. jaguar _____
9. chipmunk _____

Review Words

Write the review word that comes from each language listed below.

10. from a Dutch word meaning "a quick drawing" _____
11. from a Latin word meaning "to write" _____
12. from a French word meaning "Turkish" _____
13. from an Old English word meaning "embarkment" _____
14. from an Italian word meaning "pasteboard" _____

wharf
carton
turquoise
script
sketch

TAKE HOME

Write your spelling words in three lists: words with one syllable, two syllables, and three syllables. Use your lists to practice spelling the words at home.

Apply Spelling Skills

Dictionary Skills

Look at the entries for the list words below in the **Spelling Dictionary** on page 214. Write the origin of each word and the word's meaning.

1. igloo *from Inuit iglu, meaning "snow house"*

2. plaid ____

3. bazaar ____

4. patio ____

5. plateau ____

6. banjo ____

Proofreading

Check spelling, capital letters, and punctuation. Then rewrite the paragraph. There are six mistakes.

> Our club will be holding an international bazar to raise money. I am going to make a German choclate cake with a lot of coco Meg will play a spanish tune on her gitar.

EDITING MARKS

◯	check spelling
═	capital letter
/	lowercase letter
⊙	add a period
∧	add
ℛ	take out
¶	indent the paragraph
◯↻	move

For more help, see page 171.

Writing • About Math

PREWRITE: Pretend you are going to enter a recipe in a contest. Think about a dish you might make. List ingredients and measurements.

DRAFT: Write a recipe for the dish you chose. Include ingredients, amounts, and instructions.

REVISE: Ask a classmate if your instructions are clear. If you left out any steps, add them now.

EDIT/PROOFREAD: Use editing marks. Then rewrite your recipe.

PUBLISH: Contribute your recipe to a class cookbook.

27

WORDS FROM Foreign Languages

1. rodeo
2. alto
3. haiku
4. spaghetti
5. crochet
6. macaroni
7. cider
8. restaurant
9. solo
10. pasta
11. license
12. maneuver
13. oasis
14. enchilada
15. cabinet
16. statue
17. pajamas
18. drama
19. helmet
20. karate

Learn Spelling Patterns

LOOK & SAY Listen for the sounds in each word.

PICTURE Close your eyes. See each word in your mind.

STUDY These words come from languages other than modern English. Use your **Spelling Dictionary** on page 214 to find the origin of each word.

WRITE Sort the words. Which words come from each of the languages listed below?

French	(1)	(2)	(3)	(4)	(5)
Italian	(6)	(7)	(8)	(9)	(10)
Latin	(11)	(12)			
Japanese	(13)	(14)			
Greek	(15)	(16)			
Spanish	(17)	(18)			
Hindi	(19)				
Middle English	(20)				

CHECK Did you spell each word correctly?

Pattern Power

From what languages do we get the names of some foods? (21), (22), and (23)

Other Words

Write words you would like to add to this week's list.

_____ _____ _____ _____ _____

Practice Word Meanings

Analogies

Write list words to complete these analogies.

1. *Instrument* is to *piano* as *singer* is to _____.
2. *Orange* is to *juice* as *apple* is to _____.
3. *Passport* is to *traveler* as _____ is to *driver*.
4. *Kung fu* is to *China* as _____ is to *Japan*.
5. *Film* is to *movie theater* as *food* is to _____.
6. *Playwright* is to _____ as *sculptor* is to _____.

Challenge Words • *Social Studies*

Write the challenge word that fits each definition below.
Then write the language of origin for each word. Use the
Spelling Dictionary on page 214 to help you.

7. flat bread made of
   flour or corn   _____ _____

8. person who has inherited a high
   social position   _____ _____

9. gown with loose sleeves
   worn in Japan   _____ _____

10. intelligent ape that is smaller
    than a gorilla   _____ _____

11. naval officer of the
    highest rank   _____ _____

aristocrat
kimono
admiral
chimpanzee
tortilla

ⓢpelling Tip

Unusual words from foreign languages are easier to spell when
you sound them out one syllable at a time.

✦ Listen for the first syllable in *maneuver*. What vowel sound
  do you hear?
✦ What vowel sounds do you hear in the remaining syllables?
Write the word one syllable at a time.

ma + neu + ver = maneuver

List Words

rodeo
alto
haiku
spaghetti
crochet
macaroni
cider
restaurant
solo
pasta
license
maneuver
oasis
enchilada
cabinet
statue
pajamas
drama
helmet
karate

Challenge Words

aristocrat
kimono
admiral
chimpanzee
tortilla

Review Words

delicious
canoe
convoy
cinnamon
bacon

Build Vocabulary

Suffixes

■ You can add suffixes to base words to make new words. The suffixes -er and -ist may mean "a person who does"; -like means "resembling"; and -able means "able to be."

describe + **able** = describable   research + **er** = researcher

Add suffixes to the list words below to make new words. You may have to change the spelling of the base word.

1. solo   +   ist   =   _____
2. crochet   +   er   =   _____
3. helmet   +   like   =   _____
4. maneuver   +   able   =   _____

■ Use words you made to complete these sentences.

5. The boat was hard to steer and not very _____.

6. The _____ was alone on stage.

Review Words

Write the review word that comes from each word below.

From the Arawak word
    canoa 7. _____

From the Greek word
    kinnamomon 8. _____

From the French word
    conveier 9. _____

From the Latin word
    delicere 10. _____

From the Middle English word
    bacoun 11. _____

delicious
canoe
convoy
cinnamon
bacon

TAKE HOME

Write your words in three lists: words with two syllables, words with three syllables, and words with four syllables. Use your lists to practice spelling the words at home.

Apply Spelling Skills

Dictionary Skills

A dictionary entry tells if a word can be spelled or pronounced more than one way. It will give unusual plural forms.

Use the **Spelling Dictionary** to complete these items.

1. *Rodeo* can be pronounced _____ or _____.
2. The plural form of *oasis* is _____.
3. The plural form of *haiku* is _____.
4. *Pajamas* can also be spelled _____.
5. The plural form of *macaroni* can be spelled _____ or _____.

Pattern Power

Look at the words you just wrote.
- Circle the word that comes from the Italian language.
- Underline the word that comes from the Spanish language.

Proofreading

Check spelling, capital letters, and punctuation. Then rewrite the paragraph. There are six mistakes.

> In the united states we eat foods from many cultures. A kitchen cabinit might have spagetti or another kind of posta on one shelf and the fixings for an enchillada on another.

EDITING MARKS

⬭	check spelling
≡	capital letter
/	lowercase letter
⊙	add a period
∧	add
℘	take out
⌗	indent the paragraph
↻	move

For more help, see page 171.

Writing • *About Social Studies*

PREWRITE: List some ways in which various world cultures have contributed to our way of life.

DRAFT: Write a paragraph about one interesting contribution.

REVISE: Have you included enough details to support your main idea? Use the **Spelling Thesaurus** on page 182 as you revise.

EDIT/PROOFREAD: Create a class collection called "Our American Mosaic."

28

Abbreviations

1. p.m.
2. mph
3. inc.
4. Dr.
5. Nov.
6. misc.
7. Ms.
8. Mr.
9. radar
10. Sept.
11. scuba
12. etc.
13. a.m.
14. Mrs.
15. St.
16. Ave.
17. P.S.
18. ml
19. RSVP
20. Jr.

Learn Spelling Patterns

LOOK & SAY Listen for the sounds in each word.

PICTURE Close your eyes. See each word in your mind.

STUDY These spelling words are **abbreviations**. Some of them are **acronyms**, words formed from the first letter or letters of a group of words.

WRITE Which abbreviations contain capital letters?

(1) (2) (3) (4)
(5) (6) (7) (8)
(9) (10) (11)

Which words are acronyms?

(12) (13)

Which abbreviations have only lowercase letters?

(14) (15) (16) (17)
(18) (19) (20)

CHECK Did you spell each word correctly? Circle the capital letters and periods.

Pattern Power

What do most abbreviations have at the end? (21) What do many abbreviations have at the beginning? (22)

Other Words

Write words you would like to add to this week's list.

_____ _____ _____ _____ _____

Practice Word Meanings

Context Sentences

Write the abbreviation or acronym for the underlined words in each sentence.

1. <u>Mister</u> Kopecki and I went sailing. ___
2. The date was <u>September</u> 2. ___
3. It was only 6:00 <u>in the morning</u>. ___
4. We walked down Bridge <u>Avenue</u> towards the dock. ___
5. We passed the office of Whamo, <u>Incorporated</u>. ___
6. Together, we put the <u>self-contained underwater breathing apparatus</u> gear on the boat. ___
7. Philip Taylor, <u>Junior</u>, joined us. ___
8. The wind blew at 17 <u>miles per hour</u>. ___
9. We returned home at 7:00 <u>in the evening</u>. ___

Challenge Words • Science

Write the challenge word that matches each definition below. Use the **Spelling Dictionary** on page 214 to help you.

10. a global network of computers ___
11. acronym for *compact disc read only memory* ___
12. abbreviation for *facsimile* ___
13. acronym for *random access memory* ___
14. a device that allows computer data to be carried over telephone lines ___

fax
CD ROM
Internet
RAM
modem

Spelling Tip

If you have trouble spelling abbreviations, ask yourself these questions:

✦ Is it a person's title, a month, or part of an address? If so, it starts with a capital letter and ends with a period.

✦ Is it an acronym or metric measurement? If so, there is no capital letter or period.

List Words

p.m.

mph

inc.

Dr.

Nov.

misc.

Ms.

Mr.

radar

Sept.

scuba

etc.

a.m.

Mrs.

St.

Ave.

P.S.

ml

RSVP

Jr.

Challenge Words

fax

CD ROM

Internet

RAM

modem

Review Words

they're

we'd

you'll

hasn't

must've

Build Vocabulary

Abbreviations for Measurements

■ The prefix *kilo-* means "one thousand" (1,000) in Greek. The letter *k* is the abbreviation for *kilo-*.

The prefix *milli-* means "one thousandth" (1/1,000) in Latin. The letter *m* is the abbreviation for *milli-*.

Write the list word that includes an abbreviation for the prefix *milli-*.

1. _____

Write the abbreviations for the metric units below. These abbreviations are not capitalized and are written without periods. Use a dictionary or your math book to help you.

2. one thousand grams _____

3. one thousandth of a meter _____

■ Write the abbreviations for these measurements that are not metric. These abbreviations end with periods. Use a dictionary or your math book to help you.

4. foot _____   6. quart _____

5. yard _____   7. gallon _____

■ Use abbreviations you wrote to complete these equations.

8. 3 ft. = 1 _____   10. 1,000 g = 1 _____

9. 4 qts. = 1 _____   11. 1 cm = 10 _____

Review Words

Write the review word that each pair of words stands for.

12. they are _____   15. has not _____

13. we would _____   16. must have _____

14. you will _____

they're
we'd
you'll
hasn't
must've

TAKE HOME

Write your words in two lists: abbreviations that use periods and abbreviations that do not use periods. Circle the capitals and periods in the abbreviations. Use your lists to practice at home.

Apply Spelling Skills

Dictionary Skills

Some abbreviations stand for more than one word. Use the **Spelling Dictionary** on page 214 to find what these abbreviations stand for. Then write each word.

1. Dr. ____ ____

2. St. ____ ____ ____

Write the correct abbreviation for each definition below. Use the **Spelling Dictionary** if you need help.

3. from French "reply, if you please" ____

4. from Latin "something written afterward" ____

5. from Latin "and all the rest" ____

6. probably a blend of *Miss* and *Mrs.* ____

Proofreading

Check spelling, capital letters, and punctuation. Then rewrite the paragraph. There are five mistakes.

To: mrs. kahn   Date: Novem. 4
    Enclosed are (1) a copy of the weather data we gathered on rader today and (2) the misc information you requested about the forecast.

Writing • *About Science*

PREWRITE: List scientific events that could be used in a movie.

DRAFT: Choose the idea you like best and outline your story. Be sure to indicate the order of events and the characters.

REVISE: Is the order of events logical? Are your ideas exciting? Use the **Spelling Thesaurus** on page 182 as you revise.

EDIT/PROOFREAD: Use editing marks. Then rewrite your paragraph.

PUBLISH: Illustrate your paragraphs. Paste your paragraphs and illustrations on a class movie poster.

EDITING MARKS

⬭ check spelling

＝ capital letter

／ lowercase letter

⊙ add a period

∧ add

✐ take out

⌗ indent the paragraph

◯⤳ move

For more help, see page 171.

121

29

PLURALS

1. abilities
2. slippers
3. stockings
4. canals
5. tickets
6. chimneys
7. scissors
8. feathers
9. oats
10. themselves
11. mysteries
12. scarves
13. loaves
14. vegetables
15. dominoes
16. stereos
17. skis
18. ashes
19. echoes
20. halves

Learn Spelling Patterns

LOOK & SAY Listen for the sounds in each word.

PICTURE Close your eyes. See each word in your mind.

STUDY These words are plural nouns. Remember that some singular nouns that end with *y* or *f* change their spelling when *-es* is added.

WRITE Sort the words. Which words are made plural by adding the letters below?

s (1) (2) (3) (4)
   (5) (6) (7) (8)
   (9) (10) (11)
es (12) (13) (14)

Which words have spelling changes and end with these letters?

ies (15) (16)
ves (17) (18) (19) (20)

CHECK Did you spell each word correctly? Circle the letters that show that each word is plural.

Pattern Power

What letter or letters are used to form the plural of many words? (21) or (22) What letter might you change *y* to in a plural form? (23) What letter might you change *f* to? (24)

Other Words

Write words you would like to add to this week's list.

_____ _____ _____ _____ _____

Practice Word Meanings

Categories

Write a spelling word to complete each of these word groups.

1. wheat   barley   _____
2. hats   gloves   _____
3. leggings   tights   _____
4. radios   televisions   _____
5. grains   fruits   _____
6. rivers   streams   _____
7. comedies   dramas   _____
8. knives   clippers   _____
9. shoes   boots   _____
10. funnels   smokestacks   _____
11. thirds   fourths   _____

Challenge Words • *Social Studies*

Write the challenge word that best completes each sentence below. Use the **Spelling Dictionary** on page 214 to help you. Circle the letters that show that each word is plural.

12. There are many _____ about how to improve education.

13. The police checked the _____ of suspects.

14. The _____ for the company were busy in court.

15. We watched _____ of the town council meetings.

16. The _____ were asked to describe the robber.

videos
witnesses
alibis
theories
attorneys

Spelling Tip

To make some plural forms, you need to change the spelling of the base word.

✦ If a word ends with a consonant and *y*, change the *y* to *i* and add -*es*.

✦ For some words that end with *f*, change *f* to *v* and add -*es*.

Which spelling words follow each rule?

List Words

abilities
slippers
stockings
canals
tickets
chimneys
scissors
feathers
oats
themselves
mysteries
scarves
loaves
vegetables
dominoes
stereos
skis
ashes
echoes
halves

Challenge Words

videos
witnesses
alibis
theories
attorneys

Review Words

enemies
pants
thieves
trousers
addresses

Build Vocabulary

Base Words

Write the singular form of each plural noun below. Remember that some base words change their spellings when plural endings are added. Use your **Spelling Dictionary** beginning on page 214 if you need help.

1. tickets _____
2. echoes _____
3. ashes _____
4. halves _____
5. abilities _____
6. scarves _____
7. mysteries _____
8. loaves _____

Review Words

Write the review words that were formed by adding the letters below to the base word.

s   9. _____
     10. _____
es   11. _____

Write the review words that were formed as described below.

12. change *y* to *i* and add *es* _____
13. change a final *f* to *v* before adding *es*. _____

enemies
pants
thieves
trousers
addresses

T A K E   H O M E

Write your words in four lists: plurals that end in *-s*, plurals that end in *-es*, plurals that end in *-ies*, and plurals that end in *-ves*. Use your lists to practice spelling the words at home.

Apply Spelling Skills

Dictionary Skills

Some words have two dictionary entries. The **entry words** are numbered with small raised letters to the right of each word to show that the words have different origins.

Use the **Spelling Dictionary** on page 214 to find the entries for the word *loaf*. Write the first definition for each entry.

1. **loaf**[1] (lōf) *n., pl.* **loaves.** _____

2. **loaf**[2] (lōf) *v. i.* _____

Proofreading

Proofread the paragraph. Check for spelling, capital letters, and punctuation. Then rewrite the paragraph. There are six mistakes.

> My favorite place to shop is a garage sale. You can buy skies for a winter trip domenos for rainy days at home, or fethers to make a silly hat. Many people find something for themselfs

Writing • *About Social Studies*

PREWRITE: List some places you shop and some things you buy.

DRAFT: Choose one kind of store and product you like. Write an ad to encourage people to shop for the product at that store.

REVISE: Show your ad to a classmate. Did you use persuasive language? Use the **Spelling Thesaurus** on page 182 as you revise.

EDIT/PROOFREAD: Use editing marks. Then rewrite your ad.

PUBLISH: Paste your ad in a class Advertising Section.

E DITING MARKS

⬭ check spelling
≡ capital letter
╱ lowercase letter
⊙ add a period
∧ add
✌ take out
indent the paragraph
↻ move

For more help, see page 171.

Sort the words in each list. Write each word. Circle the prefixes in Lesson 25, the capital letters and periods in Lesson 28, and the plural endings in Lesson 29.

unnecessary
research
exchange
uneven
describe
refreshment
unusual
detail
determine
express

Lesson 25
Words with these prefixes

un 1. _____   de 6. _____
    2. _____   7. _____
    3. _____   8. _____
re 4. _____   ex 9. _____
    5. _____   10. _____

chocolate
banjo
plaid
pizza
sympathy
coyote
guitar
jaguar
myth
prairie

Lesson 26
Words from these languages

French 11. _____   Greek 16. _____
Spanish 12. _____   17. _____
Aztec   13. _____   Gaelic 18. _____
        14. _____   Tupi   19. _____
Italian 15. _____   Bantu 20. _____

rodeo
haiku
spaghetti
restaurant
solo
license
maneuver
cabinet
pajamas
karate

Lesson 27
Words from these languages

French 21. _____   Latin   26. _____
       22. _____   Japanese 27. _____
       23. _____   28. _____
Italian 24. _____   Spanish 29. _____
       25. _____   Hindi   30. _____

p.m.	
mph	
Dr.	
misc.	
radar	
scuba	
etc.	
Ave.	
P.S.	
ml	

Lesson 28
Abbreviations with capital letters

31. _____   36. _____
32. _____   37. _____
33. _____   38. _____

with lowercase letters   Acronyms

34. _____   39. _____
35. _____   40. _____

abilities
canals
tickets
scissors
themselves
mysteries
loaves
vegetables
skis
echoes

Lesson 29
Plurals ending with

s 41. _____   ies 46. _____
   42. _____   47. _____
   43. _____   ves 48. _____
   44. _____   49. _____
   45. _____   es 50. _____

Spelling Tip

Long words are easier to spell when you sound them out one syllable at a time.

✦ Listen for each syllable. What vowel sound do you hear?
✦ Remember, each syllable must have a vowel sound.
✦ Write the word one syllable at a time.

Write each word below in syllables. Use the **Spelling Dictionary** on page 214 if you need help.

1. unnecessary _____
2. chocolate _____
3. vegetables _____
4. sympathy _____

unnecessary
chocolate
vegetables
sympathy

Word Meaning Mixed Lesson Review

cabinet
refreshment
solo
themselves
tickets

Context Sentences

Use context clues to complete each sentence with a list word.

1. Ruby sang a _____ at the concert last month.
2. Dad bought _____ for the next concert.
3. They have only _____ to blame for the error.
4. You'll find an extra toothbrush in the _____.
5. Let's buy lemonade at the _____ stand.

banjo
uneven
scissors
haiku
p.m.
unusual
restaurant
Ave.
skis

Analogies

Write the spelling words to complete these analogies.

6. *Uncommon* is to *common* as _____ is to *usual.*
7. *Pens* are to *write* as _____ are to *cut.*
8. *Bumpy* is to *smooth* as _____ is to *even.*
9. *Skates* are to *ice* as _____ are to *snow.*
10. *Grains* are to *oats* as _____ are to *carrots.*
11. *Morning* is to *a.m.* as *evening* is to _____
12. *Short story* is to *fiction* as _____ is to *poetry.*
13. *Doctor* is to *Dr.* as *Avenue* is to _____
14. *Reed* is to *clarinet* as *string* is to _____.
15. *Theater* is to *movie* as _____ is to *food.*

coyote
karate
mysteries
pajamas
scuba
spaghetti

Categories

Write the spelling word that fits in each group.

16. comedies, tragedies, _____
17. wetsuit, flippers, _____
18. wolf, bear, _____
19. macaroni, pasta, _____
20. judo, kung fu, _____
21. robe, slippers, _____

Vocabulary Mixed Lesson Review

Suffixes

Add the given suffixes to these spelling words to make new words.
You may have to drop the final *e* before adding the suffix.

1. exchange   +   able   =   _____
2. maneuver   +   able   =   _____
3. express   +   ion   =   _____
4. determine +   ation   =   _____
5. myth   +   ic   =   _____

Plural Nouns

Write the plural form of each word.

6. ability   _____
7. echo   _____
8. loaf   _____
9. pizza   _____

Dictionary Skills

Write the origin of each word. Use the **Spelling Dictionary**
on page 214 to help you.

1. prairie _____
2. license _____
3. rodeo _____
4. guitar _____
5. plaid _____

Spelling and Writing

In explaining a survey, the writer reports facts in an interesting way.

MAIN FINDINGS

DATA

INTERESTING FACTS

Did you know that Spanish is the second most commonly spoken language in the United States? You probably do, because in the sixth grade survey, **45 percent** of the students said that they or a relative spoke Spanish. Another **15 percent** of students said that they were familiar with some Spanish words. Some people didn't realize that words such as *California, patio,* and *rodeo* **have Spanish roots.** Students did recognize that words such as *taco, tortilla,* and *salsa* **are Spanish words**, because they eat in Mexican and Spanish restaurants. And who doesn't know "Yo!" Why don't we have a Spanish Day at school? *¿Sí?*

WRITING TIPS!!

Report Writing

- Be sure you include the main findings supported by facts and details.
- Organize the information logically.
- Include the data you gathered and any comments that are of interest.

Now conduct your own survey and write a report. Try to use some of the spelling words in your writing.

PREWRITE: What subject could you ask your classmates about? List the questions you will ask.

DRAFT: Write a report about the results of your survey. Begin your paragraph with an introduction to the subject of your survey. Include the facts you have collected.

REVISE: Did you explain your results clearly and in order? Use the Writing Tips as you revise.

EDIT/PROOFREAD: Use editing marks to correct your capitalization, spelling, and punctuation. Rewrite your paragraph neatly.

PUBLISH: Add your survey to your school newsletter.

SPELLING FUN
CUMULATIVE REVIEW

PERPLEXING PLURALS

- Choose ten words from Lessons 1–23 that are nouns. Try to pick some that form their plurals in an unusual way, such as by dropping the final *y* and adding *-ies*.
- Write the plural form of your words on a piece of paper.
- Challenge your partner to spell the singular form of each word.
- Give your partner one point for each word spelled correctly.
- The partner with the most points wins.

heroes
identities
walruses

WORD MAP

- With two or three classmates, choose a language from which some of the spelling words from Lessons 26 and 27 originate.
- Use a map to trace the country where the language is spoken. Write the spelling words that originate in that country on the traced map.
- See how many additional words your group can think of or look up in a dictionary that come from the country you have chosen.
- Exhibit your Word Map on a bulletin board with the maps of the other groups.

pasta
ITALY
solo

SPELLING BEE

- Two teams write thirty words from Lessons 1–29 on cards. Each team takes fifteen cards.
- The first player on Team A calls out a word.
- The first player on Team B spells the word out loud.
- If the word is spelled correctly, the card is taken out of the pile. If not, the caller gives the correct spelling and returns the card to the pile.
- Then, the next Team B player calls out the word for the next Team A player. Continue until all the words are spelled correctly.
- The first team to finish the other team's pile wins!

31

COMPOUND WORDS

1. billboard
2. driveway
3. countdown
4. oatmeal
5. cheerleader
6. bathrobe
7. windmill
8. overcoat
9. checkbook
10. foolproof
11. daydream
12. applesauce
13. mainland
14. videotape
15. teammate
16. anybody
17. handkerchief
18. headache
19. newborn
20. knapsack

Learn Spelling Patterns

LOOK & SAY Listen for the sounds in each word.

PICTURE Close your eyes. See each word in your mind.

STUDY A **compound word** is made up of two or more smaller words. The words in this lesson are **closed** compound words, in which the parts are joined into a single word.

WRITE Sort the words. Which compound words have two syllables?

(1) (2) (3) (4)
(5) (6) (7) (8)
(9) (10) (11) (12)
(13) (14)

Which compound words have three syllables?

(15) (16) (17) (18)

Which compound words have four syllables?

(19) (20)

CHECK Did you spell each word correctly? Circle each word within the compound words.

Pattern Power

Two words can be joined to form a (21) word. In many compound words, the two words are written as (22) word.

Other Words

Write words you would like to add to this week's list.

_____ _____ _____ _____ _____

Practice Word Meanings

Meaning Clues

Write the spelling words that match the following clues.

1. a place to park a car   _____
2. absolutely sure   _____
3. a fantasy   _____
4. used when you sneeze   _____
5. a pain   _____
6. just brought into the world   _____
7. "3-2-1 Blast-off!"   _____
8. a hiker's equipment   _____
9. a sight-sound recording   _____
10. an outdoor garment   _____

Challenge Words • *Social Studies*

Write the challenge word that best completes each
sentence below. Use the **Spelling Dictionary**
on page 214 to help you. Circle each word within
the compound word.

11. The author will _____ her script.

12. The _____ owns stock in the company.

13. The news station hired a new _____.

14. The _____ found a few mistakes in addition.

15. The company's _____ are in Arizona.

bookkeeper
headquarters
copyright
shareholder
anchorperson

Spelling Tip

Here's a spelling rule that you can count on when choosing
between *ei* and *ie* to spell a word.

✦ Use *i* before *e* except after *c* or when sounded like
/ā/ as in *neighbor* or *weigh*.

Which spelling word follows this rule?

List Words

billboard

driveway

countdown

oatmeal

cheerleader

bathrobe

windmill

overcoat

checkbook

foolproof

daydream

applesauce

mainland

videotape

teammate

anybody

handkerchief

headache

newborn

knapsack

Challenge Words

bookkeeper

headquarters

copyright

shareholder

anchorperson

Review Words

wallpaper

goldfish

mailbox

no one

nightgown

Build Vocabulary

New Compound Words

■ New compound words can be formed by keeping one word of the compound and adding a new word.

<u>main</u>land + frame = mainframe

count<u>down</u> + town = downtown

Combine each underlined word in the compound in Column A with a word in Column B to form a new compound word.

A	B	
1. <u>check</u>book	fire	_____
2. <u>team</u>mate	guard	_____
3. <u>bath</u>robe	pine	_____
4. check<u>book</u>	work	_____
5. any<u>body</u>	cook	_____
6. <u>apple</u>sauce	room	_____
7. bill<u>board</u>	list	_____
8. fool<u>proof</u>	chalk	_____

■ Use words you made to complete these sentences.

9. The safety inspectors made sure that the exit doors were _____.

10. The president always travels with a _____ to protect him.

Review Words

Complete each review word.

11. _____box   13. _____fish

12. wall_____   14. night_____

An open compound is formed by two words that remain separate. Write the review word that is an open compound word.   15. _____

wallpaper

goldfish

mailbox

no one

nightgown

TAKE HOME

Write your spelling words in alphabetical order. Circle each word within the compound word. Use your lists to practice spelling the words at home.

Apply Spelling Skills

Dictionary Skills

Look at accent marks in the respelling for *headache* in your **Spelling Dictionary** on page 214. The accent mark in lighter print is the **secondary stress mark.** It tells you that the syllable is stressed, but is spoken with less emphasis than the syllable with the **primary stress mark.**

Look at the respellings below and say each word. Use the **Spelling Dictionary** to help you. Write the spelling word and underline the syllable that contains the secondary accent.

1. chîr′lē′dər _____

2. ōt′mēl′ _____

3. mān′land′ _____

4. wind′mil′ _____

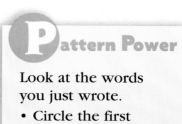

Pattern Power

Look at the words you just wrote.

• Circle the first word within each compound word.

Proofreading

Proofread the paragraph. Check spelling, capital letters, and punctuation. Then rewrite the paragraph. There are six mistakes.

Gwen and I daydrem about a trip to greece. She has a foolprof plan. We'll carry our clothes in a napsack and hike from Sparta to Athens. Then well sail from the maneland to Crete.

EDITING MARKS

⬭ check spelling

≡ capital letter

/ lowercase letter

⊙ add a period

∧ add

⤴ take out

⌗ indent the paragraph

↻ move

For more help, see page 171.

Writing • *About Social Studies*

PREWRITE: List some real or imaginary places you would like to visit.

DRAFT: Write a paragraph that gives directions from your home or school to this special place.

REVISE: Are your directions in a logical order? Use the **Spelling Thesaurus** on page 182 as you revise.

EDIT/PROOFREAD: Use editing marks. Then rewrite your paragraph.

PUBLISH: Draw a map and include it with your directions.

32

COMPOUND WORDS

1. twenty-one
2. cross-country
3. brother-in-law
4. high school
5. brand-new
6. first aid
7. ready-made
8. drive-in
9. common sense
10. question mark
11. cold front
12. one-way
13. sleeping bag
14. grown-up
15. living room
16. contact lens
17. long-distance
18. close-up
19. science fiction
20. leap year

Learn Spelling Patterns

LOOK & SAY Listen for the sounds in each word.

PICTURE Close your eyes. See each word in your mind.

STUDY These spelling words are compound words. Some are **hyphenated compounds.** Others are **open compounds**, in which the two words remain separate.

WRITE Sort the words. Which words are made of two or more words joined by a hyphen?

(1) (2) (3) (4) (5)
(6) (7) (8) (9) (10)

Which words are made up of two separate words?

(11) (12) (13) (14) (15)
(16) (17) (18) (19) (20)

CHECK Did you spell each word correctly? Circle the hyphens.

Pattern Power

Either a (21) or a (22)

can appear between two words that form

a compound word.

Other Words
Write words you would like to add to this week's list.

_____ _____ _____ _____ _____

Practice Word Meanings

Word Categories

Write the spelling word that fits best in each group of words below.

1. period, exclamation mark, *question mark*

2. device, eyeglasses, ____

3. mystery, fantasy, ____

4. bedroom, dining room, ____

5. tent, knapsack, ____

6. wisdom, knowhow, ____

7. kindergarten, junior high, ____

8. stop, yield, ____

Challenge Words • *Health*

Write the challenge word that matches each definition below. Use the **Spelling Dictionary** on page 214 to help you. Circle the hyphen in each hyphenated compound.

9. a danger in extremely hot weather ____

10. the best players from different teams playing together ____

11. control of your own actions ____

12. what you could improve by jogging or biking ____

13. the system that includes the brain and spinal cord ____

heat exhaustion
nervous system
physical fitness
self-discipline
all-star
tournament

Spelling Tip

You can help yourself remember how to spell difficult words.

✦ Figure out which part of the word gives you trouble.

✦ Pay special attention to that part every time you read or write the word.

✦ Create a sentence, a jingle, or a clue that can help you.

For example, if you think *contact lens* ends in *z*, remember that a contact lens helps a person see, and see begins with *s*.

List Words

twenty-one
cross-country
brother-in-law
high school
brand-new
first aid
ready-made
drive-in
common sense
question mark
cold front
one-way
sleeping bag
grown-up
living room
contact lens
long-distance
close-up
science fiction
leap year

Challenge Words

heat exhaustion
nervous system
physical fitness
self-discipline
all-star tournament

Review Words

all right
twenty-five
ice-skating
post office
vice president

Build Vocabulary

Plural Compounds and Irregular Plurals

■ To make most compound words plural, add -s to the end of the word.

Add -s to form the plural of each compound word below.

Singular	Plural
1. leap year	_____
2. drive-in	_____
3. grown-up	_____
4. close-up	_____
5. living room	_____
6. cold front	_____
7. question mark	_____

■ To make some compound words plural, add -s to the end of the first word part.

sister-in-law + **s** = sisters-in-law

Add -s to form the plural of this compound word.

8. brother-in-law _____

Review Words

Write the review words that are hyphenated compound words.

9. _____   10. _____

Write the review words that are open compound words.

11. _____   13. _____

12. _____

all right
twenty-five
ice-skating
post office
vice president

TAKE HOME

Write your words in three lists: compound words, with two, three, and four syllables. Circle the words within each compound word. Use your lists to practice at home.

Apply Spelling Skills

Using the Thesaurus

An **index** is an alphabetical list of material contained in a published book. The **Spelling Thesaurus** in this book has an index. All the thesaurus entry words and their synonyms and antonyms are listed in the thesaurus index, along with their part of speech.

Look up the following words in the **Spelling Thesaurus** on page 182. Find the spelling word that is a synonym for each word.

1. adult _____
2. mass-produced _____
3. fresh _____

Pattern Power

Look at the words you just wrote.
• Circle the hyphen in each word.

Proofreading

Check spelling, capital letters, and punctuation. Then rewrite the paragraph. There are six mistakes.

> Long-distence biking is very good for your health If you begin by biking crosscountry, youll need first-aide, but if you bike every day you'll soon be able to bike twenty one miles.

EDITING MARKS

⬭	check spelling
＝	capital letter
/	lowercase letter
⊙	add a period
∧	add
✁	take out
⁋	indent the paragraph
⟲	move

For more help, see page 171.

Writing • *About Health*

PREWRITE: List some things people could do to improve their physical fitness.

DRAFT: Make a physical fitness plan. Write a brochure that explains your plan and how people could benefit from it.

REVISE: Are the benefits of your fitness plan clear? Did you use facts and convincing language to make your point? Use the **Spelling Thesaurus** on page 182 as you revise.

EDIT/PROOFREAD: Use editing marks. Then rewrite your brochure.

PUBLISH: Collect your brochures in a class Fitness Guide.

33

WORDS EASILY CONFUSED

1. insure
2. councilor
3. petal
4. recipe
5. dual
6. former
7. advice
8. adapt
9. naval
10. affect
11. navel
12. effect
13. ensure
14. adopt
15. advise
16. counselor
17. duel
18. receipt
19. pedal
20. formal

Learn Spelling Patterns

LOOK & SAY Listen for the sounds in each word.

PICTURE Close your eyes. See each word in your mind.

STUDY Each spelling word is easily confused with another word on the list.

WRITE Sort the words. Which words begin with the letters below?

rec	(1)	(2)
nav	(3)	(4)
du	(5)	(6)
adv	(7)	(8)
pe	(9)	(10)
form	(11)	(12)
coun	(13)	(14)
ad	(15)	(16)

Which words end with the letters below?

| ect | (17) | (18) |
| sure | (19) | (20) |

CHECK Did you spell each word correctly? Circle the letters in each word that are not included in the beginning or ending letter patterns.

Pattern Power

Two words are easily confused when their pronunciations and spellings are almost __(21)__ .

Other Words

Write words you would like to add to this week's list.

_____ _____ _____ _____ _____

Practice Word Meanings

Words in Context

Complete the sentences below using pairs of easily confused words from the spelling list. You may want to check the words' definitions and parts of speech in the **Spelling Dictionary** on page 214.

1. The man wearing the _formal_ suit is the _former_ mayor of Canton.

2. The lawyer will _____ you to seek some good _____ from the judge.

3. Our city _____ is also a job _____ at the high school.

4. My bicycle _____ tore a rose _____ from my mother's favorite bush.

5. Mr. Diamond cannot _____ that the company will _____ all of your jewelry if you lose it.

Challenge Words • Social Studies - - - - - - - - - - - - - -

Answer each riddle with the challenge word that might be confused with the underlined word in the riddle. Use the **Spelling Dictionary** on page 214 to help you.

6. If you <u>immigrate</u> to one country or region, what do you do from another? _____

7. What could you call a <u>decent</u> landing? a smooth _____

8. What makes you <u>conscious</u> of right and wrong? _____

9. What do you need after a bad <u>anecdote</u>? an _____

10. What are we if we are <u>already</u> ready? _____

conscience
descent
emigrate
all ready
antidote

Spelling Tip

A computer Spellchecker will find words that are misspelled. If words are not misspelled, but are used incorrectly, the Spellchecker can't help you!

✦ The Spellchecker will not catch this error.

   *The flower's red **pedal** is pretty.*

The only way to check the Spellchecker is to carefully proofread your hard copy.

List Words

insure
councilor
petal
recipe
dual
former
advice
adapt
naval
affect
navel
effect
ensure
adopt
advise
counselor
duel
receipt
pedal
formal

Challenge Words

conscience
descent
emigrate
all ready
antidote

Review Words

waist
male
mail
waste
pain

Build Vocabulary

Suffixes

■ Most verbs form the past tense by adding *-ed* to the base word.

insure   insured

Form the past tense of the following verbs. You may have to drop the final *e* before adding *-ed*.

Present Tense	Past Tense
1. adapt	_____
2. effect	_____
3. pedal	_____
4. duel	_____
5. affect	_____
6. advise	_____
7. adopt	_____
8. insure	_____

■ Use words you made to complete these sentences.

9. The committee _____ the old law to address the community's current needs.

10. We _____ the building for fires and floods.

Review Words

Write the review words that are pronounced as written below. Use the **Spelling Dictionary** on page 214 to help you.

māl   **11.** _____   **12.** _____

wāst   **13.** _____   **14.** _____

pān   **15.** _____

waist
male
mail
waste
pain

TAKE HOME

Write your spelling words in word pairs. After each word, write a short definition. Refer to your **Spelling Dictionary** for help. Use your list to practice spelling the words at home.

Apply Spelling Skills

Dictionary Skills

Look up each pair of words in the **Spelling Dictionary** on page 214 to see how they are pronounced. If both words are pronounced in the same way, write *Yes*. If they are pronounced differently, write *No*.

1. dual   duel   ____
2. navel   naval   ____
3. recipe   receipt   ____
4. advice   advise   ____
5. adopt   adapt   ____

Pattern Power

Look at the word pairs.

- Circle the spellings in each word that are different from the other word in the pair.

Proofreading

Check spelling, capital letters, and punctuation. Then rewrite the paragraph. There are six mistakes.

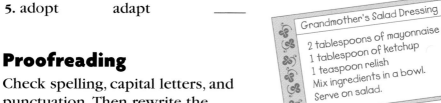

Grandmother's Salad Dressing

2 tablespoons of mayonnaise
1 tablespoon of ketchup
1 teaspoon relish
Mix ingredients in a bowl.
Serve on salad.

> Students need a place to go after school. Our teacher, ms. Daw, a formal navel officer, will speak with our city counciler We will give a former dance to raise money for a center.

Writing • *About Social Studies*

PREWRITE: List some ideas about how life could be better for the young people in your community.

DRAFT: Write a formal letter to a city councilor explaining one of your ideas and telling how to raise money to pay for it.

REVISE: Exchange papers with a partner. Your partner will ask you questions that will help you present yourself more clearly.

EDIT/PROOFREAD: Use editing marks. Then rewrite your letter.

PUBLISH: If you wish, send your letter to your city council.

EDITING MARKS

⬭ check spelling

= capital letter

/ lowercase letter

⊙ add a period

∧ add

✌ take out

indent the paragraph

↻ move

For more help, see page 171.

34

HOMOPHONES

1. hire
2. principal
3. choral
4. higher
5. real
6. miner
7. steal
8. hoard
9. steak
10. reel
11. vain
12. minor
13. stake
14. colonel
15. horde
16. steel
17. principle
18. coral
19. vane
20. kernel

Learn Spelling Patterns

LOOK & SAY Listen for the sounds in each word.

PICTURE Close your eyes. See each word in your mind.

STUDY Words that sound alike but have different spellings and meanings are called **homophones.** The spelling words in the word list are homophones.

WRITE Sort the words. Which word pairs are homophones? Write them next to each other.

(1) (2)
(3) (4)
(5) (6)
(7) (8)
(9) (10)
(11) (12)
(13) (14)
(15) (16)
(17) (18)
(19) (20)

CHECK Did you spell each word correctly? Circle the sound spellings in each word that are different from those in its homophone.

Pattern Power

How are homophones alike?

(21) How are they different? (22)

Other Words

Write words you would like to add to this week's list.

___ ___ ___ ___ ___

144

Practice Word Meanings

Words in Context

Write the homophones that correctly complete the sentence pairs below. You may want to use the **Spelling Dictionary** on page 214 to check the definition of a word.

1. Rosa took her fishing rod and ___*reel*___ to the river.

   Diana's ring has a ___*real*___ emerald.

2. I follow the ____ "Honesty is the best policy."

   Our school ____ won an award for service.

3. Ann has only ____ changes to make on her report.

   The ____ wrote an article about the coal mines.

4. That man in the uniform is a ____ in the army.

   The hungry chickens ate every ____ of corn.

Challenge Words • *Social Studies* -

Write the challenge word that is a homophone for one of the words in the sentence. Use the **Spelling Dictionary** on page 214 to help you. Circle the homophone in each sentence.

5. He wrote a letter on his new ____ while he rode his stationary exercise bike.

6. I compliment you on the way the colors of your outfit ____ each other.

7. I was sealing the ____ with plaster before painting it.

8. The ____ fighter met a gorilla in the forest.

9. Patients may need ____ to wait for doctors.

complement
guerrilla
patience
ceiling
stationery

(S)pelling Tip

You can make up a saying to help you remember how to use a homophone.

✦ This saying can help you remember when to use *principal* instead of *principle*.

The princi*pal* is my *pal*.

Try making up memory helpers for words on your spelling list.

145

List Words

hire
principal
choral
higher
real
miner
steal
hoard
steak
reel
vain
minor
stake
colonel
horde
steel
principle
coral
vane
kernel

Challenge Words

complement
guerrilla
patience
ceiling
stationery

Review Words

fowl
brake
foul
break
bury

Build Vocabulary

Rhyming Words

■ Write the spelling words that rhyme with each of the following words.

1. break _____   _____

2. cord _____   _____

3. buyer _____   _____

4. rain _____   _____

5. moral _____   _____

6. feel _____   _____

                _____   _____

7. journal _____   _____

■ Use words you wrote to complete these sentences.

8. The scuba divers carefully studied the _____ at the Great Barrier Reef.

9. The weather _____ is shaped like a rooster.

Review Words

Write the pairs of homophones that are pronounced as written below. Use the **Spelling Dictionary** on page 214 to help you.

brāk   10. _____

          11. _____

foul   12. _____

          13. _____

Write the review word that is a homophone of the word below.

berry   14. _____

fowl
brake
foul
break
bury

TAKE HOME

Write your words in homophone pairs. Write a short definition for each word, using your **Spelling Dictionary** for help. Use your lists to practice spelling the words at home.

Apply Spelling Skills

Dictionary Skills

The phrase *to break down* is an idiom that means "to stop working." An **idiom** is a group of words that has its own meaning which is different from the meanings of its separate words. In the **Spelling Dictionary** beginning on page 214, idioms appear in heavy type at the end of the entry for the most important word in the idiom.

1. Find the word *vain* in the **Spelling Dictionary**. What idiom is listed? ____

2. Look up the word *stake.* Write the first idiom listed and its definition. ____

3. Write the second idiom for *stake* and its definition. ____

Proofreading

Check the spelling, capital letters, and punctuation. Then rewrite the paragraph. There are six mistakes.

> My grandfather, John vargo, is a school principle and director of a choril group. He is also well-known for having a steal weather vaine on his roof I love to hear his stories of the past.

EDITING MARKS

◯	check spelling
═	capital letter
/	lowercase letter
⊙	add a period
∧	add
⬗	take out
⌗	indent the paragraph
◌	move

For more help, see page 171.

Writing • *About Social Studies*

PREWRITE: List some facts about a historic person you admire from the United States.

DRAFT: Write a character sketch that describes the person you chose.

REVISE: Reread your sketch and underline any areas where you feel more information is needed. Use the **Spelling Thesaurus** on page 182 as you revise.

EDIT/PROOFREAD: Use editing marks. Then rewrite your sketch.

PUBLISH: Take time to exchange papers with your classmates.

35

HOMOGRAPHS

1. lime
2. dove
3. mold
4. stern
5. hamper
6. cue
7. bass
8. jumper
9. loom
10. racket
11. refrain
12. sole
13. husky
14. flounder
15. elder
16. swallow
17. forge
18. incense
19. novel
20. poach

Learn Spelling Patterns

LOOK & SAY Listen for the sounds in each word.

PICTURE Close your eyes. See each word in your mind.

STUDY Each of these spelling words has at least two completely different meanings. Words that are spelled the same but have two or more completely different meanings are called **homographs**.

WRITE Sort the words. Which words have one syllable?

(1)　(2)　(3)　(4)　(5)

(6)　(7)　(8)　(9)　(10)

Which words have two syllables?

(11)　(12)　(13)　(14)　(15)

(16)　(17)　(18)　(19)　(20)

CHECK Did you spell each word correctly? Can you think of two different meanings for each word?

Pattern Power

How are homographs alike? (21) How are they different? (22)

Other Words

Write words you would like to add to this week's list.

_____ _____ _____ _____ _____

Practice Word Meanings

Words in Context

Write the homographs that complete these sentence pairs.

1. The gentle ___dove___ is a symbol of peace.

   The swimmer ___dove___ into the swimming pool.

2. Ming is the ____ winner of the contest.
   The chef prepared the ____ with fresh herbs.

3. Being late will certainly ____ the judge.
   The sweet smell of rose ____ filled the room.

4. Cathy bought a ____ to wear over her blouse.
   A horse that is a good ____ can clear a high gate.

5. Orange, lemon, and ____ trees grow in the orchard.
   Spreading ____ on the field will improve the soil.

Challenge Words • *Language Arts*

Each challenge word is a homograph. Write the challenge word that matches each meaning under Meaning 1. Then write the second meaning. Use the **Spelling Dictionary** on page 214 to help you.

Meaning 1	Challenge Word	Meaning 2
6. cupboard	____	____
7. brownish red	____	____
8. part of the arm	____	____
9. physical	____	____
10. association of people	____	____

corporal
forearm
buffet
league
maroon

Spelling Tip

Use words you know to help you spell new words.

✦ If you aren't sure how to spell the word *cue*, think of a familiar word that rhymes with *cue*, such as *blue*.

✦ Think about the ending spelling of the word *blue*. What letters stand for the final sound?

✦ Add these letters to the consonant letter you hear at the beginning of *cue*.

   blue - bl = ue   c + ue = cue

36 REVIEW Spelling Patterns

Sort the words in each list. Write each word. In Lesson 31, also circle each part of each compound word. In Lesson 34, write the homophone pairs next to each other.

driveway	**Lesson 31**
countdown	**Compound words with two syllables** / **with three or four syllables**
oatmeal	
overcoat	
foolproof	
applesauce	
videotape	
teammate	
headache	
knapsack	

Lesson 31

Compound words with two syllables

1. _____
2. _____
3. _____
4. _____
5. _____
6. _____
7. _____

with three or four syllables

8. _____
9. _____
10. _____

twenty-one
cross-country
brother-in-law
high school
question mark
cold front
one-way
sleeping bag
close-up
science fiction

Lesson 32

Open compound words

11. _____
12. _____
13. _____
14. _____
15. _____

Hyphenated compound words

16. _____
17. _____
18. _____
19. _____
20. _____

insure
councilor
petal
recipe
affect
effect
ensure
counselor
receipt
pedal

Lesson 33

Words that end with

ect 21. _____
      22. _____
sure 23. _____
      24. _____

Words that begin with

rec 25. _____
      26. _____
pe 27. _____
      28. _____
coun 29. _____
      30. _____

hire	**Lesson 34**
principal	**Word pairs that are homophones**
higher	
steal	31._____ 32._____
steak	33._____ 34._____
stake	35._____ 36._____
colonel	37._____ 38._____
steel	39._____ 40._____
principle	
kernel	

dove	**Lesson 35**	
mold	**One-syllable**	**Two-syllable**
cue	**homographs**	**homographs**
bass		
racket	41._____	45._____
refrain	42._____	46._____
flounder	43._____	47._____
elder	44._____	48._____
incense		49._____
novel		50._____

Spelling Tip

A **memory aid** is a sentence or phrase that helps you remember how to spell a word. Here is a memory aid that may help you when spelling *steak* or *stake*.

Eat steak!

✦ Notice that the spelling *ea* is in *eat* and *steak*.

✦ If you can't *eat* it, it is probably a *stake*.

Try writing your own memory aids for words from this lesson. Can you write one for *hire* and *higher*? How about *pedal* and *petal*? Write as many memory aids as you can and share them with your classmates.

stake
steak

Word Meaning Mixed Lesson Review

Meaning Clues

Write the spelling word that matches the clue below.

insure
ensure
councilor
counselor
receipt
recipe

1. list of ingredients and directions ＿＿＿
2. a member of a council ＿＿＿
3. to protect against risk or loss ＿＿＿
4. guarantee ＿＿＿
5. a person who gives advice ＿＿＿

Words in Context

Write the spelling word that correctly completes each sentence.

colonel
kernel
principal
principle
steal
steel

6. The builder ordered new ＿＿＿ beams for the gym.
7. The school board appointed a new ＿＿＿ for next year.
8. The soldiers saluted the ＿＿＿ when she walked past them.
9. Her decision was a matter of ＿＿＿.

Word Categories

Write the spelling word that fits best in each group of words.

flounder
pedal
elder
oatmeal
effect
racket
steak
sleeping bag
science fiction
videotape

10. net, ball, ＿＿＿
11. handlebar, wheel, ＿＿＿
12. movie, film, ＿＿＿
13. mystery, adventure, ＿＿＿
14. tent, backpack, ＿＿＿
15. hamburger, meatloaf, ＿＿＿
16. sole, tuna, ＿＿＿
17. toast, eggs, ＿＿＿
18. outcome, result, ＿＿＿
19. youth, adult, ＿＿＿

Vocabulary Mixed Lesson Review

Compound Words

Combine each underlined word in the compound in column A with a word in column B to form a new compound word.

	A	B	
1.	<u>brother</u>-in-law	room	*brotherhood*
2.	<u>high</u> school	hood	____
3.	<u>head</u>ache	walks	____
4.	apple<u>sauce</u>	way	____
5.	count<u>down</u>	school	____
6.	<u>cross</u>-country	line	____
7.	over<u>coat</u>	pan	____
8.	team<u>mate</u>	touch	____

Dictionary Skills

Write the spelling word for each respelling below. Use your **Spelling Dictionary** on page 214 for help. Then circle the syllables that have primary accents and underline the syllables that have secondary accents.

1. (twen′tē wun′) ____
2. (nap′sak′) ____
3. (drīv′wā′) ____
4. (wun′wā′) ____
5. (ri sēt′) ____
6. (fül′prüf′) ____

Thesaurus Skills

Use the index of your **Spelling Thesaurus** on page 182 to find the spelling word that is a synonym for each word below.

1. tale ____
2. influence ____
3. essence ____

Spelling and Writing

A movie review is a form of persuasive writing. The writer gives reasons for the reader to see the movie or not.

CONVINCING WORDS AND PHRASES

101 Dalmatians is a **high stakes, action-packed thriller.** Will the rich, greedy Cruella De Vil and her hired goons succeed in their terrible plan to steal the spotted dogs? **Even grown-ups can not refrain from laughing** at the many close-ups of the adorable puppy Dalmatians. The cutest puppy has spots shaped like a question mark. The puppies are great actors, and say all their lines on cue. When I saw it, kids thought it was hilarious when Cruella De Vil dove into a vat of molasses. The animated version of *101 Dalmatians* is great, but this one breaks the mold. I am giving this movie even higher marks than I gave *Babe* last year. **I give *101 Dalmatians* a ten!**

CLEARLY STATE AN OPINION

WRITING TIPS!!

Persuasive Writing

- Use convincing words and phrases.
- Clearly state an opinion.
- Give facts that support your opinion.
- Present the facts and reasons in a clear order.

Now write your own persuasive review. Try to use some of the spelling words in your review.

PREWRITE: What movie have you seen that you would like to recommend to your friends? List some interesting points about the movie.

DRAFT: Write a paragraph about the movie. Begin with a topic sentence that states your opinion. Give reasons to support your opinion.

REVISE: Exchange paragraphs with a classmate. Use your classmate's comments and the Writing Tips as you revise.

EDIT/PROOFREAD: Use editing marks to correct your capitalization, spelling, and punctuation. Rewrite your paragraph neatly.

PUBLISH: Publish your paragraph as a commercial for the movie you have reviewed.

SPELLING FUN
CUMULATIVE REVIEW

CROSSWORD PUZZLE

- Choose eight to ten words from Lessons 1–29 that could be included in a crossword puzzle.
- Use graph paper, or draw vertical lines on lined paper. Work out your crossword puzzle so that some of the letters of your words are used twice.
- Write one clue for each word.
- Use a pen to neatly rewrite your crossword.
- Invite a classmate to use a pencil and solve your crossword puzzle.

PLAY COMPOUNDS

- Choose twelve compound words from Lessons 31–35. Use compounds that are made up of two separate words.
- Write each word within the compound on a separate index card.
- Mix up the cards, and place them face down in a pattern of 6 cards across, and 4 cards down.

- Take turns turning over two cards at a time. If you can make a compound word with the cards, keep the cards. If not, return the cards to the array in the same position.
- The player who has the most cards when all the cards have been collected wins.

SPELLING BEE

- Members of two teams each choose one word from each lesson in Units 1–6 and list their words on a piece of paper.
- The first player on Team A calls out the first word on the team's list.
- The first player on Team B spells the word. If the word is spelled correctly,

the word is crossed out on the list. If not, the word is asked again later.

- Then the next Team B player calls out a word for the next Team A player. Continue until all the words have been used.
- The first team to finish spelling the other team's words wins.

Spelling Resources

Writing Handbook

Common Spelling Patterns

This list shows different ways sounds are spelled. Use this list when you can't find words in the dictionary to see how else the sound may be spelled.

/a/	a	active, apple	/n/	gn	design, sign		oo	shampoo, tool
/ā/	a	ache, agent		kn	knowledge, kneel		u	truly, lunar
	a-e	stake, amaze					ue	true, glue
	ai	trail, drain		n	novel, banjo		ui	cruise, fruit
/är/	ar	partner, cart		nn	banner, channel		ou	youth, coupon
/âr/	air	despair, haircut	/o/	o	lock, hobby	/ū/	ew	nephew, few
	ar	vary, wary	/ō/	o	old, Oklahoma		iew	view, review
	are	flare, dare		o-e	overthrow, owe		u	union, musical
	ere	there, anywhere		oa	poach, oak		ue	value, argue
/ch/	ch	cheat, starch		oe	foe, hoe	/ûr/	ear	earthquake, rehearse
	tch	stitch, watch		ow	own, slow			
/chər/	ture	creature, lecture	/ô/	a	although, all right		er	fertile, preserve
/e/	e	effect, pressure					ir	firm, birth
/ē/	ea	teammate, eagle		au	laundry, caution		or	worthy, work
	ee	screen, agree		aw	dawn, awful		our	courtesy, journey
	ie	believe, fields		o	loss, coffee			
/i/	i	igloo, window		ou	thoughtless, fought		ur	turn, nurse
/ī/	i	idle, triumph				/yu̇/	ur	curious, bureau
	i-e	advice, scribe	/oi/	oi	broil, appoint	/əl/	al	petal, royal
	igh	sigh, mighty		oy	loyalty, annoyance		el	shovel, travel
	y	reply, shy					il	evil, council
/îr/	eer	pioneer, peer	/ôr/	or	corduroy, order		ile	fertile, futile
	ere	severe, mere		ore	ignore, Baltimore		le	apple, purple
	ier	pier, pierce		orr	corridor, horrible	/ən/	ain	certain, fountain
/k/	ch	choral, character		our	mourn, court			
	c	coin, act	/ou/	ou	outfit, house		an	urban, island
	ck	track, knuckle		ow	towel, coward		en	chicken, broken
	k	kitchen, weak	/sh/	sh	shade, flash			
	lk	walk, talk		ch	parachute, chef		on	ribbon, apron
/m/	lm	palm, calm		ti	partial, impatient	/ər/	ar	grammar, polar
	m	macaroni, plum		ci	facial, ancient		er	copper, sweater
	mb	numb, plumber	/th/	th	thankful, thumb		or	honor, flavor
	mm	immigrant, hammer	/t͟h/	th	these, they			
	mn	autumn, condemn	/u/	u	under, upset			
			/ü/	u-e	rule, flute			
				o-e	prove, lose			

Spelling Tips: Rules

Learning these spelling rules can help you spell many words.

1. When words end in silent *e*, drop the *e* when adding an ending that begins with a vowel. *(pursue + ed = pursued)* When adding an ending that begins with a consonant, keep the silent *e*. *(agile + ly = agilely)*

2. When a base word ends with a consonant followed by *y*, change the *y* to *i* when adding any ending except endings that begin with *i*. *(cry + es = cries; cry + ing = crying)*

3. When a base word ends with a vowel followed by *y*, do not change the ending when adding suffixes or endings. *(monkey = monkeys)*

4. When a one-syllable word ends in one vowel followed by one consonant, double the consonant before adding an ending that begins with a vowel. *(run + ing = running)*

5. The letter *q* is always followed by *u*. *(quilt, quiet)*

6. No English words end in *j*, *q*, or *v*.

7. Add *-s* to most words to form plurals or to change the tense of verbs. Add *-es* to words ending in *x*, *z*, *s*, *sh*, or *ch*. *(cup = cups; laugh = laughs; glass = glasses)*

8. To make plurals of words that end with one *f* or *fe*, you often need to change the *f* or *fe* to *v* and add *-es*. *(wife = wives)*

9. When choosing *ei* or *ie*, remember that *i* comes before *e* except after *c* or when sounded like /ā/ as in *neighbor* or *weigh*.

10. When /s/ is spelled *c*, *c* is always followed by *e*, *i*, or *y*. *(peace, citizen, fancy)*

11. When /j/ is spelled *g*, *g* is always followed by *e*, *i*, or *y*. *(gem, engine, energy)*

12. If /ch/ immediately follows a short vowel in a one-syllable word, it is spelled *tch*. *(clutch, sketch)* There are a few exceptions in English: *much*, *such*, *which*, and *rich*.

13. The /f/ sound at the end of a word may be spelled *f*, *ph*, or *gh*. *(chief, graph, laugh)*

Spelling Tips

Spelling Tips: Strategies

These strategies can help you become a better speller.

1. Learn common homophones and make sure you have used the correct homophone in your writing.
   They brought *their* own books.
   Move the books over *there*.
   It's a sunny day.
   The earth gets *its* light from the sun.

2. Think of a word you know that has the same spelling pattern as the word you want to spell, such as a rhyming word. *(blue, clue, glue)*

3. Use words that you know how to spell to help you spell new words. *(flower + clock = flock)*

4. Make up clues to help you remember the spelling. *(ache = a cat has ears; u and i build a house; a piece of pie; the principal is your pal)*

5. Think of a related word that can help you spell a word with a silent letter or a hard-to-hear sound. *(sign—signal; relative–related)*

6. Divide the word into syllables. *(sub scrip tion)*

7. Learn how to spell prefixes and suffixes you use often in writing.

8. Look for word chunks or smaller words that help you remember the spelling of the word. *(hippopotamus = hippo pot am us)*

9. Change the way you say the word to yourself to help with the spelling. *(knife = /kə nīf/; beauty = /bē ə ü tē/)*

10. Think of times you may have seen the word in reading, on signs, or in another textbook. Try to remember how it looked. Write the word in different ways to see which one looks correct. *(havy, hevy, heavy)*

11. Become familiar with the dictionary and use it often. If you are working on a computer, use the spell-check program. Remember, though, that spell-checkers are not perfect. They cannot tell whether or not you have used a word correctly.

Computer Tip:
Use the spell-check, but read your writing carefully, too. The computer can't tell if you used a wrong word, such as *your* instead of *you're* or *it's* instead of *its*.

12. In a notebook, keep an alphabetical Personal Word List. List words you often have trouble spelling.

Spelling and Meaning Connections

Many words, like *cycle* and *cyclical,* are close in meaning. They are also close in spelling. Such words are called related words. Sometimes two related words can have different pronunciations but the same spelling. You can use this fact to help you remember how to spell many related words.

1. The underlined letter in the first word in each group below stays the same in other words in the group. How does the sound change?

electri<u>c</u>
electri<u>c</u>ity—a form of energy that uses electric power
electri<u>c</u>ian—a person who repairs electrical objects

mathemati<u>c</u>s
mathemati<u>c</u>ian—someone who studies and teaches mathematics

musi<u>c</u>
musi<u>c</u>ian—someone who plays music

practi<u>c</u>al
practi<u>c</u>e—the act or process of doing something

publi<u>c</u>
publi<u>c</u>ity—information given to attract public attention to a person or thing

In each group above, the sound that the letter *c* stands for changes from /k/ to /s/ or /sh/.

■ To remember how to spell *electricity,* think of the related word *electric*.

■ If you know that *electric* ends with the letter *c*, it can help you remember to spell /s/ in *electricity* with the letter *c*.

■ Use this tip with other related words that follow the same pattern as *electric* and *electricity*.

2. Here's another sound-letter pattern. What changes about the underlined letter in each word in the group?

crea<u>te</u>
crea<u>t</u>ion—the act or process of creating something

decora<u>te</u>
decora<u>t</u>ion—the act or process of decorating

depar<u>t</u>
depar<u>t</u>ure—the act of departing

direc<u>t</u>
direc<u>t</u>ion—the act or process of directing or instructing

except
exception—something that is
excepted; something to which a
rule does not apply

fact
factual—having the quality of
being based on facts

habit
habitual—being done by habit

invent
invention—something that is
invented

narrate
narration—the act or process of
narrating or telling something

operate
operation—the act or process of
operating or working

part
partial—being only a part; not full
or total

regulate
regulation—the act or process of
regulating, managing, or
controlling something

In all the words you just read, the
sound that the letter *t* stands for
changes from /t/ to /sh/ or /ch/.

■ To remember how to spell
creation, think of the related word
create.

■ If you know that *create* contains
the letter *t,* it can help you
remember to spell /sh/ in *creation*
with the letter *t.*

■ Use this tip with other related
words that follow the same pattern
as *create* and *creation.*

3. Look at the letter that is underlined
in the words in each group below.
How does the sound of that letter
change from the first word in the
group to the other word or words?

autumnal —having to do with
autumn
autumn
autumns

columnist—someone who writes a
column for a newspaper or
magazine
column
columns

condemnation—the act of
condemning or giving disapproval
condemn
condemning

crumble—to break into pieces or
crumbs
crumb
crumbs

fas<u>t</u>—firmly attached; securely
  fastened
fas<u>t</u>en
fas<u>t</u>ener
unfas<u>t</u>en

has<u>t</u>e—speed or hurry
has<u>t</u>en

in<u>h</u>erit—to receive money or
  property when someone else dies
<u>h</u>eir

mus<u>c</u>ular—having strong or well-
  developed muscles
mus<u>c</u>le
mus<u>c</u>les

rece<u>p</u>tion—the act of receiving
  something
recei<u>p</u>t

sof<u>t</u>—easy to shape; not hard
sof<u>t</u>en
sof<u>t</u>ener

In each group, the underlined letter is
sounded in the first word and silent
in the word or words that follow.

■ To remember how to spell
autumn, think of the sound of the
related word *autumnal.*

■ You can hear the *n* in *autumnal.*
That sound can help you remember
to spell the final /m/ in *autumn*
with *mn.*

■ Use this tip with other related
words that have silent and sounded
letters.

4. Each word in this group has one or
more vowels underlined. Decide
how the vowels change in other
words in the group.

br<u>ea</u>the—to draw air, or breath,
  into the lungs and let it out again
br<u>ea</u>th
br<u>ea</u>thless

c<u>a</u>ve—a hole or hollow in the
  ground or in a mountainside
c<u>a</u>vity
c<u>a</u>vern

cl<u>ea</u>n—not dirty
cl<u>ea</u>nse
cl<u>ea</u>nser

comp<u>e</u>te—to try to win or gain
  something
comp<u>e</u>tition
comp<u>e</u>titive

dr**ea**m—to see images and events in one's sleep
dr**ea**mt

h**ea**l—to get better or make something get better
h**ea**lth
h**ea**lthy

m**i**nus—less, decreased by
m**i**nimum

n**a**tion—a country that has its own government
n**a**tional
intern**a**tional

n**a**ture—all plants, animals, and other things not produced by people
n**a**tural
unn**a**tural

pl**ea**se—to give pleasure to
pl**ea**sure
pl**ea**sant

s**o**le—only; lone
s**o**litary
s**o**litude

un**i**te—to join into a single unit
un**i**t
un**i**ty

A long vowel sound in one word can sometimes change to a short vowel sound in a related word, without a change in spelling.

- *Breathe* and *breath* are related in meaning.
- *Breathe* has the long vowel sound spelled *ea*.
- *Breath* has the short vowel sound spelled *ea*.
- Remembering how to spell *breathe* can help you spell *breath*.
- Can you think of a word that will help you spell *dreamt*?

5. The underlined letter in the first word in each pair stands for /ə/. What sound does that letter stand for in the other word?

ability—the condition of being able
able

def**i**nition—a phrase or sentence that defines a word
def**i**ne

equ**a**l—the same or even
equ**a**tion

rel**a**tive—a person like a sister or cousin who is related to you
rel**a**te

supp**o**sition—something that is assumed or supposed
supp**o**se

In related words, /ə/ in one word can sometimes change to a long vowel sound in a related word, without a change in spelling.

■ The letter *a* stands for /ə/ in *ability* and a long vowel sound in *able.*

■ Remembering how to spell *able* can help you spell *ability.*

6. The underlined letter in the first word in each pair stands for /ə/. What sound does that letter stand for in the other word?

democr<u>a</u>cy—a form of government that recognizes people's rights
democr<u>a</u>tic

fin<u>a</u>l—last
fin<u>a</u>lity

hum<u>a</u>n—having to do with people
hum<u>a</u>nity

individu<u>a</u>l—one person
individu<u>a</u>lity

leg<u>a</u>l—done according to the law
leg<u>a</u>lity

person<u>a</u>l—having to do with a particular person; private
person<u>a</u>lity

In related words, /ə/ in one word can sometimes change to a short vowel sound in a related word, without a change in spelling.

■ The letter *a* stands for /ə/ in *democracy* and a short vowel sound in *democratic.*

■ Remembering how to spell *democratic* can help you spell *democracy.*

7. Many English words have word parts that come from ancient Greek or Latin. Words that contain the same Greek or Latin root are often related in spelling or meaning. Here are a few examples.

Greek roots

ast, meaning "star"
astronomy
astronaut
asterisk

bio, meaning "life"
biography
biology
autobiography

gon, meaning "angle"
polygon
trigonometry
diagonal

gram, meaning "letter" or "written"
telegram
diagram
grammar

meter, meaning "measure"
diameter
metric
centimeter

photo, meaning "light"
photograph
telephoto lens
photosynthesis

phys, meaning "nature"
physical
physics
physician

syn or *sym*, meaning "together" or "the same"
synonym
symbol
symmetrical

Latin roots

aud, meaning "hear"
audience
audible
auditorium

dict, meaning "speak"
predict
dictate
diction

fac, meaning "make or do"
factory
manufacture
facsimile

loc, meaning "place"
locate
relocate
local

mis or *mit*, meaning "send"
mission
submit
dismiss

port, meaning "carry"
portable
import
transportation

vac, meaning "empty"
vacate
vacuum
evacuate

vid or *vis*, meaning "see"
video
evidence
vision

- What other words can you think of that contain these Greek or Latin roots?

- How can you use what you know about Greek or Latin roots to explain the meaning of the word *location*?

Difficult Words

Easily Confused Words are words that are often mistaken for one another because they are spelled similarly or sound alike. These words have different definitions and can mix up the meaning of a sentence. Use this list to make sure you know the meaning of the words in each pair.

accent	alley	breath	desert	later	respectively
ascent	ally	breathe	dessert	latter	respectfully
accept	*all ready	cease	device	lay	suppose
except	already	seize	devise	lie	supposed
access	all together	cloth	emigrant	loose	than
excess	altogether	clothe	immigrant	lose	then
accuse	angel	coma	envelop	moral	though
excuse	angle	comma	envelope	morale	through
*adapt	any more	command	expand	picture	use
*adopt	anymore	commend	expend	pitcher	used
*advice	any way	continual	expect	quiet	vary
*advise	anyway	continuous	suspect	quite	very
*affect	bazaar	costume	farther	recent	your
*effect	bizarre	custom	further	resent	you're

*These words appear in Lesson 33.

Troublesome Words Some words are more difficult to spell than others. Use this list to check your spelling or to test yourself to see how many of these words you can spell correctly.

ache	college	field	let's	really	there's
again	cousin's	finally	library	reason	they're
a lot	different	foreign	license	receive	through
always	doesn't	forty	lightning	religious	together
anything	early	grabbed	met	restaurant	umbrella
argument	elementary	guess	meteor	schedule	until
around	entertainment	happened	myself	separate	upstairs
awhile	environment	happiness	no	since	usually
beautiful	especially	heard	now	someone	wear
because	everybody	height	off	something	we're
beginning	everything	he's	one	sometimes	what's
bored	except	into	our	started	which
business	exciting	it's	outside	than	whole
canoe	favorite	I've	planet	their	wouldn't
clothes	February	laboratory	probably	themselves	

Words printed in color appear in Spelling lessons.

Common Homophones

Homophones are words with the same pronunciation as one another, but with a different spelling, meaning, and origin. *Aisle* and *isle* are homophones. Use this list of homophones to help you decide which word to use.

air	bolder	*foul	missed	rain	*steal
heir	boulder	*fowl	mist	reign	*steel
aisle	capital	*higher	pain	rein	throne
isle	capitol	*hire	pane	rap	thrown
allowed	*choral	*hoard	passed	wrap	*vain
aloud	*coral	*horde	past	*real	*vane
band	cite	horse	*patience	*reel	vein
banned	sight	hoarse	patients	ring	wade
bass	site	lessen	peace	wring	weighed
base	coarse	lesson	piece	shone	wail
beat	course	lie	peer	shown	whale
beet	*colonel	lye	pier	*stake	waist
birth	*kernel	mail	pole	*steak	waste
berth	council	male	poll	stationary	
bite	counsel	*miner	*principal	*stationery	
byte	die	*minor	*principle		
	dye				

*These words appear in Lesson 34.

Writing Plan

prewrite → draft → revise → edit/proofread → publish

Writing is a way for you to share facts, ideas, or feelings. Follow these steps to create good, clear writing.

Prewrite

Decide on a topic.
Think about who your audience will be.
What is your writing purpose?

- to express feelings
- to describe
- to inform
- to persuade

Jot down what you already know about your topic. Then see what more you can learn.

- Read books, magazines and newspapers, or use the Internet.
- Talk to other people. If possible, interview an expert.
- Take a look at the real thing. If you need to, take a field trip.

How will you remember details and organize information?

- Take notes.
- Make a list or outline.
- Draw a chart or graph.
- Create a story map.
- Draw pictures.
- Make a diagram.
- Make a word web.

Draft

Now that you have gathered and organized your information, write it in sentence form. For now, just write. You'll correct problems later.

Revise

Read over your writing. Keep your audience and purpose in mind.

- Are all the important points covered?
- Did you present your ideas in a logical order? Do you need to move, take out, or add anything?
- Does your writing have a clear beginning, middle, and end?
- Do all the sentences express complete thoughts?

You could also ask a friend to look over your writing.

Writing Plan

Edit/Proofread

As you reread your writing, look carefully at these things:

- spelling
- punctuation—commas, apostrophes, quotation marks, end marks
- capital letters—to start a sentence and for proper nouns
- indenting of paragraphs
- handwriting—dotting **i**'s and **j**'s, crossing **t**'s and **x**'s

Use these editing marks as you revise, edit, and proofread.

¶Ice-skating is my favrit sport to watch on TV. The Costumes are beautiful, and the skating is exciting. a triple jump in skating can be as amazing to watch as is a run home in baseball.

Ice-skating is my favorite sport to watch on TV. The costumes are beautiful, and the skating is exciting. A triple jump in skating can be as amazing to watch as a home run in baseball.

EDITING MARKS

⬭ check spelling
≡ capital letter
/ lowercase letter
⊙ add a period
∧ add
⌇ take out
¶ indent the paragraph
⟳ move

Publish

Now you're ready to put your writing into final form. Here are some ways for you to share your work with your audience.

- Read it aloud.
- Record it on tape.
- Hang it on the wall.
- Give it to a friend.
- Illustrate it.
- Create a book.
- Act it out.
- Mail it.

Writing Plan

Types of Writing

Here are things to think about for different types of writing you may do.

Narrative Writing

Narrative writing is writing that tells a story. The story can be fictional or based on real life.

- Does the story have memorable characters who face an interesting problem? Is the solution to their problem believable?
- Will the action hold readers' attention?
- Are the events related in time order? Do any flashbacks work logically within the order of events?
- Does the characters' dialog help move the story forward?
- Have you written in a style that is uniquely your own?

Report

A report gives information about a subject. It presents facts about that subject in a clear, well-organized way.

- Do you present the main idea of your report in an introduction?
- Does the body of the report contain facts that are logically organized?
- Do you conclude your report with a clear summary of the facts?

Explanatory Writing

Explanatory writing gives information about something or tells how to make or do something.

- Did you start by clearly expressing your purpose?
- Have you presented information and details in the right order?
- Do you need to add details to make your explanation clearer?
- Should your explanation be accompanied by pictures or diagrams?

Persuasive Writing

Persuasive writing presents the writer's view and tries to get readers to share it or to take some action. Examples of persuasive writing include ads, film reviews, letters to a newspaper, and book reports.

- Did you make your point by using facts and persuasive language?
- What is the most convincing part of your writing?
- Are readers likely to adopt your opinion on this issue?

Comparison/Contrast Writing

Comparison/contrast writing presents information about two things to show how they are alike and how they are different.

- Do you start by expressing your main idea?
- Do you make clear comparisons and contrasts? Are they in an order that makes them easy to understand?
- Do the comparisons and contrasts help express the main idea?
- Did you end with a clear conclusion?

Descriptive Writing

Descriptive writing paints a picture with words. This word picture can describe a person, place, thing, or event. Sensory details—details that appeal to the five senses—help put your readers in the scene.

- Have you used sensory details to create a vivid word picture?
- When appropriate, have you used figurative language such as similes and metaphors?
- Does your writing express a feeling about your subject?

Capitalization and Punctuation Tips

Abbreviation An abbreviation is a short form of a word. Most abbreviations begin with a capital letter and end with a period. An abbreviation for *inch* is *in.,* and an abbreviation for *department* is *dept.*

Use abbreviations for titles of people, addresses, days of the week, and months of the year.

Mr. and Mrs. Rivera   **56 Shore Ave.**   **Sat.**   **Apr.**

Some abbreviations, such as the U.S. Postal Service abbreviations for the names of states, contain all capital letters and no periods.

Alabama—AL	Missouri—MO
Alaska—AK	Montana—MT
Arizona—AZ	Nebraska—NE
Arkansas—AR	Nevada—NV
California—CA	New Hampshire—NH
Colorado—CO	New Jersey—NJ
Connecticut—CT	New Mexico—NM
Delaware—DE	New York—NY
District of	North Carolina—NC
Columbia—DC	North Dakota—ND
Florida—FL	Ohio—OH
Georgia—GA	Oklahoma—OK
Hawaii—HI	Oregon—OR
Idaho—ID	Pennsylvania—PA
Illinois—IL	Rhode Island—RI
Indiana—IN	South Carolina—SC
Iowa—IA	South Dakota—SD
Kansas—KS	Tennessee—TN
Kentucky—KY	Texas—TX
Louisiana—LA	Utah—UT
Maine—ME	Vermont—VT
Maryland—MD	Virginia—VA
Massachusetts—MA	Washington—WA
Michigan—MI	West Virginia—WV
Minnesota—MN	Wisconsin—WI
Mississippi—MS	Wyoming—WY

Apostrophe
An apostrophe is a punctuation mark used with *s* to show possession.

When an apostrophe with *s* is used after a person's name, it shows that something belongs to that person.

Jake's bike the bike that belongs to Jake

Use an apostrophe alone to form the possessive of a plural noun that ends in *-s*.

the doctors' offices the offices that belong to the doctors

Use an apostrophe to show where letters have been left out in a contraction.

wouldn't would not

Capitalization
Capitalization is the writing of the first letter of a word in its upper case form.

Capitalize the first word in a sentence.

This is the way to draw a tree.

Capitalize the first letter of a proper noun.

Yoshiko Dr. Valdez New Zealand

Capitalize days of the week, months, and holidays.

Sunday October Presidents' Day

Colon
A colon is a punctuation mark used to introduce a list, an explanation, or an example.

I can play the following instruments: the piano, the guitar, and the recorder.

A colon is also used to separate hours and minutes when writing time in numerals.

I will leave promptly at 3:30.

Comma A comma is a punctuation mark that indicates a pause or separation between parts of a sentence.

Use a comma between the city and the state in an address.

Augusta, Maine

Use a comma between the day and the year in a date.

November 2, 1998

Use commas to separate three or more items in a series.

That store sells videos, CD ROMs, and music tapes.

Use a comma after the greeting in a friendly letter and the closing in all letters.

Dear Iris,   Yours truly,

Use commas to set off an appositive phrase.

My sister, a doctor, says that garlic is good for you.

Use a comma after a dependent clause if the clause comes first in a sentence.

Although it is very cold, rain instead of snow is falling.

Use a comma before the coordinating conjunction that separates two independent clauses in a sentence.

Vera went hiking yesterday, but Dennis stayed home.

End Punctuation The punctuation mark at the end of a sentence tells you what kind of sentence it is.

A **period** is used at the end of a statement, a mild command, or a polite request.

Inez is running for class president.   Please be seated.

An **exclamation point** is used at the end of a strong command or an exclamatory sentence.

Don't look down!   That was amazing!

A **question mark** is used at the end of an interrogative sentence, or question.

Who is working at that desk?

Hyphen Use a hyphen to show the division of a word at the end of a line. Divide the word between syllables.

A hyphen is one kind of punctu-ation mark.

A hyphen can also be used to form some compound words.

self-confidence   world-class   double-decker

Initial An initial is the first letter of a name. A period is used after an initial.

E.B. White

Quotation Marks In a direct quotation, quotation marks go before and after the exact words that someone said.

DeeDee said, "I'm going to try out for the play."

Semicolon Use a semicolon to join the parts of a compound sentence when a coordinating conjunction such as *and, but,* or *or* is not used.

The sun has almost set; the sky is getting dark.

Grammar Glossary

Adjective An adjective is a word that can be used to describe a noun or pronoun. It tells what kind, how many, or which one.

> The <u>new</u> shoes are <u>comfortable</u>.

Adverb An adverb is a word that can describe a verb, an adjective, or another adverb. It tells how, when, where, or how much.

> He <u>immediately</u> answered my call.

Appositive Phrase An appositive phrase is a group of words that identifies or explains a nearby noun or pronoun.

> Mr. and Mrs. Garcia, <u>the people who live next door</u>, are both lawyers.

Article An article is a special adjective. *A* and *an* are called **indefinite articles** because they refer to any of a group of people, places, things, or ideas. *The* is called a **definite article** because it identifies a particular person, place, thing, or idea.

Comparative Adjective A comparative adjective is a form of an adjective that can compare two or more persons or things. To compare two persons or things, form the comparative by adding *-er* to some adjectives. To compare more than two persons or things, form the superlative by adding *-est* to some adjectives.

> Bears are <u>large</u>, but elephants are <u>larger</u>.

> Bears and elephants are <u>large</u>, but blue whales are the world's <u>largest</u> animals.

For some other adjectives, add the word *more* or *less* to form the comparative, and the word *most* or *least* to form the superlative.

> Drawing was the <u>most difficult</u> skill I ever tried to learn, and singing was the <u>least difficult</u>.

Comparative Adverb The comparative form of an adverb compares two actions or qualities. Form a comparative by adding *-er* to some adverbs. To compare more than two actions or qualities, form the superlative by adding *-est* to some adverbs.

> Ilya arrived <u>late</u>, but Mei Lee arrived <u>later</u>.

> Of the three, Diego arrived <u>latest</u>.

For some adverbs, add *more* or *less* to form the comparative, and the word *most* or *least* to form the superlative.

> Isabela speaks <u>more rapidly</u> when she is nervous and <u>less rapidly</u> when she is calm.

Complete Predicate The complete predicate is the simple predicate and all the words in a sentence that tell what the subject is or does.

> Cats <u>sleep in the sun</u>.

Complete Subject The complete subject is the simple subject and all the words in a sentence that tell what or whom the sentence is about.

> <u>The large, golden-eyed owl</u> turned its head.

Compound Predicate A compound predicate occurs when a sentence contains more than one equally important predicate, or verb phrase. The coordinating conjunctions *and, but,* or *or* can be used to join a compound predicate.

> The race <u>began and ended</u> quickly.

Compound Sentence A compound sentence is formed by joining two or more sentences with a coordinating conjunction such as *and, but,* or *or.* A comma is placed before the conjunction that joins the sentences.

I live in Ohio, *but* **you live in Texas.**

Compound Subject A compound subject occurs when a sentence contains more than one equally important subject. The coordinating conjunctions *and, but,* or *or* can be used to join a compound subject.

Flowers and vegetables grow in my garden.

Compound Word A compound word is formed by putting two or more words together to make a new word. A compound word can be a hyphenated compound, an open compound, or a closed compound.

water-repellent   water mill   waterfall

Conjunction A conjunction is a word that is used to join words or groups of words. **Coordinating conjunctions** such as *and, but,* and *or* can be used to make compound sentences, subjects, and predicates.

Contraction A contraction is a short form of two words. An apostrophe replaces letters that are left out.

Didn't is a contraction for did not.

Declarative Sentence A declarative sentence is a statement. It ends with a period.

Australia is both an island and a continent.

Dependent Clause A dependent clause is a group of words with a subject and a verb that cannot stand on its own as a separate sentence.

Because I like music, I went to a concert last week.

Double Negatives Some adverbs, like *no* and *not,* are called negatives because they negate the meaning in the rest of a sentence. Using two negatives in the same sentence is considered a mistake because they cancel one another.

Some negative words: **no not nobody none no one nothing**

Correct: **No one was there.**
Correct: **There wasn't anyone there.**
Mistake: **There wasn't no one there.**

Exclamatory Sentence An exclamatory sentence shows excitement, surprise, or strong feeling. It ends with an exclamation mark.

Watch out for the traffic!

Homographs Homographs are words that have the same spelling but completely different meanings. *Counter* is a homograph because it can mean "a long table, like the selling area in a store" or "opposite."

Homophones Homophones are words that sound the same but are spelled differently and have different meanings. The words *pear* and *pair* are homophones.

Imperative Sentence An imperative sentence gives a command or request. It ends with a period or an exclamation mark.

Don't turn off the light.
Get out of the way!

Grammar Glossary

Independent Clause An independent clause is a group of words with a subject and a verb that can stand on its own as a separate sentence.

Margaret wants to paint a mural, but Greg wants to make a mobile.

Interrogative Sentence An interrogative sentence asks a question. It ends with a question mark.

Does that toy need batteries to run?

Irregular Verb An irregular verb is a verb that does not follow the rule of forming the past tense and the past participle by adding -ed or -d to the base form of the word.

base form: **begin**
past tense: **began**
past participle: **begun**

Noun A noun is the name of a person, place, thing, or idea.

student	**village**
computer	**helpfulness**

Paragraph A paragraph is a group of sentences that tells about one main idea. The first word in a paragraph is indented, or set in from the margin.

Parts of Speech The English language is divided into eight parts of speech. Each word is a part of speech: a noun, a verb, an adjective, an adverb, a conjunction, a pronoun, an interjection, or a preposition. Some words can be used as more than one part of speech.

Guess can be a noun or a verb.

Plural Plural means "more than one." The plurals of most nouns are formed by adding -s or -es to the noun. Some plurals are formed by changing the spelling of the noun. Some nouns can be both singular and plural.

bird birds	**wax waxes**
man men	**sheep sheep**

Possessive A possessive is a word that shows ownership. There are possessive forms of both pronouns and nouns.

Here are the possessive forms of the pronouns:

my	**your**	**his**	**her**	**its**
our	**their**			
mine	**yours**	**his**	**hers**	**its**
ours	**theirs**			

To form the possessive of most singular nouns, add an apostrophe and -s.

the cow's horns   Sara's coat

To form the possessive of most regular plural nouns, add an apostrophe.

the boys' gloves

To form the possessive of most irregular plural nouns, add an apostrophe and -s.

the children's room
the women's voices

Prefix A prefix is a meaningful unit of letters added to the beginning of a base word to form a new word.

dis- + agree = disagree

Preposition A preposition is a word that links a noun or pronoun to the rest of the sentence.

Some common prepositions:

for	**to**	**around**	**in**	**by**	**at**
out	**under**	**against**	**on**		

Pronoun A pronoun is a word or group of words that takes the place of a noun or a group of words acting as a noun.

Dr. Rao is in Utah. She is visiting relatives.

Grammar Glossary

Proper Noun A proper noun is the name of a particular person, place, or thing.

**Barbara Jordan   Montana
Mount Everest**

Question A question, or interrogative sentence, asks about something. It ends with a question mark.

What happens next in the story?

Quotation A quotation includes the words that someone says. A direct quotation is the exact words that someone says. Quotation marks are used before and after it, and commas are used to set it off from the rest of the sentence. The first word is capitalized. If a direct quotation is broken up, the first word in the second part of it is *not* capitalized if it does not start a complete sentence.

Sophie said, "Please sit down."

"Please, " said Sophie, "sit down."

Sentence A sentence is a group of words that tells one complete thought. The first word in a sentence begins with a capital letter. A sentence may end with a period, a question mark, or an exclamation mark.

Simple Predicate The simple predicate, or verb, is the main word or words in the complete predicate of a sentence. It tells what the subject of the sentence is or does.

Tall pine trees <u>grow</u> in the forest.

Simple Subject The simple subject is the main word or words in the complete subject of a sentence. It tells what the sentence is about.

A small <u>box</u> is in the store window.

Subject/Verb Agreement The form of verbs changes depending on the number of people or things performing the action. This is called subject/verb agreement. If one person or thing is performing the action, the verb is **singular.** If more than one person is performing the action, the verb is **plural.**

The skater <u>glides</u>.

The skaters <u>glide</u>.

Suffix A suffix is a meaningful letter or group of letters added to the end of a word to change its meaning or part of speech.

kind + <u>ness</u> = kindness

Verb A verb is a word that expresses action or state of being. The simple predicate in a sentence is a verb. The principal parts of verbs are the forms the verb has to show present, past, or future tense.

**climb   climbed   will climb
seem   seemed   will seem**

Grammar Glossary

How to Use the Spelling Thesaurus

Thesaurus Entry

Have you ever looked for just the right word to make a sentence more interesting or exciting? You could find that word in a thesaurus. A **thesaurus** is a collection of synonyms and antonyms. It can help you with your writing. Read this sentence:

> The group of friends walked *happily* down the street, *happily* singing a song.

The sentence would be better if the word *happily* wasn't used twice. You need another word that means the same or almost the same as *happily*. You can find one in your **Spelling Thesaurus**.

Read the thesaurus entry below. There are four synonyms for *happily*. You can use one or more of those synonyms to rewrite the sentence like this:

> The group of friends walked *blithely* down the street, *merrily* singing a song.

Look at this entry for *happily*.

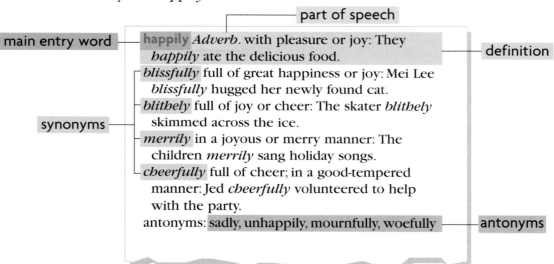

part of speech

main entry word →

happily *Adverb.* with pleasure or joy: They *happily* ate the delicious food.

definition

blissfully full of great happiness or joy: Mei Lee *blissfully* hugged her newly found cat.
blithely full of joy or cheer: The skater *blithely* skimmed across the ice.

synonyms

merrily in a joyous or merry manner: The children *merrily* sang holiday songs.
cheerfully full of cheer; in a good-tempered manner: Jed *cheerfully* volunteered to help with the party.

antonyms: sadly, unhappily, mournfully, woefully

antonyms

A few **Spelling Thesaurus** entries have so many synonyms that you'll find a box full of synonyms instead of sentences. The box may also have some antonyms. Here's the box for *racket*.

racket

Noun. a loud or confusing noise.

blast	reverberation
clamor	roar
clatter	stir
din	tumult
hullabaloo	uproar
pandemonium	

antonyms: quiet, calm, silence, hush

Thesaurus Index

The index can help you find what is in your **Spelling Thesaurus**. The index is a listing of every word in the **Spelling Thesaurus**, including every synonym and every antonym. All the words are in alphabetical order.

Each **entry word** is listed in red:
> happily *Adverb*

To find this entry word, look in the **Spelling Thesaurus** under **H.** Use the guide words at the top of each page to help you.

Each *synonym* is listed in italic print. Next to the synonym is the synonym's entry word.
> *merrily* **happily** *Adverb*

To find the meaning of the word *merrily,* look up the thesaurus entry for **happily**.

Each antonym is listed in black print. Next to the antonym is its entry word.
> sadly **happily** *Adverb*

To find this word, look up the entry for **happily.**

Shades of Meaning

Take a moment to look through your **Spelling Thesaurus**. You'll find something interesting about synonyms. While some synonym pairs have exactly the same meaning, others don't. For example, two synonyms of **vacant** are *unoccupied* and *abandoned. Unoccupied* means "containing no one; unused." *Abandoned* means "once used but now left behind." You might describe an empty kitchen as *unoccupied,* but you wouldn't describe it as *abandoned.* The definitions and sample sentences with each word will help you figure out whether the synonyms have slightly different meanings.

Try This: Replace each underlined word with a more exact word. Use your **Spelling Thesaurus** to help you. Then write your new sentence.

1. The key is <u>absent</u> from the hook I keep it on.

2. The food that was cooking on the stove gave off a delicious <u>perfume</u>.

3. I need to get rid of the <u>quantity</u> of weeds growing in the garden.

4. As soon as the singer leaves the stage, the audience will <u>enclose</u> him.

5. If you do your work too <u>rapidly</u>, you'll make mistakes.

Spelling Thesaurus Index

A

abandoned vacant *Adjective*
abilities *Noun*
abnormal natural *Adjective*
absent *Adjective*
absurd foolish *Adjective*
abundance quantity *Noun*
accept deny *Verb*
accord quarrel *Noun*
accurate exact *Adjective*
accurate mistaken *Adjective*
achieve gain *Verb*
acquaintance knowledge *Noun*
active inactive *Adjective*
acute keen *Adjective*
adjust vary *Verb*
admire respect *Verb*
adopt Verb
adult grown-up *Adjective*
advice Noun
affect Verb
agreement quarrel *Noun*
alarm frighten *Verb*
allow permit *Verb*
alter vary *Verb*
altogether barely *Adverb*
angry calm *Adjective*
annoy bother *Verb*
appear vanish *Verb*
approve adopt *Verb*
approved official *Adjective*
aptitudes abilities *Noun*
argument quarrel *Noun*
aroma perfume *Noun*
array variety *Noun*
association union *Noun*
assortment variety *Noun*
assumption notion *Noun*

assurance promise *Noun*
at once immediately *Adverb*
attain gain *Verb*
attentive careless *Adjective*
atypical natural *Adjective*
authorized official *Adjective*
away absent *Adjective*

B

ban permit *Verb*
ban require *Verb*
banquet *Noun*
bar permit *Verb*
bar require *Verb*
barely *Adverb*
belief opinion *Noun*
bevy horde *Noun*
blast racket *Noun*
blaze flare *Noun*
blissfully happily *Adverb*
blithely happily *Adverb*
bolted fled *Verb*
book novel *Noun*
bore charm *Verb*
bother *Verb*
bound *Verb*
brand-new *Adjective*
brawny mighty *Adjective*
bumpy uneven *Adjective*

C

calm *Adjective*
calm racket *Noun*
captivate charm *Verb*
careful careless *Adjective*
careless *Adjective*

certain uncertain *Adjective*
change vary *Verb*
characteristic quality *Noun*
charm *Verb*
charm bother *Verb*
cheerfully happily *Adverb*
clamor racket *Noun*
clatter racket *Noun*
clattering silent *Adjective*
commonplace pedestrian *Adjective*
companion *Noun*
compelling urgent *Adjective*
completely barely *Adverb*
conceit pride *Noun*
concoct maneuver *Verb*
confine limit *Verb*
conflict quarrel *Noun*
consequence effect *Noun*
constant frequent *Adjective*
continual frequent *Adjective*
conviction opinion *Noun*
correct exact *Adjective*
correct mistaken *Adjective*
counsel advice *Noun*
courteous impolite *Adjective*
courtesy *Noun*
cover shelter *Verb*
crimson scarlet *Adjective*
critical urgent *Adjective*
crowd horde *Noun*
crowded vacant *Adjective*
crucial unnecessary *Adjective*
custom-made ready-made *Adjective*

D

danger threat *Noun*
dawdle loiter *Verb*
decided uncertain *Adjective*

decline decrease *Verb*
decline deny *Verb*
decrease *Verb*
defect flaw *Noun*
delay hesitate *Verb*
delight bother *Verb*
demand require *Verb*
deny *Verb*
depict describe *Verb*
describe *Verb*
deserving worthy *Adjective*
device instrument *Noun*
devise maneuver *Verb*
diary journal *Noun*
dillydally loiter *Verb*
diminish decrease *Verb*
diminutive tall *Adjective*
din racket *Noun*
dinner banquet *Noun*
disappear vanish *Verb*
disapprove adopt *Verb*
discharge dismiss *Verb*
discourteous impolite *Adjective*
dismiss *Verb*
disperse scatter *Verb*
display shelter *Verb*
displease charm *Verb*
disrespectful impolite *Adjective*
disseminate scatter *Verb*
disturb bother *Verb*
dominant major *Adjective*
doubtful uncertain *Adjective*
drove horde *Noun*
dull keen *Adjective*
dull pedestrian *Adjective*
dwindle decrease *Verb*

Spelling Thesaurus

ease hamper *Verb*
easily *Adverb*
ebb decrease *Verb*
effect *Noun*
effortlessly easily *Adverb*
embrace adopt *Verb*
empty vacant *Adjective*
encircle enclose *Verb*
enclose *Verb*
enclose shelter *Verb*
encompass enclose *Verb*
encourage frighten *Verb*
enemy companion *Noun*
energetic inactive *Adjective*
enterprise venture *Noun*
entirely barely *Adverb*
escaped fled *Verb*
essence kernel *Noun*
essential unnecessary *Adjective*
esteem respect *Verb*
evaporate vanish *Verb*
even uneven *Adjective*
exact Adjective
exasperate bother *Verb*
excited calm *Adjective*
excited inactive *Adjective*
exciting pedestrian *Adjective*
excuse dismiss *Verb*
expand decrease *Verb*
expand limit *Verb*
expect require *Verb*

fade vanish *Verb*
falter hesitate *Verb*
fascinate charm *Verb*
feast banquet *Noun*
feature quality *Noun*
federation union *Noun*
feeble mighty *Adjective*
feed nourish *Verb*
filled vacant *Adjective*
find locate *Verb*
fine keen *Adjective*
flare *Noun*
flash flare *Noun*
flaw *Noun*
fled *Verb*
flock horde *Noun*
fluctuate vary *Verb*
foe companion *Noun*
foolish *Adjective*
forbid permit *Verb*
forbid require *Verb*
forceful mighty *Adjective*
fragrance perfume *Noun*
frail mighty *Adjective*
freedom independence *Noun*
frequent *Adjective*
fresh brand-new *Adjective*
friend companion *Noun*
frighten *Verb*
frivolous foolish *Adjective*
full vacant *Adjective*
fully barely *Adverb*
functional practical *Adjective*

G

gain *Verb*
gather marshal *Verb*
gather scatter *Verb*
gathering horde *Noun*
gesture signal *Noun*
gist kernel *Noun*
glare flare *Noun*
good manners courtesy *Noun*
grant deny *Verb*
gratify bother *Verb*
greater major *Adjective*
grow decrease *Verb*
grown-up *Adjective*
guard shelter *Verb*
guidance advice *Noun*

H

hamper *Verb*
handcrafted ready-made *Adjective*
handily easily *Adverb*
handmade ready-made *Adjective*
happily *Adverb*
hardly barely *Adverb*
hardy mighty *Adjective*
hastily rapidly *Adverb*
heap *Noun*
hearten frighten *Verb*
heckle bother *Verb*
help hamper *Verb*
here absent *Adjective*
hesitate *Verb*
hide shelter *Verb*
higher major *Adjective*
hinder hamper *Verb*
hodgepodge variety *Noun*

horde *Noun*
horrify frighten *Verb*
hover loom *Verb*
hullabaloo racket *Noun*
humility pride *Noun*
hurry loiter *Verb*
hush racket *Noun*

I

ignore adopt *Verb*
imaginative pedestrian *Adjective*
immature grown-up *Adjective*
immediately *Adverb*
impede hamper *Verb*
imperfection flaw *Noun*
implement instrument *Noun*
impolite *Adjective*
impoliteness courtesy *Noun*
impractical practical *Adjective*
imprecise exact *Adjective*
in attendance absent *Adjective*
inaccurate exact *Adjective*
inactive *Adjective*
inattentive careless *Adjective*
incorrect exact *Adjective*
incorrect mistaken *Adjective*
increase decrease *Verb*
increase limit *Verb*
independence *Noun*
inexact exact *Adjective*
inflate limit *Verb*
influence affect *Verb*
infrequent frequent *Adjective*
insensitive keen *Adjective*
insignificant major *Adjective*
insist upon require *Verb*
instantly immediately *Adverb*
instrument *Noun*
intelligent foolish *Adjective*

Spelling Thesaurus

interfere with hamper *Verb*
invincible mighty *Adjective*
irk bother *Verb*
irrational foolish *Adjective*
irregular uneven *Adjective*
irritate bother *Verb*

join scatter *Verb*
journal *Noun*

keen *Adjective*
kernel *Noun*
key major *Adjective*
knowledge *Noun*

languid inactive *Adjective*
laughable foolish *Adjective*
leading major *Adjective*
leap bound *Verb*
lessen decrease *Verb*
let permit *Verb*
lethargic inactive *Adjective*
liberty independence *Noun*
limit *Verb*
limited keen *Adjective*
linger loiter *Verb*
listless inactive *Adjective*
locate *Verb*
lofty tall *Adjective*
log journal *Noun*

loiter *Verb*
loom *Verb*
lose gain *Verb*
lose locate *Verb*
loud silent *Adjective*
loudly quietly *Adverb*
ludicrous foolish *Adjective*

made-to-order ready-made *Adjective*
major *Adjective*
maneuver *Verb*
mannerly impolite *Adjective*
manufactured ready-made *Adjective*
marshal *Verb*
mass heap *Noun*
mass horde *Noun*
mass-produced ready-made *Adjective*
mature grown-up *Adjective*
meander roam *Verb*
mechanism instrument *Noun*
menace threat *Noun*
merrily happily *Adverb*
mighty *Adjective*
minor major *Adjective*
minute tall *Adjective*
misinformed mistaken *Adjective*
miss locate *Verb*
missing absent *Adjective*
mistaken *Adjective*
mistaken foolish *Adjective*
mob horde *Noun*
modesty pride *Noun*
modify vary *Verb*
motion signal *Noun*
mournfully happily *Adverb*
multiply limit *Verb*
multitude horde *Noun*
muscular mighty *Adjective*
myriads horde *Noun*

N

nag bother *Verb*
narrow limit *Verb*
natural *Adjective*
necessary unnecessary *Adjective*
needed unnecessary *Adjective*
needless unnecessary *Adjective*
noiseless silent *Adjective*
noisily quietly *Adverb*
noisy silent *Adjective*
nonsensical foolish *Adjective*
normal natural *Adjective*
notion *Noun*
nourish *Verb*
novel *Noun*
numerous frequent *Adjective*

O

occasional frequent *Adjective*
occupied vacant *Adjective*
odor perfume *Noun*
official *Adjective*
old brand-new *Adjective*
opinion *Noun*
organize marshal *Verb*
original pedestrian *Adjective*
outcome effect *Noun*
overshadow loom *Verb*

P

pack horde *Noun*
paint describe *Verb*
pal companion *Noun*
pandemonium racket *Noun*
pause hesitate *Verb*

peaceful calm *Adjective*
pedestrian *Adjective*
perfume *Noun*
permit *Verb*
perturb bother *Verb*
pester bother *Verb*
petrify frighten *Verb*
pile heap *Noun*
pinpoint locate *Verb*
please bother *Verb*
pledge promise *Noun*
plot maneuver *Verb*
polite impolite *Adjective*
politeness courtesy *Noun*
portion section *Noun*
portray describe *Verb*
potent mighty *Adjective*
powerful mighty *Adjective*
practical *Adjective*
precise exact *Adjective*
present absent *Adjective*
pressing urgent *Adjective*
pride *Noun*
primary major *Adjective*
profusion quantity *Noun*
prohibit permit *Verb*
prohibit require *Verb*
promise *Noun*
promptly immediately *Adverb*
protect shelter *Verb*
provoke bother *Verb*

Q

quality *Noun*
quantity *Noun*
quarrel *Noun*
quickly rapidly *Adverb*
quiet racket *Noun*
quiet silent *Adjective*

Spelling Thesaurus

quietly *Adverb*
quiver tremble *Verb*

racket *Noun*
ramble roam *Verb*
ranking major *Adjective*
rapidly *Adverb*
rare frequent *Adjective*
readily immediately *Adverb*
ready-made *Adjective*
realistic practical *Adjective*
reappear vanish *Verb*
reasonable practical *Adjective*
reassure frighten *Verb*
rebuff deny *Verb*
red scarlet *Adjective*
refuse deny *Verb*
regular uneven *Adjective*
reject adopt *Verb*
reject deny *Verb*
remained fled *Verb*
remarkable pedestrian *Adjective*
repeated frequent *Adjective*
repel charm *Verb*
require *Verb*
required unnecessary *Adjective*
respect *Verb*
respectful impolite *Adjective*
responsible careless *Adjective*
restrict limit *Verb*
result effect *Noun*
reverberation racket *Noun*
ridiculous foolish *Adjective*
ring enclose *Verb*
roam *Verb*
roar racket *Noun*
rough uneven *Adjective*
rove roam *Verb*

ruby scarlet *Adjective*
rude impolite *Adjective*
rudeness courtesy *Noun*
rush loiter *Verb*

sadly happily *Adverb*
safeguard shelter *Verb*
sanction adopt *Verb*
scarcely barely *Adverb*
scarlet *Adjective*
scatter *Verb*
scent perfume *Noun*
scheme maneuver *Verb*
scorn respect *Verb*
screen shelter *Verb*
seasoned grown-up *Adjective*
section *Noun*
segment section *Noun*
senseless foolish *Adjective*
sensible practical *Adjective*
serviceable practical *Adjective*
settled uncertain *Adjective*
settlement quarrel *Noun*
shake tremble *Verb*
shape affect *Verb*
sharp keen *Adjective*
shelter *Verb*
shield shelter *Verb*
shift vary *Verb*
shiver tremble *Verb*
short tall *Adjective*
shortcoming flaw *Noun*
sign signal *Noun*
signal *Noun*
silence racket *Noun*
silent *Adjective*
silently quietly *Adverb*

Spelling Thesaurus

silly foolish *Adjective*
sizable tall *Adjective*
skills abilities *Noun*
slice section *Noun*
slowly immediately *Adverb*
slowly rapidly *Adverb*
sluggish inactive *Adjective*
sluggishly rapidly *Adverb*
smart foolish *Adjective*
smooth uneven *Adjective*
smoothly easily *Adverb*
sound practical *Adjective*
soundless silent *Adjective*
soundlessly quietly *Adverb*
speed loiter *Verb*
speedily rapidly *Adverb*
spin twirl *Verb*
spot locate *Verb*
spring bound *Verb*
spurn adopt *Verb*
squabble quarrel *Noun*
stack heap *Noun*
stale brand-new *Adjective*
stayed fled *Verb*
stealthily quietly *Adverb*
stir racket *Noun*
story novel *Noun*
stranger companion *Noun*
strew scatter *Verb*
strong mighty *Adjective*
substance kernel *Noun*
superfluous unnecessary *Adjective*
superhuman mighty *Adjective*
superior major *Adjective*
sure uncertain *Adjective*
surround enclose *Verb*
surround shelter *Verb*
sustain nourish *Verb*
swarm horde *Noun*
sway affect *Verb*
swiftly rapidly *Adverb*

tale novel *Noun*
talents abilities *Noun*
tall *Adjective*
tardily immediately *Adverb*
terrify frighten *Verb*
theory notion *Noun*
thoughtful careless *Adjective*
thoughtless careless *Adjective*
threat *Noun*
threaten loom *Verb*
throng horde *Noun*
tiny tall *Adjective*
took flight fled *Verb*
tool instrument *Noun*
tough mighty *Adjective*
towering tall *Adjective*
trait quality *Noun*
tranquil calm *Adjective*
transform vary *Verb*
tremble *Verb*
tumult racket *Noun*
twirl *Verb*
typical natural *Adjective*

unauthorized official *Adjective*
uncertain *Adjective*
uncover shelter *Verb*
undecided uncertain *Adjective*
understanding knowledge *Noun*
understanding quarrel *Noun*
undertaking venture *Noun*
uneven *Adjective*
unexpected natural *Adjective*
unhappily happily *Adverb*

KEY

entry word

synonym

antonym

part of speech

Spelling Thesaurus

unimportant **major** *Adjective*
union *Noun*
unite **scatter** *Verb*
unnatural **natural** *Adjective*
unnecessary *Adjective*
unoccupied **vacant** *Adjective*
unrealistic **practical** *Adjective*
unruffled **calm** *Adjective*
unseasoned **grown-up** *Adjective*
unsettled **uncertain** *Adjective*
unthinking **careless** *Adjective*
unused **brand-new** *Adjective*
unwise **foolish** *Adjective*
unworkable **practical** *Adjective*
unyielding **mighty** *Adjective*
uproar **racket** *Noun*
urgent *Adjective*
usable **practical** *Adjective*
used **brand-new** *Adjective*
useful **unnecessary** *Adjective*
useless **unnecessary** *Adjective*
useless **worthy** *Adjective*

vacant *Adjective*
valuable **worthy** *Adjective*
value **respect** *Verb*
vanish *Verb*
vanity **pride** *Noun*
variety *Noun*
vary *Verb*
vault **bound** *Verb*
venture *Noun*
vex **bother** *Verb*
vibrant **inactive** *Adjective*
view **opinion** *Noun*

waited **fled** *Verb*
weak **mighty** *Adjective*
welcome **deny** *Verb*
well-informed **mistaken** *Adjective*
whirl **twirl** *Verb*
whole **section** *Noun*
wholly **barely** *Adverb*
wise **foolish** *Adjective*
woefully **happily** *Adverb*
word **promise** *Noun*
workable **practical** *Adjective*
worry **bother** *Verb*
worthless **worthy** *Adjective*
worthwhile **worthy** *Adjective*
worthy *Adjective*
wrong **exact** *Adjective*

youthful **grown-up** *Adjective*

Spelling Thesaurus

abilities

*Noun, plural of **ability**.* powers to do or to act: My teacher believes that all people have artistic *abilities*.

skills powers or abilities to do something: Marta's writing *skills* helped her win the poetry contest.

aptitudes natural abilities or talents: Barry shows *aptitudes* for music and math.

talents special natural abilities or aptitudes: The *talents* of many actors contributed to the movie's success.

absent

Adjective. not in a place at a certain time: Two senators were *absent* from the meeting.

away in another place; absent: Mercedes called Ron, but he was *away* from home at the time.

missing absent or lacking: One of the pieces from the toy is *missing* from the box.

> antonyms: present, here

adopt

Verb. to accept or approve, especially by formal vote: The mayor hopes the citizens will *adopt* the plan.

approve to have a favorable opinion toward or give consent to: Most of the club members *approve* the list of rules.

sanction to give approval or support to: Many businesses *sanction* the use of recycled paper.

embrace to take up as one's own, to adopt: Today, many countries *embrace* the idea of conserving the environment.

> antonyms: reject, disapprove, spurn, ignore

advice

Noun. an opinion that helps someone make a decision or take action: Helen asked her aunt's *advice* about the problem.

counsel thoughtful opinion: The man's wise *counsel* gave the villagers hope.

guidance something that guides or gives direction: Jeremy asked Mrs. Quinn for *guidance* in choosing next year's classes.

affect

Verb. to act upon: Vitamins *affect* people's health in a good way.

influence to produce an effect: A good teacher can *influence* the way a student feels about learning.

shape to give a definite direction or character to: The books I read and admire often *shape* the way I write.

Spelling Thesaurus

sway to cause to be directed in a certain way: Guillermo did not let the TV ads *sway* his opinions of the candidates.

banquet

Noun. a large, elaborate, or formal meal: My family had a *banquet* to celebrate my great-grandmother's ninetieth birthday.

feast a fancy, plentiful meal, especially one prepared for a special occasion: There were sixty guests at the Kwans' wedding *feast*.

dinner a formal meal in honor of a special occasion: The mayor attended the *dinner* held to celebrate the new bridge.

barely

Adverb. not much at all: Kevin *barely* heard the whispered words.

hardly only just; barely: The audience *hardly* noticed the player's nervousness.

scarcely hardly: Open the new carton of milk because this carton has *scarcely* enough milk in it for one bowl of cereal.

> antonyms: completely, entirely, fully, altogether, wholly

bother

Verb. to give trouble to.

annoy	*nag*
disturb	*perturb*
exasperate	*pester*
heckle	*provoke*
irk	*vex*
irritate	*worry*

antonyms: please, charm, delight, gratify

bound

Verb. to move quickly by jumping: A kangaroo can *bound* out of danger.

leap to make a big jump: You can *leap* across the narrow stream.

spring to move forward or jump up quickly: When Wu says "Surprise," we will *spring* from our hiding places.

vault to jump over: Laura's speed and strength helped her *vault* the railing.

brand-new

Adjective. entirely new; newly made or obtained: Some of my clothes are hand-me-downs from my big sisters, but I just got *brand-new* jeans.

unused never used before: I knew by looking at the soles that these sneakers were your *unused* pair and not your old ones.

fresh newly done, made, gathered, or obtained. Instead of writing on that yellowed old paper, open a *fresh* package.

antonyms: used, stale, old

calm

Adjective. free from excitement or other strong feeling: The teacher's *calm* manner put the students at ease.

tranquil free from disturbance: Because there was no wind, the surface of the pond was smooth and *tranquil.*

peaceful calm: The children were very excitable in the morning and argued constantly, but after lunch they were in a far more *peaceful* mood and played together quietly.

unruffled not disturbed: Ray's *unruffled* reply showed that he was not angry at all.

antonyms: excited, angry

careless

Adjective. not paying enough attention; not cautious: The baseball player's *careless* swing resulted in a foul ball.

thoughtless careless: A *thoughtless* mistake in a math problem will give you an incorrect answer.

inattentive not paying attention: The *inattentive* boy almost walked into the closed door.

unthinking not thinking or not careful: *Unthinking* visitors left litter in the park.

antonyms: careful, attentive, thoughtful, responsible

charm

Verb. to attract or please greatly: My little brother can *charm* most adults just by smiling at them.

fascinate to attract and hold the close interest of: Mobiles with bright shapes usually *fascinate* young babies.

captivate to capture and hold the attention or affection of: I have seen my grandfather *captivate* an audience with stories of his life.

antonyms: bore, repel, displease

companion

Noun. a person who keeps company with another; a friend: In stories, the hero or heroine often has a *companion* with whom to share adventures.

friend a person who is known well and regarded with fondness: Carlota has been my *friend* since preschool.

pal an informal word for a friend: Fred's *pal* Nathan lives next door to him.

antonyms: enemy, foe, stranger

Spelling Thesaurus

courtesy

Noun. courteous behavior; politeness: Parents can encourage their children to treat other people with *courtesy.*

politeness having good or correct social behavior: The shopkeeper's *politeness* made her store very popular with customers.

good manners a good way of acting or behaving: People with *good manners* tend to get along well with each other.

antonyms: rudeness, impoliteness

decrease

Verb. to become less.

decline	*lessen*
diminish	*shrink*
dwindle	*subside*
ebb	*wane*
fade	*waste away*

antonyms: increase, grow, expand

deny

Verb. to refuse to give or grant: No one can *deny* her the right to speak.

reject to refuse to accept, believe, or grant: He may *reject* the job offer.

refuse to withhold acceptance of; turn down: I don't know anyone who would *refuse* a million dollars.

decline to refuse politely: I'm sorry, but I must *decline* the invitation to the party.

rebuff to reject bluntly or rudely: Don't *rebuff* your friend's offer to help.

antonyms: grant, accept, welcome

describe

Verb. to give a picture in words; to tell or write about: In my letter, I will *describe* the buildings of Savannah to my friends back home.

portray to describe: When he writes stories, Victor likes to *portray* his main characters as brave and adventurous.

depict to represent in words. Hassan's magazine article will *depict* the old house his grandparents built.

paint to describe vividly in words: My aunt's old letters *paint* a humorous picture of her life.

dismiss

Verb. to send away or allow to leave: The coach will *dismiss* the team members as soon as practice ends.

discharge to let go or clear out: The team leader will *discharge* the volunteers as soon as their job is done.

excuse to release from duty or attendance: Because of the blizzard, the principal plans to *excuse* the students early so they can get home safely.

Spelling Thesaurus

easily

Adverb. without difficulty or effort: Our team *easily* won the game.

smoothly free from obstacles or difficulties: The ship passed *smoothly* through the rough water.

handily in a handy or easy way: His wheelchair *handily* passed through the doorway.

effortlessly without effort or difficulty: The pianist seemed to play *effortlessly*.

effect

Noun. something brought about by a cause or agent: One *effect* of the rain was that the grass began to turn from brown to green.

result something brought about by an action, process, or condition: As a *result* of the election, he became president.

consequence something that results from an earlier action: As a *consequence* of not studying, she did not do well on the test.

outcome a result or consequence: The damaged trees are an *outcome* of the hurricane.

enclose

Verb. to close in on all sides: We may *enclose* the yard with a fence.

surround to be on all sides of: The fans *surround* the actress.

encircle to form a circle around: In the game, the children *encircle* someone who is "it."

encompass to form a circle around: The wall will *encompass* the entire garden.

ring to put a ring around; enclose with a ring: The gravel path will *ring* the cottage.

exact

Adjective. very accurate: Do you need an *exact* answer for this addition problem, or is a rounded answer close enough?

precise very accurate or definite: The captain's *precise* directions led us to the treasure.

correct free from error: The recipe gave the *correct* amounts for all the ingredients.

accurate making few or no errors or mistakes: Most of her answers on the test were *accurate*.

> antonyms: inexact, imprecise, incorrect, wrong, inaccurate

flare

Noun. a sudden bright light, especially one that lasts for only a short time. Jay saw a *flare* of light in the dark sky.

blaze a bright, intense light: The spotlights all came on at once, creating a *blaze* of brilliant white light.

Spelling Thesaurus

flash a sudden, short burst of light: I saw a *flash* of lightning about five seconds before I heard the thunder roll.

glare a strong, usually unpleasant light: In the *glare* of the sun, even the sidewalks seemed to shrivel up.

flaw

Noun. something that spoils or takes away from perfection or completeness: There is a *flaw* in the leather of those boots.

defect an imperfection or weakness: A *defect* in the software kept the computer from running.

imperfection not perfect; having a flaw. The jewel was on sale because it had a slight *imperfection*.

shortcoming a fault or defect: Carelessness is a serious *shortcoming*.

fled

*Verb, past tense and past participle of **flee**.* to have run away: We *fled* before the hurricane arrived.

escaped got away or got free: Once again our cat *escaped* from the house.

took flight left quickly: The crowd *took flight* when the ground began to shake.

bolted made a sudden spring or start: The antelope *bolted* when it saw the lion.

antonyms: remained, waited, stayed

foolish

Adjective. showing a lack of understanding or good sense.

absurd	mistaken
frivolous	nonsensical
irrational	ridiculous
laughable	silly
ludicrous	unwise

antonyms: wise, intelligent, smart

frequent

Adjective. taking place again and again: He is a *frequent* guest at our house.

repeated done or happening again and again: They have made *repeated* visits to the town.

continual happening over and over again without stop: *Continual* dry weather caused the crops to fail.

constant continuing without a break: The *constant* noise kept me awake all night.

numerous forming a large number; many: The phone rang *numerous* times.

antonyms: infrequent, occasional, rare

frighten

Verb. to make suddenly alarmed or scared: Spiders *frighten* me.

alarm to cause to feel sudden fear: Did the loud noise *alarm* you?

horrify to cause to feel horror: The sight of a snake can *horrify* some people.

Spelling Thesaurus

terrify to frighten or alarm greatly: The silly ghost story did not *terrify* me.

petrify to paralyze with fear: A dog's loud growl can *petrify* some cats, but my cat just growls back.

> antonyms: reassure, encourage, hearten

gain

Verb. to get through work or effort: If she sticks with her training program, Shaniqua will *gain* skill and strength.

achieve to do or reach successfully: Next year, Carlos will *achieve* his goal of becoming a pilot.

attain to achieve or gain through work or effort: Some people *attain* stardom through hard work and good luck.

> antonym: lose

grown-up

Adjective. characteristic of adults: The child tried to speak in a *grown-up* way.

adult relating to or for adults: At dinner, the children were expected to behave in an *adult* manner.

mature showing characteristics of a fully grown person: The young baseball player had a *mature*

approach to fame.

seasoned made suitable for use by experience and age: He was a *seasoned* city official.

> antonyms: youthful, immature, unseasoned

hamper

Verb. to interfere with the action or progress of: The runner's sore leg will *hamper* him in the race.

impede to get in the way of or to delay: We are eager to start our trip, and we hope the storm won't *impede* us.

interfere with to cause an interruption or hindrance: The cold weather did not *interfere with* our plans to go swimming.

hinder to delay or make difficult the movement or progress of: The fog could *hinder* the arrival of the plane.

> antonyms: help, ease

happily

Adverb. with pleasure or joy: They *happily* ate the delicious food.

blissfully full of great happiness or joy: Mei Lee *blissfully* hugged her newly found cat.

blithely full of joy or cheer: The skater *blithely* skimmed across the ice.

merrily in a joyous or merry manner:

Spelling Thesaurus

The children *merrily* sang holiday songs.

cheerfully full of cheer; in a good-tempered manner: Jed *cheerfully* volunteered to help with the party.

> antonyms: sadly, unhappily, mournfully, woefully

heap

Noun. a collection of things piled together: A *heap* of dirty clothes lay beside the washer.

pile a number of things laid or lying on one another: Somewhere in this *pile* of socks, there must be a matching pair.

stack a pile of things arranged in an orderly way: The *stack* of books lay on the night table.

mass a large quantity, amount, or number: A *mass* of money was stacked inside the huge vault.

hesitate

Verb. to wait or stop a moment: If you *hesitate* before hitting the ball, you may miss it.

pause to stop for a short time: The marching band will *pause* before the reviewing stand before continuing down the parade route.

delay to put off or slow down action: People who *delay* when faced with a decision might end up with fewer choices.

falter to act with hesitation or uncertainty: People who rehearse their parts well are less likely to get nervous and *falter* midway through a speech.

horde

Noun. a large group.

bevy	*mob*
crowd	*multitude*
drove	*myriads*
flock	*pack*
gathering	*swarm*
mass	*throng*

immediately

Adverb. done or happening without delay: The ambulance went *immediately* to the hospital.

at once immediately; without delay: When the storm began, we closed the windows *at once*.

promptly done or given without delay. She answered his letter *promptly*.

readily quickly or promptly: He answered my questions *readily*, without hesitating.

instantly without delay: I recognized his face *instantly*.

> antonyms: tardily, slowly

impolite

Adjective. not having or showing good manners: The *impolite* remark made him angry.

rude not polite or courteous: Such *rude* behavior deserved to be punished.

disrespectful rude or impolite: *Disrespectful* audiences sometimes boo loudly.

discourteous not courteous; not polite: A *discourteous* tone of voice can offend people even if the actual words you say are not rude.

> antonyms: polite, courteous, mannerly, respectful

inactive

Adjective. not active; not full of activity: Many desert animals are *inactive* during the day when temperatures soar.

sluggish showing little activity: Our pace was *sluggish* because we were tired.

languid showing a lack of energy or force: He answered slowly with a sleepy, *languid* voice.

lethargic sluggish: Their *lethargic* singing almost caused me to fall asleep.

listless lacking energy or desire to do anything: Joaquin's *listless* walk showed his disappointment.

> antonyms: active, energetic, excited, vibrant

independence

Noun. the ability to govern oneself or make one's own decisions: A job gives people *independence* because they don't need to count on others to fill their basic needs.

freedom the state of not being under the control of others: The citizens of our country value the *freedom* to live where and how they please.

liberty political independence; the state of being free from the control of a harsh government: Britain was forced to grant *liberty* to the American colonists.

instrument

Noun. a tool used for precise or careful work: A telescope is an *instrument* for observing distant objects.

tool something used for doing work: A hammer is a *tool* for driving nails into wood.

device something made for a particular purpose: A screen saver is a *device* to keep a computer screen from burning out.

implement something used in performing a task or other work. The sculptor used a long, thin *implement* to carve the mouth and the eyes.

mechanism an instrument used for doing something: A clock is a *mechanism* for keeping track of time.

journal

Noun. a record, especially one kept daily, of events, experiences, or thoughts: Juan writes in his *journal* every evening.

diary a daily record of events, especially of the writer's personal experiences and thoughts: Keiko writes her *diary* on her word processor.

log any record of progress, performance, or events: The explorers kept a *log* of what happened during their sea voyage.

keen

Adjective. very sensitive or acute: Deborah has a *keen* sense of fashion.

sharp having the ability to perceive or feel quickly: His *sharp* ears recognized the disguised voice.

acute very sensitive; keen: Her *acute* sense of touch helped her find the key in the dark.

fine sharp; keen: Great cooks usually have a *fine* sense of smell.

> antonyms: dull, insensitive, limited

kernel

Noun. the central, most valuable or most important part: The first paragraph of a newspaper report often presents the *kernel* of the report.

gist a main idea or central point: Read the television listing to find out the *gist* of the new show.

essence a necessary and basic part: The *essence* of the plot is a missing jewel.

substance the real or essential thing or part, especially of something written or spoken: The *substance* of the chapter was a discussion of how to use a thesaurus.

knowledge

Noun. what is known from experience, study, or awareness: Carlos has a vast *knowledge* of history.

understanding thorough knowledge or mastery: Mrs. Burke's *understanding* of computers helped her become familiar with the Internet.

acquaintance knowledge of something, especially as a result of personal experience or contact: Randy's years of living in Montreal gave him a thorough *acquaintance* with the French language.

limit

Verb. to keep within bounds: The rules *limit* each speaker to five minutes.

restrict to keep within specified limits: The plaster cast will *restrict* the movement of her hand.

confine to keep within limits; restrict: The fence will *confine* the dog to our yard.

narrow to make smaller in width or extent: You need to *narrow* the topic of your paper.

> antonyms: expand, inflate, increase, multiply

locate

Verb. to discover the exact place of: I can't *locate* the town on this map.

pinpoint to find precisely: The building plan will help you *pinpoint* the location of each window.

find to discover the location of: You will *find* a pencil in the desk drawer.

spot to pick out by sight: The binoculars will help you *spot* the nest in the tree.

> antonyms: lose, miss

loiter

Verb. to move slowly or with frequent pauses: Tourists often *loiter* along the paths of the ancient ruined city.

linger to go or act at a slow pace: We decided to *linger* on the way to the museum so that we could see the sidewalk art show.

dawdle to waste time; linger: My young sisters often *dawdle* as they walk home.

dillydally to waste time: Those students don't *dillydally* after school but instead go straight home.

> antonyms: hurry, rush, speed

loom

Verb. to appear as a large, menacing shape: The huge trees *loom* over the tiny house.

threaten to hang over dangerously; to loom: Heavy dark clouds *threaten* on the horizon.

overshadow to cast a shadow over, as a larger object does to a smaller one: The giant office towers *overshadow* the three-story apartment building squeezed between them.

hover to remain suspended in the air over a particular spot or object: The giant blimps *hover* over the field.

major

Adjective. greater than others in importance or rank.

dominant	leading
greater	primary
higher	ranking
key	superior

antonyms: minor, unimportant, insignificant

maneuver

Verb. to use skillful or clever moves or plans: The driver had to *maneuver* her car carefully on the icy roadway.

plot to form a plan or scheme: His friends will *plot* to surprise him on his birthday.

scheme to make a plan; plot: Sherlock Holmes will often *scheme* to catch a villain.

devise to plan or think out: Officials should *devise* a more efficient public transportation system.

concoct to put together; devise: You always *concoct* such funny stories!

marshal

Verb. to arrange in proper or logical order: To write the paper, he will *marshal* information from several sources.

organize to arrange in an orderly way: If you *organize* your ideas, the speech you give will be much clearer and more persuasive.

gather to bring together in one place or group: The students will *gather* information from the Internet.

mighty

Adjective. having or showing great power, strength, or ability.

brawny	*powerful*
forceful	*strong*
hardy	*superhuman*
invincible	*tough*
muscular	*unyielding*
potent	

antonyms: weak, feeble, frail

mistaken

Adjective, formed from the past participle of the verb **mistake.** based on error: Ilya had the *mistaken* belief that the game began at noon.

misinformed in error because of false or wrong information: Harry's *misinformed* ideas about computers are a result of ignorance.

incorrect not correct or right: A lot of people have *incorrect* notions about healthful eating.

antonyms: well-informed, accurate, correct

natural

Adjective. to be expected: It is *natural* to be excited about winning a contest.

normal logical or natural: Stage fright is a *normal* reaction for actors to have.

typical usual, to be expected: Running around noisily is *typical* behavior for young children.

antonyms: unnatural, abnormal, atypical, unexpected

notion

Noun. a thought that something might be true: Mariko had the *notion* that the movie would end happily.

theory a supposition that is based on some evidence but is not proved: Len's *theory* is that the book's characters are based on real people.

assumption something that is taken for granted to be true: Our *assumption* was that you wanted to eat with us.

Spelling Thesaurus

nourish

Verb. to provide food or other substances that promote health and growth: The honey in one beehive can *nourish* thousands of bees.

sustain to supply with nourishment: Freeze-dried foods are easy to pack and can *sustain* hikers for many days.

feed to provide food or nourishment: This powdered formula is designed to *feed* babies.

novel

Noun. a long work of narrative writing, usually fiction: The author published his first *novel* when he was fifty years old.

book a long work of fiction or nonfiction: I just read a wonderful *book* by Yoshiko Uchida.

story a long or short narrative work, usually fiction: The last *story* I read took place in Australia.

tale a story, usually fictional, that can be short or long: This adventure *tale* kept me reading until late at night.

official

Adjective. coming from or permitted by a proper authority: These are the *official* T-shirts worn by athletes for City Sports Week.

approved permitted by the proper authority: In our apartment we must use only an *approved* air conditioner that doesn't overload the wiring.

authorized officially approved: The *authorized* life story of my favorite TV star will be published next spring.

antonym: unauthorized

opinion

Noun. a conclusion based on judgment and feelings as well as facts: It is my *opinion* that everyone should have the chance to take music lessons.

belief an opinion: I hold the *belief* that anyone can become a good athlete.

conviction a firm belief or opinion: It is Danny's *conviction* that people will do the right thing if they are treated right.

view a particular way of looking at something; an opinion: What is your *view* on the way our state's environment is being protected?

pedestrian

Adjective. lacking originality, imagination, or excitement: Farida thinks that this author has a *pedestrian* style of writing.

commonplace not original or remarkable: This picture seems *commonplace* to me because it looks like dozens of others I've seen.

dull not interesting: Your stories

Spelling Thesaurus

won't be *dull* if you set them in some of the unusual places you have visited.

antonyms: original, imaginative, exciting, remarkable

perfume
Noun. a sweet or pleasant smell, usually of flowers or the like: The delicate *perfume* of roses filled the room.

fragrance a sweet or delicate smell—usually of flowers, pine trees, other plants, spices, and similar smells: Lilacs keep their *fragrance* even after they are cut from the bush.

aroma an agreeable smell—used more broadly than perfume: The *aroma* from the steaming soup pot made Graciela's mouth water.

scent a smell, often an agreeable or delicate one: The breeze held the *scent* of the ocean.

odor any smell, good or bad: Eli detected the *odor* of detergent on the freshly washed towel.

permit
Verb. to give someone leave to do something: Our city does not *permit* people to park their cars on downtown streets.

allow to give permission: Does the arena's management *allow* people to take pictures while the game is going on?

let to allow: *Let* me help you move that sofa.

antonyms: forbid, prohibit, bar, ban

practical
Adjective. having the possibility of being used or carried out; making sense.

functional	*serviceable*
realistic	*sound*
reasonable	*usable*
sensible	*workable*

antonyms: impractical, unrealistic, unworkable

pride
Noun. an exaggerated sense of one's own worth or importance: Rod's *pride* keeps him from seeing that other people might know more than he does.

conceit a very high opinion of oneself or one's achievements: Oswald was filled with *conceit* after he won three talent contests.

vanity too much concern with one's looks, abilities, deeds, or the like: That movie star is famous for her *vanity* and is always being photographed in a different outfit.

antonyms: humility, modesty

Spelling Thesaurus

promise

Noun. a guarantee given that one will or will not do something: My mother made a *promise* to be at all of our team's softball games.

assurance a declaration or guarantee: Mr. Fong gave his *assurance* that the repair would be finished by Friday.

word a promise: Maria always keeps her *word* when she says she'll do something.

pledge a formal promise: I made a *pledge* to my parents to keep my room tidy and my bed made.

quality

Noun. something that makes a person or thing what it is: Patience is a *quality* that athletes need as they train.

feature an important part or quality of something or someone: Dependability is a *feature* of all the machines our company makes.

trait a feature or quality: Jana's most obvious *trait* is her creativity.

characteristic a feature: A strong beat is a *characteristic* of danceable music.

quantity

Noun. a number or amount, often large: A vast *quantity* of food is always left over at our family dinners.

profusion a plentiful amount: A *profusion* of papers covered Andy's desk.

abundance a quantity that is more than enough: Because Gerry always has an *abundance* of ideas for stories, her worst problem is deciding which idea to write about.

quarrel

Noun. an angry disagreement: The neighbors had a *quarrel* about parking space.

argument a discussion of something by people who do not agree: It is possible for people to have an *argument* without getting angry.

conflict a strong disagreement: The two groups tried to resolve their *conflict* peacefully.

squabble a dispute or argument over something small and unimportant: Two of my uncles are always having a *squabble* about who gets to choose the TV channel.

> antonyms: agreement, accord, settlement, understanding

quietly

Adverb. with little or no noise: Cats walk *quietly* on their padded paws.

soundlessly without noise: The hands of my electric clock move *soundlessly* across its face.

silently with no noise: The snake moved *silently* across the sand.

Spelling Thesaurus

stealthily sneakily, so as not to be noticed: He tiptoed *stealthily* toward the refrigerator.

antonyms: loudly, noisily

racket

Noun. a loud or confusing noise.

blast	reverberation
clamor	roar
clatter	stir
din	tumult
hullabaloo	uproar
pandemonium	

antonyms: quiet, calm, silence, hush

rapidly

Adverb. with great speed: A hummingbird's heart beats much more *rapidly* than a human's heart.

quickly fast: The chef sliced the vegetables so *quickly* that her hand movements were almost a blur.

speedily rapidly: The clock's second hand turned *speedily* as I rushed to finish the test before the bell rang.

swiftly with great speed: In a 100-meter dash, the runners move so *swiftly* that the race seems to end as soon as it begins.

hastily quickly, often urgently or carelessly: Lee gathered his papers up *hastily* and stuffed them into his bookbag.

antonyms: slowly, sluggishly

ready-made

Adjective. made in quantity and not to order: Long ago, people sewed their own clothes, but now most of us buy *ready-made* clothes.

mass-produced made in large quantities, usually by machine: *Mass-produced* toys don't have the beauty or personality of handmade ones.

manufactured made by machines, especially on a large scale: Hand-carved chairs take longer to make than *manufactured* ones.

antonyms: handmade, made-to-order, custom-made, handcrafted

require

Verb. to order or compel: My teachers *require* me to have neat handwriting.

demand to require as necessary or useful: This film will *demand* your full attention so that you don't miss any clues.

insist upon to demand firmly and strongly: Our coaches *insist upon* our attendance at each practice.

expect to consider as necessary or right: Once you join this club, we *expect* you to volunteer an hour each week for community service.

antonyms: forbid, prohibit, bar, ban

Spelling Thesaurus

respect

Verb. to feel or show a high regard for: My friends *respect* someone who always tells the truth.

esteem to consider good or important: I *esteem* your opinion of my writing, so I'm glad you like this story.

value to prize: People *value* Carlos's advice because he thinks carefully before giving it.

admire to feel high regard for: I *admire* people who can stay calm in an emergency.

antonym: scorn

roam

Verb. to go around, especially over a large area, without any purpose or destination: When the family tours a new city, Dad decides on his route beforehand, but Mom likes to *roam* around with no special plan.

ramble to go about aimlessly: Early evening is a nice time to *ramble* through a museum.

rove to wander aimlessly from place to place: The campers *rove* around the field, examining the plants and wildflowers.

meander to wander here and there: The tourists *meander* through the downtown shopping area.

scarlet

Adjective. a bright red or orange-red color: Mimi's *scarlet* coat was a bright contrast to the dreary gray sky.

red the color of objects such as stoplights, blood, and many fire engines: The flashing *red* lights alerted us to the ambulance's approach.

crimson a deep red: Some people think that *crimson* lipstick is very elegant.

ruby a deep red, like the jewel of the same name: Betty's *ruby* velvet dress made her stand out in the crowd.

scatter

Verb. to spread or throw about here and there: If you *scatter* birdseed, the birds won't have to crowd together to eat it.

strew to spread or throw about at random: The flower girls *strew* rose petals in the bride's path.

disperse to break up and send off in different directions: Put the leaves in a bag, or the wind will *disperse* them and we'll have to rake again.

disseminate to scatter things or ideas widely: Volunteers will *disseminate* these leaflets throughout the city.

antonyms: unite, join, gather

Spelling Thesaurus

section

Noun. a part of a whole: After the game, Yuki ate an orange *section* as a snack.

portion a part of a larger whole: Everyone received a *portion* of the profits from the sale at the street fair.

segment any of the parts into which an object may be divided: Each *segment* of the apple should be the same size.

slice a thin, flat piece cut from a larger object: Doug cut a *slice* of pizza.

antonym: whole

shelter

Verb. to provide cover or protection for.

cover	*safeguard*
enclose	*screen*
guard	*shield*
hide	*surround*
protect	

antonyms: display, uncover

signal

Noun. something used to warn, direct, inform, or instruct: The coach used a hand *signal* to let us know where to throw the ball.

sign an action or hand movement used as communication: Corazon waved her hand as a *sign* that she had seen Mickey.

gesture a movement of the head, body, or limbs to express or communicate something: Peg's shrug was a *gesture* that showed her confusion.

motion the act of moving the body or one of its parts: Mr. Park used an arm *motion* instead of words to get the chorus to sing more loudly.

silent

Adjective. making no sound: One dog barked loudly, but the other was *silent*.

soundless making no sound: In my sneakers, I have a *soundless* walk even if I don't tiptoe.

noiseless not making noise: Some machines hum, click, or buzz, but others are *noiseless*.

quiet making little or no noise: The audience was *quiet* except for a few coughs and rustles.

antonyms: noisy, loud, clattering

tall

Adjective. having more than average height: That tree is so *tall* that it reaches above the roof of the house.

lofty reaching high into the air: The *lofty* mountaintops seemed to pierce the clouds.

towering very tall: The streets were lined with *towering* oak trees.

sizable somewhat large or tall: A *sizable* flagpole stood in the center of the yard.

antonyms: short, tiny, diminutive, minute

Spelling Thesaurus

threat

Noun. a person or thing that is a source of injury or harm: Air pollution is a *threat* to people's health.

danger a person or thing that is a source of harm, injury, or loss: An ice storm can be a *danger* to drivers who try to drive too fast.

menace a person or thing that is a harm: A wild dog on the loose can be a *menace* to children.

tremble

Verb. to shake as with cold, weakness, fear, or anger: As I lifted my cat onto the vet's examining table, I felt her entire body *tremble*.

shake to move quickly to and fro, up and down, or from side to side: I tried to keep my voice firm as I addressed the audience, but I was so nervous I could feel my knees *shake*.

shiver to shake, as with cold or fear: The swimmers *shiver* as they get out of the pool.

quiver to shake slightly, often with fear or excitement: The children seemed to *quiver* with excitement, as though they couldn't hold still.

twirl

Verb. to turn rapidly: When tops *twirl*, their colors seem to flow together.

spin to turn quickly: If I twirl this coin, it will *spin* so fast that its flat shape will blur into a sphere.

whirl to spin: The pinwheel's blades *whirl* in the wind.

uncertain

Adjective. not known for sure: The outcome of the election is still *uncertain* because all the votes haven't been counted.

doubtful not clear or sure: Megan's plans for tomorrow are *doubtful* because she still doesn't feel well.

undecided not agreed upon: The outcome of the competition will remain *undecided* until the judges finish reviewing the entries.

unsettled not agreed upon: The family's vacation plans are still *unsettled* because no one can agree on either choice.

> antonyms: certain, decided, sure, settled

uneven

Adjective. not smooth or flat: The sidewalk's surface was so *uneven* that the children couldn't skate on it.

rough not smooth or level: The tree's bark was *rough* and scratchy.

bumpy full of bumps, not smooth: The car bounced along on the *bumpy* road.

irregular not even or uniformly shaped: The moon has an *irregular* surface that is full of craters.

> antonyms: even, smooth, regular

Spelling Thesaurus

union

Noun. something formed by joining two or more people or units for a common purpose: Several countries formed an economic *union* that had special trade agreements for members.

federation a union formed by agreement between states, nations, or other groups: Many countries joined the new business *federation*.

association a group of people or organizations that get together for a purpose: Local artists formed an *association* to promote their work.

unnecessary

Adjective. not needed or useful: This car is full of *unnecessary* features that add to its price without improving its quality.

needless unnecessary: If you don't make a plan beforehand, you will waste your energy and time doing *needless* tasks.

useless serving no purpose: The important-looking knobs on that machine are *useless* and are there just for decoration.

superfluous more than is needed or wanted: Many toys are sold in showy display boxes that use a lot of *superfluous* packaging materials.

> antonyms: necessary, needed, useful, essential, crucial, required

urgent

Adjective. calling for immediate action or attention: The leaking sink pipe is an *urgent* matter that the plumber should know about now.

pressing requiring action or attention right away: Rescue workers in that town have a *pressing* need for blankets and canned food.

compelling driving; urgent: The shortage of classroom space is a *compelling* problem that must be dealt with at once.

critical at a point of crisis: A high fever in a child is a *critical* situation that needs a doctor's attention.

vacant

Adjective. containing nothing or no one: After the movers left with the family's furniture, Imelda took a last look at the *vacant* rooms.

empty having nothing or no one inside: The carton was so light that Greg knew it was *empty*.

unoccupied containing no one, unused: There was only one *unoccupied* seat on the benches in the crowded waiting room.

abandoned once used but now left behind: The *abandoned* shed was falling to ruins.

> antonyms: filled, full, occupied, crowded

Spelling Thesaurus

vanish

Verb. to cease to exist: When you press this button, whatever is on your computer screen will *vanish* if you don't save it first.

disappear to vanish: When I scrub hard, the stains on the floor will *disappear* completely.

evaporate to vanish: Her fears always *evaporate* as soon as she turns on a light.

fade to disappear gradually: The sound of the radio will *fade* as the batteries grow weaker.

> antonyms: appear, reappear

variety

Noun. a number or collection of different things: The store sells a *variety* of greeting cards.

assortment a collection of different things: A bowl on the table held an *assortment* of fruits.

array a large, impressive collection of things: The *array* of shoes in my mother's closet could stock an entire shoe store.

hodgepodge a disorderly collection of things: The drawer held a *hodgepodge* of writing tools.

vary

Verb. to be or become different.

adjust	*modify*
alter	*shift*
change	*transform*
fluctuate	

venture

Noun. an attempted project or task that involves some risk or danger: Don't take part in a risky business *venture* unless you can afford to lose the money.

enterprise an attempted project or task, especially a difficult or important one: Sending astronauts to Mars is an *enterprise* that could have great benefits for humankind.

undertaking something that is tried or worked on: Learning to speak a second language is a difficult but worthwhile *undertaking*.

worthy

Adjective. Having worth or value: Is this book *worthy* of a good review?

deserving worthy of: The principal will give the scholarship to a *deserving* student.

worthwhile having enough value or importance to be worth the time or effort: Music is a *worthwhile* activity as well as an enjoyable one because it sharpens math and memory skills.

valuable of great use, worth, or importance: Typing is a *valuable* skill because these days everyone uses computers.

> antonyms: worthless, useless

Spelling Thesaurus

A **dictionary** helps you use a word correctly. You will see **guide words** at the top of each page. The guide word on the left shows the first word on that page. The one on the right shows the last word on that page.

An **example phrase or sentence** helps you know how to use a meaning of the word.

The word you look up is a **main entry** word. All entry words are in alphabetical order.

If the word is a homograph, you will find two separate entries.

sta•ble¹ (stā′bəl) *n.* a building in which horses or cattle are kept and fed. — *v.t.,* **sta•bled, sta•bling.** to keep in a stable.

sta•ble² (stā′bəl) *adj.* **1.** not easily moved, shaken, or overthrown: *a stable platform, a stable government.* **2.** dependable, steady: *a stable personality.* **3.** continuing without much change: *to enjoy stable health.* **—sta′bly,** *adv.*

Other **forms** of the entry word are given to show how to add an ending if you need to.

The **part of speech** of each meaning is given, usually as an abbreviation. See page 215 for a list of abbreviations.

A **respelling** shows you how to pronounce the word. You also see how to break the word into syllables. Look at the pronunciation key on each right-hand page in this Dictionary, or look at the table of Common Spelling Patterns on page 159.

A **run-on entry** tells how some entry words can be changed to make different words.

A **definition** tells what the entry word means. Each meaning will be numbered.

Spelling Dictionary

Parts of Speech

In this dictionary, many parts of speech or other labels are written as abbreviations. Here are the abbreviations used in the dictionary:

abbr. abbreviation

adj. adjective

adv. adverb

contr. contraction

conj. conjunction

n. noun

prep. preposition

pron. pronoun

v. verb

v.t. transitive verb

v.i. intransitive verb

The words *transitive* and *intransitive* reflect the way a verb is used in a sentence.

A transitive verb is an action verb that has a direct object. The verb is transferring its action onto someone or something else.

Maris sang a song.

An intransitive verb is an action verb that has no direct object.

Maris sang. Maris sang happily.

Many verbs can be used as either transitive or intransitive verbs, as *sing* is above.

Your Spelling Dictionary will help you identify transitive verbs (*v.t.*) and intransitive verbs (*v.i.*).

A

ab•bre•vi•a•tion (ə brē′vē ā′shən) *n.* **1.** a shortened form of a word or phrase. **2.** the act of making briefer or shorter.

a•bil•i•ty (ə bil′i tē) *n., pl.* **a•bil•i•ties.** **1.** the power to do or perform something: *The student's ability to persuade others amazed everyone.* **2.** talent or skill: *Her athletic ability earned her many awards.*

-able *suffix* able to be: *countable.*

ab•sent (ab′sənt) *adj.* **1.** not present; away. **2.** not existing; missing: *Gills are absent in an adult frog.* —**ab′sent•ly,** *adv.* —**ab′sen•tee′,** *n.*

ac•cent (*n.,* ak′sent; *v.,* ak′sent, ak sent′) *n.* **1.** greater force or emphasis given to a particular syllable or word in speech. In the word *alone,* the accent is on the second syllable. **2.** a special manner of pronouncing words that is characteristic of a certain part of a country, or a person speaking a foreign language: *a New York accent. My grandparents speak English with a German accent.* **3.** stress on certain words or syllables marking the rhythm of a line of verse. **4.** *Music.* **a.** stress or emphasis given to certain notes or chords. **b.** a mark used to indicate this. —*v.t.* to pronounce (a syllable, word, or words) with particular stress or emphasis: *to accent the first syllable of the word "accident."*

ac•count (ə kount′) *n.* **1.** a record of money paid and received. **2.** regard for someone or something's importance or worth: *She is held in high account by all who know her.* **3.** a spoken or written statement: *She gave a detailed account of her actions.* **4.** a sum of money deposited in a bank. —*v.t.* **1.** to give an explanation. **2.** to be the cause: *Slippery roads account for many motor vehicle accidents.* —**ac•count′a•ble,** *adj.*

ache (āk) *n.* continuous, usually dull pain. —*v.i.* **ached, ach•ing.** to have or be in pain: *My teeth ached from the cold.* —**ach′y,** *adj.*

ac•tiv•i•ty (ak tiv′i tē) *n., pl.* **ac•tiv•i•ties.** **1.** the act of moving about. **2.** a brisk or vigorous action; liveliness. **3.** a thing done or to be done: *I am involved in many school activities.*

ac•tor (ak′tər) *n.* one who acts, especially a theatrical performer.

a•dapt (ə dapt′) *v.t.* to change to make more suitable.

ad•dress (*n.,* ə dres′, ad′res; *v.,* ə dres′) *n., pl.* **ad•dress•es. 1.** a formal speech: *The president's address to the nation will be on television.* **2.** the place at which a person lives or an organization is located: *Our address is 90 Pine Lane.* **3.** *Computers.* **e-mail address.** a set of symbols through which a user can receive and send messages on a computer network.

ad•mi•ral (ad′mər əl) *n.* **1.** a naval officer of the highest rank. **2.** in the U.S. Navy, any officer ranking above a captain. **3.** either of two species of brightly colored butterflies. [From Arabic *amir-al,* meaning "commander."]

a•do•be (ə dō′bē) *n.* **1.** a brick made by baking clay in the sun, used as a building material. **2.** the clay from which such bricks are made. —*adj.* constructed or made of adobe: *an adobe house.*

ad•o•les•cent (ad′ə les′ənt) *n.* a person between childhood and adulthood, especially one between the ages of twelve and eighteen. —*adj.* of or relating to adolescence or an adolescent; youthful; immature: *adolescent behavior.*

a•dopt (ə dopt') *v.t.* to take legally as one's own.

ad•vice (ad vīs') *n.* helpful information; a suggestion.

ad•vise (ad vīz') *v.,* **ad•vised, ad•vis•ing.** —*v.t.* **1.** to give advice; to give an opinion. **2.** to inform; to tell. —**ad•vis′er** or **ad•vi′sor,** *n.*

af•fair (ə fâr') *n.* a matter of business done or to be done: *Moving to a new home can be a tiring affair.*

af•fect (ə fekt', a fekt') *v.t.* to influence; to have an effect on: *Bart's poor health may affect his work.*

af•ford (ə fôrd') *v.t.* **1.** to have enough money to pay for. **2.** to be able to do or bear without serious harm: *I can afford to take that risk if I have to.*

al•ge•bra (al′jə brə) *n.* the branch of mathematics in which quantities and the relationships between them are shown by letters, numerals, and abstract symbols. For example: *If 2x + y = 7, and x = 3, then y = 1.* [From Arabic *al + jabr* meaning "reduction."]

al•i•bi (al′ə bī′) *n., pl.* **al•i•bis. 1.** a claim or proof of having been somewhere else when a crime or other act was committed. **2.** an excuse: *Do you have an alibi for being late?*

a•lign (ə līn') *also,* **a•line.** *v.t.* **1.** to bring into line. **2.** to ally (oneself) with others.

al•low•ance (ə lou′əns) *n.* **1.** a definite amount of money given at regular times: *I get an allowance of two dollars each week.* **2.** a reduction in price given in return for something: *The dealer gave us an allowance of $500 on our old car when we traded it in for a new one.*

all read•y (ôl red′ē) all prepared: *The order is all ready to be shipped.*

all right (ôl rīt') *adj.* **1.** acceptable, good enough. **2.** well; safe; not hurt or ill: *I hope everyone is all right.* —*adv.* **1.** well enough: *James does all right in school.* **2.** yes: *All right, I'll go along.* **3.** for certain: *That's the answer, all right!*

all-star tour•na•ment (ôl′stär′tùr′nə mənt *or* tùr′nə mənt) *n.* a competition or series of competitions involving exceptional or star players.

al•to (al′tō) *n., pl.* **altos. 1.** the second-highest of the four voice parts in a chorus: *She sings alto in the school choir.* **2.** the second-highest member of a family of musical instruments. [From Italian *alto,* meaning "high voice."]

a.m. *abbr.* the time between midnight and noon; morning. [From Latin *ante,* meaning "before," and *meridiem,* meaning "noon."]

am•bu•lance (am′byə ləns) *n.* a vehicle specially designed and equipped to carry injured or sick people.

-ance *suffix.* **1.** the process or action of. **2.** the quality or state of.

at, āpe, fär, câre; end, mē; it, īce, pîerce; hot, ōld, sông, fôrk, oil, out; up, ūse, rüle, pùll, tûrn; chin, sing, shop; thin, this; hw in white; zh in treasure. The symbol ə stands for the unstressed vowel sound in about, taken, pencil, lemon, and circus.

Spelling Dictionary

an•chor•per•son (ang′kər pûr′sən) *n.* a person who is the main announcer on a news broadcast.

an•nounce (ə nouns′) *v.,* **an•nounced, an•nounc•ing.** —*v.t.* **1.** to tell the public. **2.** to inform in writing about the coming, arrival, or presence of: *A large banner was displayed to announce the upcoming sale.* **3.** to act as an announcer. —**an•nounce′ment, an•noun′cer,** *n.*

an•noy•ance (ə noi′əns) *n.* **1.** the act of annoying. **2.** irritation; the feeling of being annoyed. **3.** nuisance; something that annoys.

an•nu•al (an′ū əl) *n.* **1.** a publication appearing once a year. **2.** a kind of plant completing its life cycle in one year. —*adj.* happening once a year. —**an′nu•al•ly,** *adv.*

-ant *suffix.* **1.** a person or thing that does: *servant.* **2.** doing or being: *defiant.*

an•ti•dote (an′ti dōt′) *n.* **1.** a medicine or other remedy to counteract the effects of a poison. **2.** any remedy: *An interesting book is an antidote to boredom.*

an•y•bod•y (en′ē bod′ē, en′ē bud′ē) *pron.* anyone; any person at all.

ap•ple•sauce (ap′əl sôs′) *n.* a food made of sweetened stewed apples.

ap•proach (ə prōch′) *v.i.* to come near or nearer: *The car approached swiftly.*—*v.t.* to come near or close to: *The girl approached the house.* —*n., pl.* **ap•proach•es.** the act of coming near or nearer.

ap•prove (ə prüv′) *v.,* **ap•proved, ap•prov•ing.** —*v.t.* **1.** to say yes to; to think well of. **2.** to consent to officially. —*v.i.* to have or give a favorable opinion (often with *of*). —**ap•prov′ing•ly,** *adv.*

a•ris•to•crat (ə ris′tə krat′) *n.* a person who has inherited a high social position. [From Greek *aristos,* meaning "best," and *kratia,* meaning "rule," meaning that aristocrats were thought of as "rulers from the best class of people."]

arm•chair (ärm′châr′) *n.* a chair with arms.

ar•rive (ə rīv′) *v.i.,* **ar•rived, ar•riv•ing.** to reach a place where one is going: *Frank will arrive there at six o'clock.*

ar•ti•cle (är′ti kəl) *n.* **1.** a nonfiction piece of writing in a magazine or newspaper. **2.** a thing. **3.** a word such as *a, an,* or *the,* used before a noun to limit its meaning.

art•ist (är′tist) *n.* a person skilled in one of the arts, such as painting, sculpture, music, or dance.

ash[1] (ash) *n., pl.* **ash•es. 1.** the gray-white, powdery substance left after something has been burned. **2.** fine particles of lava.

ash[2] (ash) *n., pl.* **ash•es. 1.** a tree with thin bark and winged seeds. **2.** the wood of this tree.

as•tro•naut (as′trə nôt′) *n.* a person who is trained to fly in or navigate a spaceship.

-ation (ā′shən) *suffix.* **1.** the action or process of. **2.** the condition or state of being: *isolation.*

at•tempt (ə tempt′) *v.t.* to make an effort to do (something): *They attempted the climb up Mount Washington.* —*n.* a putting forth of effort to do something: *They made an attempt to learn to ski.*

at•ten•dant (ə ten′dənt) *n.* one who helps, waits on, or accompanies another, for example in a ceremony: *In a wedding, bridesmaids are the bride's attendants.*

at•tor•ney (ə tûr′nē) *n., pl.* **at•tor•neys.** a person whose profession is representing people in lawsuits or in court, and advising them of their rights; lawyer.

au•di•ence (ô′dē əns) *n.* **1.** a group of people who attend a play, concert, or other performance. **2.** a group of people who give attention to something said, done, or written: *The advertisers hope to reach a large audience.*

au•to•graph (ô′tə graf′) *n.* a person's signature. —*v.t.* to sign one's name: *I asked the author to autograph the book.*

Ave. *abbr.* Avenue.

a•ware (ə wâr′) *adj.* conscious; having or showing realization or knowledge. —**a•ware•ness,** *n.*

back•ground (bak′ground′) *n.* **1.** the part of a picture or scene that is, or appears to be, farthest from the viewer's eye: *The artist painted a waterfall in the background of the picture.* **2.** past events or facts that help to explain some later event or situation: *the background of World War II.*

ba•con (bā′kən) *n.* salted and smoked meat from the back and sides of a hog. [From Middle English *bacoun,* with the same meaning.]

bam•boo (bam bü′) *n.* a tall, woody grass with strong, hollow stalks that can be used to make furniture. [From the Malay word *bambu,* with the same meaning.]

bamboo

ban•jo (ban′jō) *n., pl.* **ban•jos** or **ban•joes.** a musical instrument played like a guitar, with a long neck and small, round body. [From a Bantu (African) word, *mbanza,* a stringed musical instrument.]

ban•ner (ban′ər) *n.* a flag or strip of cloth with a design or words on it.

ban•quet (bang′kwit) *n.* a big, formal meal for a large number of people.

bar•be•cue (bär′bi kū′) *n.* a social gathering, usually outdoors, where food is roasted and eaten. —*v.t.,* **bar•be•cued, bar•be•cu•ing. 1.** to roast on a rack or revolving spit over hot coals. **2.** to cook in a spicy sauce.

bare•ly (bâr′lē) *adv.* hardly; slightly. *The bird was barely old enough to fly.*

bar•gain (bär′gin) *n.* **1.** an agreement. **2.** something bought or offered for sale at a low price. —*v.i.* to discuss the terms of a purchase or agreement, especially to try to gain the most profitable terms: *to bargain over a price.*—**bar′gain•er,** *n.*

ba•sic (bā′sik) *adj.* **1.** of, at, or forming the base; fundamental: *Food is a basic human need.* **2.** *Chemistry.* **a.** of or containing a base. **b.** alkaline. —*n.* **1.** *usually,* **basics.** something that is basic: *to learn the basics of cooking.* **2.** *Computers:* **BASIC,** a programming language that uses simple English words to represent computer commands. [Short for *B*(eginner's) *A*(ll-purpose) *S*(ymbolic) *I*(nstruction) *C*(ode).]

at, āpe, fär, câre; end, mē; it, īce, pîerce; hot, ōld, sông, fôrk, oil, out; up, ūse, rüle, pùll, tûrn; chin, sing, shop; thin, this; hw in white; zh in treasure. The symbol ə stands for the unstressed vowel sound in about, taken, pencil, lemon, and circus.

Spelling Dictionary

bass¹ (bās) *n., pl.* **bass•es. 1.** a male singing voice with the lowest range; below baritone. **2.** a musical instrument with a similar range. —*adj.* able to sing or play the bass: *a bass voice, a bass clarinet.*

bass² (bas) *n., pl.* **bass** or **bass•es.** Any of various edible, freshwater fishes.

bathe (bā<u>th</u>) *v.,* **bathed, bath•ing.** —*v.i.* **1.** to take a bath. **2.** to go swimming. —*v.t.* **1.** to give a bath to: *to bathe a baby.* **2.** to cover or surround as a liquid does: *The sun will bathe the flowers in warmth.* —**bath′er,** *n.*

bath•robe (bath′rōb′) *n.* a loose, coatlike garment worn before or after bathing or while dressing or resting.

ba•zaar (bə zär′) *n.* **1.** an Eastern market with many shops or stalls. **2.** a place where many types of wares are sold. **3.** a fair for the sale of various articles. [From Persian *bazar,* meaning "market."]

bead (bēd) *n., pl.* **beads. 1.** a small, usually round object with a hole for threading on a string or wire. **2.** a small, ball-shaped body: *Not a single bead of perspiration crossed her face.* —*v.* **bead•ing.** —*v.t.* To cover with beads. —*v.i.* **1.** To form into a bead: *Liquid mercury will bead if you pour it onto a flat surface.*

be•come (bi kum′) *v.,* **be•came, be•come, be•com•ing.** —*v.i.* to come or grow to be: *Tadpoles become frogs.* —*v.t.* to look attractive on; suit: *That blue shirt becomes you.* —**be•com′ing•ly,** *adv.*

beef (bēf) *n.* the meat of a steer, cow, or bull.

beg•gar (beg′ər) *n.* one who begs, especially one who begs for a living.

be•neath (bi nēth′) *adv.* in a lower place: *Look beneath for any storage space.* —*prep.* **1.** lower than, below, under. **2.** unworthy of: *It was beneath his dignity to ask for help.*

ben•e•fit (ben′ə fit) *n.* **1.** something that helps or betters a person or thing; advantage: *the benefits of a good education.* **2.** *usually,* **benefits.** money or other services given by an insurance company, government agency, or other institution, as to sick, disabled, or aged persons: *health insurance benefits.* **3.** a social or theatrical event held to raise money for some charity or cause. —*v.t.* to be useful or helpful to: *Rain will benefit the crops.* —*v.i.* to gain or profit; receive help: *to benefit from a teacher's knowledge.*

bill•board (bil′bôrd′) *n.* a large board on which signs or advertisements are painted or displayed.

bit•ter (bit′ər) *adj.* **1.** having a sharp, unpleasant taste. **2.** painful; hard to bear. —**bit′ter•ly** *adv.* —**bit′ter•ness** *n.*

blame (blām) *n.* responsibility for something that goes wrong: *I had to take the blame for the lost library books.* —*v.,* **blam•ing.** to hold responsible. *Does she blame him for the accident?* —**blame′less,** *adj.*

blight (blīt) *n.* any of several diseases that wither or kill plants. —*v.t.* to cause to wither or decay: *Too much rain blighted the corn.*

blouse (blous, blouz) *n.* a loose shirt or smock.

boast (bōst) *v.i.* to brag; to praise oneself or one's possessions: *Brad likes to boast about his trophies.* —*n.* the act of praising oneself. —**boast′ful,** *adj.* —**boast′er,** *n.*

book•keep•er (bůk′kē′pər) *n.* a person who keeps records of business accounts or transactions.

boom•er•ang (bü′mə rang′) *n., pl.* **boom•er•angs.** a curved piece of wood that when properly thrown will return to the thrower. —*v.i.* to act as a boomerang. [This word comes from a native Australian language, where it has the same meaning.]

bor•der (bôr′dər) *n.* an outer part or edge. —*v.t.* **1.** to put an edge on: *I'll border the sleeves of your dress with lace.* **2.** to touch or lie near an edge. —**bor′dered,** *adj.*

both•er (bo<u>th</u>′ər) *v.t.* **1.** to give trouble to; annoy. **2.** to cause worry or concern to. —*v.i.* to take pains; to make a special effort: *Don't bother to knock.* —*n.* something that causes trouble or annoyance.

bot•tom (bot′əm) *n.* the lowest part of anything: *The snowball rolled to the bottom of the hill.* —*adj.* at or on the bottom: *the bottom drawer of a dresser.*

bough (bou) *n.* a branch of a tree, especially a large or main branch.

bound¹ (bound) *v.* a past tense and past participle of **bind.** —*adj.* **1.** made fast; tied. **2.** certain; sure: *We're bound to do well if we train hard.* **3.** under obligation; obliged: *to feel bound by a promise.*

bound² (bound) *v.i.* to move by a series of leaps; spring; jump: *The children went bounding over the hill.* —*n.* a long or high leap: *With one bound the deer cleared the stream.*

bound³ (bound) *n.* also, **bounds.** a limiting line; boundary: *You're out of bounds.* —*v.t.* to form the boundary of: *A river bounds this land on the north.*

bound⁴ (bound) *adj.* going or intending to go; on the way: *The train is bound for California.*

boy•cott (boi′kot) *n.* a refusal to do business or have contact with. —*v.* to refuse to buy, usually from a certain person or place: *We will boycott that store because of its unfair treatment of workers.*

braid (brād) *n.* a length of hair or cloth woven from three or more strands. —*v.t.* to weave together three or more strands into a braid.

braid

brake (brāk) *n.* a device that slows down or stops the motion of a wheel, vehicle, or engine. —*v.,* **braked, brak•ing.** —*v.t.* to stop or slow down with a brake. —*v.i.* to apply a brake: *The driver braked when the deer crossed the road.*

brand-new (brand′nü′ *or* brand′ nü′) *adj.* obviously new and unused.

break (brāk) *n.* **1.** the action or result of breaking. **2.** a rest from work. **3.** a broken place, a gap: *The break in the cement allowed grass to grow.* —*v.,* **broke, bro•ken, break•ing.** —*v.t.* **1.** to cause to separate into pieces; shatter. **2.** to open the surface of; cut. —*v.i.* **1.** to come apart by force: *The mirror broke when I dropped it.* **2.** to become useless because of damage. **3.** to move suddenly. **4.** to divide up or scatter. —**break′a•ble,** *adj.*

bright•en (brī′tən) *v.* to make or become bright or brighter.

broth•er-in-law (bru<u>th</u>′ər in lô) *n., pl.* **broth•ers-in-law. 1.** the husband of one's sister. **2.** the brother of one's husband or wife.

at, āpe, fär, câre; end, mē; it, īce, pîerce; hot, ōld, sông, fôrk, oil, out; up, ūse, rüle, pu̇ll, tûrn; chin, sing, shop; thin, <u>th</u>is; hw in white; zh in treasure. The symbol ə stands for the unstressed vowel sound in about, taken, pencil, lemon, and circus.

Spelling Dictionary

browse (brouz) *v.t.,* **browsed, brows•ing.** to read or look here and there: *Nancy loves to browse in bookstores.* —**brows•er** *n.*

bub•ble (bub′əl) *n.* a thin film of liquid having the shape of a ball, filled with air or other gas. *v.i.,* **bub•bled, bub•bling. 1.** to rise in or form bubbles: *The boiling water bubbled rapidly.* **2.** to show emotion in a bright, happy manner: *to bubble with joy.*

buf•fet[1] (buf′it) *v.t.* **1.** to beat or strike with the hand or fist. **2.** to knock about: *The rough water buffeted the raft.* —*n.* **1.** a blow with the hand. **2.** something that hits with the force of a blow; violent shock: *the buffet of a hurricane.*

buf•fet[2] (bə fā′, bŭ fā′) *n.* **1.** a meal laid out on a buffet or table so that guests may serve themselves. **2.** a counter where refreshments or light meals are served.

bu•gle (bū′gəl) *n.* a brass wind instrument similar to a trumpet. —*v.i.* **bu•gled, bu•gling.** to play the bugle. —**bu′gler,** *n.*

bugle

burnt (bûrnt) *v.* past tense and past participle of **burn.** —*v.t.,* **1.** set on fire. **2.** made by fire, heat, or acid: *The iron burnt a hole in the dress.* —*v.i.* gave off light or heat: *The streetlights burnt all night.*

bur•y (ber′ē) *v.t.,* **bur•ied, bur•y•ing. 1.** to put (a dead body) in the earth, a tomb, or the sea. **2.** to cover up or hide: *to bury a bone, to bury your face in your hand.* **3.** to interest (oneself) in completely: *to bury yourself in a book.*

bus•i•ly (biz′ə lē) *adv.* in an occupied way; actively: *Joel was busily writing letters.*

C

cab•i•net (kab′ə nit) *n.* **1.** a case or cupboard, usually with doors and shelves. **2.** *also* **Cabinet.** a group of advisers to a government leader. [From French *cabine,* meaning "a small room."]

ca•ble (kā′bəl) *n.* **1.** a strong, thick, rope especially one made of wires twisted together. **2. cable TV,** a system for transmitting television programs by cable to the individual sets of subscribers who pay for such a service. —*v.t.* **1.** to transmit (a message) by underwater cable.

cal•cu•late (kal′kyə lāt′) *v.,* **cal•cu•lat•ed, cal•cu•lat•ing.** —*v.t.* **1.** to determine by using mathematics; to compute: *The scientists calculated the time required for a trip to the moon.* **2.** to figure out beforehand by reasoning; estimate: *The athletes calculated their chances of winning the tournament.* [From Latin *calculatus* meaning "reckon" and *calculus* meaning "pebble," probably because pebbles were used for counting and tallying.]

calm (käm) *n.* **1.** a time with no wind or rough water. **2.** a time of quiet or stillness. —*adj.* **1.** not moving; still. **2.** not excited: *Can you keep calm in an emergency?* —**calm′ly** *adv.*

ca•nal (kə nal′) *n., pl.* **ca•nals. 1.** a tube-shaped passage or channel in the body. **2.** an artificial waterway for boats or for draining or watering land.

ca•noe (kə nü′) *n., pl.* **canoes.** a light, narrow boat, usually pointed at both ends, propelled with a paddle. —*v.,* **ca•noed, ca•noe•ing.** —*v.i.* to paddle or go in a canoe. —**ca•noe′ist,** *n.* [From the Arawak (Native

American) word *canoa,* with the same meaning.]

car•bo•hy•drate (kär′bō hī′drāt) *n.* a compound of carbon, hydrogen, and oxygen produced by green plants. Cellulose, sugars, and starches are carbohydrates.

car•bon (kär′bən) *n.* a nonmetallic element found in diamonds, coal, petroleum, and other substances.

care•ful•ly (kâr′fə lē) *adv.* **1.** with caution and close attention; watchfully, cautiously: *Walk carefully so as not to trip on that last step.* **2.** in a thorough manner: painstakingly: *to have researched carefully.*

care•less (kâr′lis) *adj.* **1.** not paying enough attention: *The careless guest spilled the water.* **2.** caused by or done with a lack of care or attention: *a careless error.* —**care′less•ly,** *adv.* —**care′less•ness,** *n.*

car•i•bou (kar′ə bü′) *n., pl.* **car•i•bou** or **car•i•bous.** any of a group of large deer that live in the northern regions of the world.

car•ni•vore (kär′nə vôr′) *n.* **1.** an animal or plant that feeds chiefly on flesh. Sharks, eagles, dogs, and Venus's-flytraps are carnivores. **2.** any member of the order of Carnivora, flesh-eating mammals having long, sharp teeth, such as dogs, bears, and lions.

car•ton (kär′tən) *n.* a container made of any of various materials, such as cardboard, wood, or plastic: *an egg carton, a milk carton.* [From Italian *cartone,* meaning "pasteboard."]

carve (kärv) *v.t.,* **carved, carv•ing. 1.** to cut with exactness, especially artistically: *We carved the wood into chess pieces.* **2.** to cut into pieces or slices. —**carv′er,** *n.*

CD ROM (sē dē rom′) *n.* a disk that stores sounds and images that can be called up on a computer. CD ROMs store so much information that an entire encyclopedia can fit on a single disk. [Short for *C*(ompact) *D*(isk) *R*(ead) *O*(nly) *M*(emory).]

ce•dar (sē′dər) *n.* **1.** a tall tree related to the pine and noted for its fragrant, long-lasting wood. **2.** the wood of a cedar.

ceil•ing (sē′ling) *n.* **1.** the interior overhead covering or surface of a room. **2.** the highest or upper limit set on anything: *The government set a ceiling on prices.*

cen•sus (sen′səs) *n., pl.* **cen•sus•es.** an official count of the people of a country or district, made in order to obtain certain statistics, such as age, occupation, or economic status.

cham•pi•on (cham′pē ən) *n.* **1.** a person or thing that is the winner. **2.** someone who is better than everyone else in a game or sport.

chan•de•lier (shan′də lîr′) *n.* a lighting fixture hung from a ceiling.

chan•nel (chan′əl) *n.* **1.** the deepest part of a river, harbor, or other waterway, often dredged and maintained as a passage for boats and ships. **2.** a proper or official route or means, especially of communication: *The request for a new typewriter had to go through the proper channels.* **3.** a frequency or band of frequencies assigned to a radio or television station for the transmission of electronic signals: *This old television set can only pick up one channel.*

at, āpe, fär, câre; end, mē; it, īce, pîerce; hot, ōld, sông, fôrk, oil, out; up, ūse, rüle, pùll, tûrn; chin, sing, shop; thin, this; hw in white; zh in treasure. The symbol ə stands for the unstressed vowel sound in about, taken, pencil, lemon, and circus.

chap•ter (chap′tər) *n.* **1.** a main part of a book or law code. **2.** a local branch of a club or society.

char•ac•ter (kar′ik tər) *n.* **1.** nature; the qualities that make up a person: *Jeremy has a very gentle character.* **2.** an unusual or odd person: *Gus was quite a character.* **3.** a person in a story: *Rani is the story's main character.*

char•i•ty (char′i tē) *n., pl.* **char•i•ties.** **1.** good will and love toward others. **2.** the giving of aid to those who are in need. **3.** an organization or fund for helping those in need: *Please give to your favorite charity.* —**char′i•ta•ble,** *adj.*

charm (chärm) *n.* **1.** an attractive or pleasing quality. **2.** a small object worn on a chain or bracelet for decoration. —*v.t.* to delight. —**charm′er,** *n.*

cheat (chēt) *v.i.* to act in a dishonest manner, as on a test or in a game. —*n.* **1.** the act of cheating. **2.** a person who cheats. —**cheat′er,** *n.*

check•book (chek′bủk′) *n.* a book of blank checks.

cheer•lead•er (chîr′lē′dər) *n.* a person who directs cheering at a sports event.

chef (shef) *n., pl.* **chefs.** a cook, especially the chief cook in a restaurant.

chem•i•cal (kem′i kəl) *n.* **1.** a natural or manufactured substance or combination of substances: *Soap is a substance made up of different chemicals.* **2.** a substance that acts on something else to change it: *The chemical that makes iron rust is oxygen.* —*adj.* **1.** of, used in, related to, or produced by chemistry. **2.** acting, operating, or produced by chemicals: *a chemical reaction.* —**chem′i•cal•ly,** *adv.*

chest•nut (ches′nut′) *n.* **1.** the smooth-shelled, sweet nut of a tree belonging to the beech family. **2.** the tree producing this nut. **3.** a reddish brown color. —*adj.* having the color chestnut; reddish brown.

chim•ney (chim′nē) *n. pl.* **chim•neys.** a passage for smoke, especially an upright brick or stone structure reaching above a building's roof.

chim•pan•zee (chim′pan zē′, chim pan′zē) *n.* an ape native to western and central Africa. Chimpanzees are smaller than gorillas and highly intelligent. [From a Bantu (African) word naming this ape.]

chip•munk (chip′mungk) *n., pl.* **chip•munks.** a small, striped squirrel. [From an Algonquin (Native American) word naming this animal.]

chipmunk

chlo•ro•phyll (klôr′ə fil′) *n.* an organic compound of carbon, hydrogen, nitrogen, oxygen, and magnesium. It is the green coloring matter of plants and is needed by them for making food materials by changing carbon dioxide and water into sugar.

choc•o•late (chô′kə lit, chok′ə lit) *n.* **1.** a food made from ground, roasted cacao beans. **2.** A drink made from mixing chocolate with milk or water. **3.** A candy made of or coated with chocolate. —*adj.* containing a food made from ground, roasted cacao beans. [From Nahuatl (the Aztec language) *chocolatl*, a word with the same meaning.]

choir (kwīr) *n.* an organized group of singers, especially one used in a religious service.

choral (kôr′əl) *adj.* **1.** of or relating to a choir or chorus. **2.** performed by or written for a choir or chorus: *choral music.*

chord[1] (kôrd) *n.* a combination of three or more musical tones or notes sounded at the same time to produce a harmony.

chord[2] (kôrd) *n.* a straight line segment joining any two points on the circumference of a circle.

cho•re•o•graph (kôr′ē ə graf′) *v.t.* to create, arrange, or direct (dance movement), as for ballet.

cho•rus (kôr′əs) *n., pl.* **cho•rus•es. 1.** choir; a large group of singers. **2.** a part of a song that is repeated. **3.** something uttered at the same time by a number of people: *a chorus of cheers.*

chrome (krōm) *n.* a metal often used as a shiny trim or panel: *The car's bumpers were plated with chrome.*

ci•der (sī′dər) *n.* the juice of apples used as a drink or for making other products, such as vinegar. [From Middle English *sidre,* their name for this drink.]

cin•na•mon (sin′ə mən) *n.* **1.** a reddish brown spice made from the dried bark of a tree grown in tropical regions. **2.** a light, reddish brown color. [From the Greek word *kinnamomon,* with the same meaning.]

cir•cum•fer•ence (sər kum′fər əns) *n.* **1.** a line bounding any rounded plane figure, especially a circle. **2.** the measurement of this line; the distance around something: *the circumference of the earth.*

clas•sic (klas′ik) *adj.* **1.** serving or used as a standard, model, or guide because of its high quality: *That cathedral is a classic example of Gothic architecture.* **2.** typical or traditional: *the classic symptoms of a*

disease.—*n.* a work of art or literature considered to be of such high quality or excellence that it serves as a standard or model: *Many of the plays of Shakespeare are classics.*

cli•mate (klī′mit) *n.* **1.** the typical weather conditions in a particular place. **2.** mood: *The survey tried to find out the climate of public opinion.*

clo•set (kloz′it) *n.* a room or recess, usually with a door, for storing clothing or other items.

close-up (klōs′-up′) *n.* **1.** a photograph taken at close range or with a telescopic lens: *The toothpaste advertisement showed a close-up of two smiling people.* **2.** a close or detailed view or look: *a close-up of a problem.*

co- *prefix.* see **com-**.

co•coa (kō′kō) *n.* **1.** A fat-free powder that is ground from cacao beans. **2.** A drink made by heating cocoa powder with water or milk. [From Nahuatl (the Aztec language) *cucahuatl,* meaning "cacao beans."]

co•coon (kə kün′) *n.* **1.** a protective case that encloses the pupa of certain insects, such as the silkworm, while it is developing into an adult. **2.** any similar protective covering.

co•ex•ist (kō′eg zist′) *v.i.* **1.** to exist together or at the same time. **2.** to live at peace with one another. —**co′ex•ist•ence,** *n.*

col- *prefix.* see **com-**.

at, āpe, fär, câre; end, mē; it, īce, pîerce; hot, ōld, sông, fôrk, oil, out; up, ūse, rüle, pull, tûrn; chin, sing, shop; thin, this; hw in white; zh in treasure. The symbol ə stands for the unstressed vowel sound in about, taken, pencil, lemon, and circus.

Spelling Dictionary

cold front (kōld′ frunt′) *n.* the border between an advancing mass of cold or cool air and a mass of warmer air.

col•lab•o•ra•tion (kə lab′ə rā′shən) *n.* cooperation; the act or process of work with another or others in some project or effort: *That discovery was the result of a collaboration between two scientists.*

col•lapse (kə laps′) *v.,* **col•lapsed, col•laps•ing.** —*v.i.* **1.** to fail suddenly: *Many businesses collapse during bad times.* **2.** to fall in; to fall down: *Did any buildings collapse during the tornado?* **3.** to become ill or exhausted suddenly. —*v.t.* to fold together: *to collapse a folding table and put it away.* —**col•laps′i•ble,** *adj.*

col•lec•tion (kə lek′shən) *n.* **1.** a group of objects that belong together: *I have a large collection of seashells.* **2.** any gathering: *A collection of people stood around the statue.* **3.** a gathering of money: *A collection was taken for the family.*

col•lide (kə līd′) *v.i.,* **col•lid•ed, col•lid•ing.** to come together with force.

colo•nel (kûr′nəl) *n.* a military officer ranking just below a brigadier general.

colt (kōlt) *n.* foal; a young horse, especially a male. —**colt′ish,** *adj.*

colt

col•umn (kol′əm) **1.** a supporting post, especially one that is round **2.** one of two or more sections of typed lines side by side on a page and separated by blank space. **3.** an article that appears regularly in a newspaper or magazine: *She writes a column for a newspaper.*

com- or **col-** or **con-** or **cor-** or **co-** *prefix.* with; together; jointly.

com•mand (kə mand′) *n.* **1.** an order given. **2.** control or mastery: *She has an excellent command of the German language.* **3.** the possession of authority: *She took command of the whole project.* —*v.t.* **1.** to give an order. **2.** to demand as one's due: *The doctor commanded high fees.*

com•mis•sion (kə mish′ən) *n.* **1.** a group of persons appointed or elected to perform certain duties: *The president set up a commission to investigate the causes of crime.* **2.** a fee for services or work done, usually a percentage of the total price: *The salesclerk received a commission of fifty dollars on the sale*—*v.t.* **1.** to give military rank and authority to: *to commission an officer.* **2.** to order a work of art: *The city commissioned a mural for the new library.*

com•mit•tee (kə mit′ē) *n.* a group of people appointed or elected to consider some matter. *The committee voted to increase public spending.*

com•mon sense (kom′ən sens′) *n.* good sense and wisdom based on experience rather than on special knowledge; sound practical judgment.

com•pan•ion (kəm pan′yən) *n.* **1.** a friend. **2.** a person or thing that goes with another: *The companion to this glove is lost.*

com•pa•ny (kum′pə nē) *n., pl.* **com•pa•nies. 1.** one or more guests: *We had company for* dinner. **2.** a business firm. **3.** companionship; fellowship.

com•pare (kəm pâr′) *n.* comparison: *The beauty of the Rocky Mountains is beyond compare.* —*v.t.,* **com•pared, com•par•ing. 1.** liken; to describe as similar: *Our assignment was to compare the anthill to a community of humans.* **2.** to inspect for similarities or differences: *If you compare the two trees, you will notice that one is much fuller.*

com•pat•i•ble (kəm pat′ə bəl) *adj.* **1.** capable of existing well together; in harmony: *The two roommates were no longer compatible.* **2.** *Technology.* capable of being connected to each other or operating together: *This printer is compatible with my computer.*

com•pete (kəm pēt′) *v.i.,* **com•pet•ed, com•pet•ing.** to try to win or do well in a competition or contest.

com•pe•ti•tion (kom′pi tish′ən) *n.* **1.** the act of competing; rivalry: *The competition for scholarships was keen.* **2.** something that tests or proves skill or ability; contest: *a skating competition.*

com•plain (kəm plān′) *v.i.* **1.** to express unhappiness. **2.** to accuse; to make a charge.

com•ple•ment (*n.,* kom′plə mənt; *v.,* kom′plə ment′) *n.* **1.** something that makes complete or perfect: *The new table is just the right complement for the room.* **2.** the required number or amount: *The football team now has its full complement of players.* —*v.t.* to make complete or perfect: *The background music complements the action in the movie.*

com•plete (kəm plēt′) *v.t.,* **com•plet•ed, com•plet•ing. 1.** finish; to achieve fully. **2.** to make whole or perfect, especially to provide all needed parts. —*adj.* **1.** having all

parts; whole: *The complete kit is very expensive.* **2.** total; absolute:*The bake sale was a complete success.* —**com•plete′ly,** *adv.*

com•pose (kəm pōz′) *v.t.,* **com•posed, com•pos•ing. 1.** to form by putting together: *to compose a seating plan.* **2.** to make something original: *Kristen wants to compose a symphony.* **3.** to make calm: *Try to compose yourself before you go on stage.* —**com•pos′er,** *n.*

com•po•si•tion (kom′pə zish′ən) *n.* **1.** the act of forming parts into a whole; the act of composing, as a work of writing, art, or music: *The musician spent several years in the composition of the opera.* **2.** the parts that make up a whole: *The chemist analyzed the moon rock to determine its composition.* **3.** Something composed, especially a work of writing, art, or music.

com•pound (*adj.,* kom′pound; *v.,* kəm pound′; *n.,* kom′pound) *adj.* made by combining or putting parts together:*a compound word.* —*v.t.* **1.** to combine; to put together: *The pharmacist will compound the medicine for you.* **2.** to increase: *You will only compound the problem by being rude.* —*n.,* **1.** a word made by joining two or more words. **2.** a chemical consisting of two or more substances: *Water is a compound of hydrogen and oxygen.*

con- (kon, kən) *prefix.* see **com-**.

con•cen•tra•tion (kon′sən trā′shən) *n.* **1.** the act of giving complete attention to a single

at, āpe, fär, câre; end, mē; it, īce, pîerce; hot, ōld, sông, fôrk, oil, out; up, ūse, rüle, pùll, tûrn; chin, sing, shop; thin, **th**is; **hw** in white; zh in treasure.The symbol ə stands for the unstressed vowel sound in about, taken, pencil, lemon, and circus.

Spelling Dictionary

object: *The President placed all his concentration on public education.* **2.** strength: *The concentration of some medicines can make them toxic in large doses.*

con•cern (kən sûrn′) *n.* **1.** something that one has to do or be involved in. **2.** care or anxiety. —*v.t.* **1.** to relate to; to be about: *These stories concern young people seeking their fortunes.* **2.** to be the business of: *Litter is a problem that should concern everyone.* **3.** to make anxious or worried: *The dangers concern all of us.*

con•cer•to (kən cher′tō) *n., pl.* **con•cer•tos** or **con•cer•ti** (kən cher′tē). a musical composition for one or more solo instruments accompanied by an orchestra.

con•crete (kon′krēt, kon krēt′) *n.* a mixture of crushed stone or gravel, sand, cement, and water that becomes hard when it dries. —*adj.* **1.** made of concrete: *a concrete driveway.* **2.** of or relating to things or events that can be seen, felt, or experienced, rather than merely thought about: *A chair is a concrete object.*

con•demn (kən dem′) *v.t.* **1.** to declare to be wrong or guilty: *No one can condemn you for doing your best.* **2.** to declare to be unfit or not safe for use: *The city council wants to condemn the old warehouse.* —**con′dem′na′tion**, *n.*

con•di•tion (kən dish′ən) *n.* **1.** a thing on which something else depends; a requirement: *Lisa met every condition for being on the baseball team.* **2.** a state of usability: *The car was in good condition.* **3.** state of fitness or health. —*v.t.* to put into good condition.

con•duc•tor (kən duk′tər) *n.* **1.** a person who leads; director; guide; leader. **2.** *Music.* the director of an orchestra, chorus, or other musical group. **3.** a material or body that carries heat, electricity, or sound.

conductor

con•fuse (kən fūz′) *v.t.,* **con•fused, con•fus•ing. 1.** to mix up; to make uncertain. **2.** to fail to tell two or more things apart: *Don't confuse yards with meters.* —**con•fus•ed•ly, con•fus′ing•ly,** *adv.* —**con•fu′sion,** *n.*

con•nec•tion (kə nek′shən) *n.* **1.** the act of joining one thing to another. **2.** relationship. **3.** a thing that joins: *The lamp did not work because of a loose connection.* **4.** a way to continue a journey by changing to another vehicle: *They made a connection for Dallas in Atlanta.*

con•science (kon′shəns) *n.* a sense or understanding of what is right and what is wrong that prompts a person to do right.

con•ser•va•tion (kon′sər vā′shən) *n.* the protection and preservation of something, especially our natural resources.

con•sid•er (kən sid′ər) *v.t.* **1.** to think over carefully: *Sue wants to consider the plan.* **2.** to have an opinion of or on: *Does Allan consider her the greatest athlete he has ever known?* **3.** to be thoughtful of: *Terri tries to consider the feelings of others.* —**con•sid′er•a′tion,** *n.*

Spelling Dictionary

con•sist (kən sist′) *v.i.* to be made up of: *Our new menu will consist of only the most natural foods.*

con•so•nant (kon′sə nənt) *n.* **1.** a speech sound produced by blocking the passage of air through the mouth with the lips, teeth, or tongue. **2.** any letter of the alphabet representing such a sound.

con•tact lens (kon′takt lenz′) *n., pl.* **con•tact lens•es.** a thin lens that fits directly over the eye to improve sight.

con•tain (kən tān′) *v.t.* **1.** restrain; to hold back; to keep within limits. **2.** hold; to have within. **3.** to include as a part of: *Two gallons of milk contain eight quarts.* —**con•tain′a•ble,** *adj.* —**con•tain′ment,** *n.*

con•test (*n.,* kon′test; *v.,* kən test′) *n.* **1.** something that tests or proves skill or ability, such as a game or race; competition for a prize, honor, or position. **2.** a struggle or conflict: *a contest between nations.* —*v.t.* **1.** to struggle in order to win (something). **2.** to challenge or dispute: *The pitcher contested the decision of the umpire.*

con•tin•ue (kən tin′ū) *v.,* **con•tin•ued, con•tin•u•ing.** —*v.i.* **1.** not to stop in an action: *The rain continued for an hour.* **2.** to remain in a place or position. **3.** to start again after a break: *The meeting will continue after lunch.* —*v.t.* to not stop: *We will continue our work.*

con•tract (*v.,* kən trakt′, *n.,* kon′trakt) *v.t.* to draw together (the parts of a thing); make shorter or smaller: *Tighten and contract your arm muscles.* —*v.i.* **1.** to draw together; become shorter or smaller: *The leather strap contracted as it dried.* **2.** to enter into a legally binding agreement: *The farmer contracted to lease his land.*—*n.* **1.** a legally binding agreement between people or groups of people. **2.** a document stating terms of an agreement.—**con•trac′tion,** *n.*

con•trol (kən trōl′) *n.* **1.** power; authority: *This department is under the control of the treasurer.* **2.** a means or device for controlling: *She could not operate the machine because of a broken control.* —*v.t.,* **con•trolled, con•trol•ling,** to exercise or have power over: *You should control your temper.* —**con•trol′la•ble,** *adj.*

con•ver•sa•tion (kon′vər sā′shən) *n.* informal or friendly talk between people.

con•vic•tion (kən vik′shən) *n.* **1.** the act of finding or proving (someone) guilty of a criminal charge. **2.** a firm belief or opinion: *the conviction that all people are equal.*

con•voy (*n.,* kon′voi; *v.* kon′voi, kən voi′) *n.* **1.** a group of ships or vehicles traveling with a protective escort: *a convoy of tankers.* **2.** a group, as of warships, troops, or aircraft, that acts as a protective escort: *A convoy of destroyers escorted the aircraft carrier.* **3.** any group of persons or vehicles traveling together: *A convoy of trucks passed us on the highway.* —*v.t.* to accompany or escort in order to provide protection. [From the French word *conveier,* meaning "to convey or transport."]

co•op•er•ate (kō op′ə rāt′) *v.i.,* **co•op•er•at•ed, co•op•er•at•ing.** to act or work with others, especially in a way that helps everyone: *The classes cooperated in planning the party.* —**co•op′er•a′tion,** *n.*

at, **ā**pe, fär, câre; end, mē; **it**, **ī**ce, pîerce; h**o**t, ōld, sông, fôrk, **oil**, **out**; **up**, **ū**se, r**ü**le, p**ů**ll, tûrn; **ch**in, si**ng**, **sh**op; **th**in, **th**is; **hw** in **wh**ite; **zh** in treasure. The symbol ə stands for the unstressed vowel sound in ab**ou**t, tak**e**n, penc**i**l, lem**o**n, and circ**u**s.

Spelling Dictionary

cop•y•right (kop′ē rīt′) *n.* the sole right to produce, publish, or sell a literary, musical, or artistic work, granted by law for a certain number of years. —*v.t.* to get a copyright for: *to copyright a song.*

cor•al (kôr′əl) *n.*

coral

1. a hard substance resembling limestone, usually found in tropical waters. It is secreted by certain tiny sea animals, called polyps. **2.** any of the polyps that secrete this substance. **3.** a mass or structure formed by the skeletons of these animals, such as a reef. **4.** a pinkish red color. —*adj.* **1.** made of coral: *a coral reef.* **2.** having the color coral.

cor•du•roy (kôr′də roi′) *n.* a ribbed material: *Yvette's skirt was made of corduroy.*—*adj.* made of corduroy.

cor•po•ral[1] (kôr′pər əl) *adj.* of or relating to the human body; physical: *corporal punishment.*

cor•po•ral[2] (kôr′pər əl, kôr′prəl) *n.* the lowest noncommissioned officer in the U.S. Army or Marine Corps, ranking below a sergeant.

cor•rec•tion (kə rek′shən) *n.* **1.** the act of fixing something: *Correction of the car's engine problem took an hour.* **2.** a change made to fix an error: *Make these corrections on your homework.*

cos•tume (*n.*, kos′tüm, kos′tūm; *v.*, kos tüm′) *n.* **1.** the clothes typical of a period or country. **2.** a set of clothes, especially those worn for a play or party.—*v.t.,* **cos•tumed, cos•tum•ing.** to provide with a costume. —**cos•tum′er,** *n.*

couch (kouch) *n., pl.* **couch•es.** sofa; a piece of furniture that two or more people can sit on at the same time.—*v.t.* to word in a specific manner: *Please couch your message in pleasant terms.*

coun•cil (koun′səl) *n.* **1.** a group of people who meet to give advice and discuss questions. **2.** a group of elected people who make laws for and manage a town.

coun•ci•lor (koun′sə lər) *n.* a member of a council.

coun•se•lor (koun′sə lər) *n.* **1.** someone who gives advice. **2.** a supervisor at a summer camp.

count•down (kount′doun′) *n.* a counting backwards before an event, such as a rocket launch.

count•er (koun′tər) *n.* **1.** a piece used in counting or games. **2.** a level surface on which food is served or goods are displayed. **3.** a person or device that counts or keeps the count.

cou•pon (kü′pon, kū′pon) *n.* a ticket, certificate, or printed advertisement that can be presented in exchange for something: *You will be admitted at half price if you show this coupon.*

cour•te•sy (kûr′tə sē) *n., pl.* **cour•te•sies.** **1.** politeness; a thoughtful way of behaving. **2.** a kind act; a favor.

cow•ard (kou′ərd) *n.* one who lacks courage, or who runs away from any form of danger or trouble.—**cow′ard•ly,** *adv.*

coy•o•te (kī ō′tē, kī′ōt) *n., pl.* **coy•o•tes** or **coy•o•te.** a small prairie wolf. [From Nahuatl (the Aztec language) *coyotl,* with the same meaning.]

cra•dle (krā′dəl) *n.* **1.** a bed for a baby, usually on rockers. **2.** a framework providing support, such as the cradle of a telephone. —*v.t.* **cra•dled, cra•dling.** to put, rock, or hold in or as if in a cradle.

crawl (krôl) *n.* **1.** the act of moving slowly: *The traffic was so heavy that it slowed to a crawl.* **2.** a swimming stroke. —*v.i.* to creep; to move slowly and close to the ground, as a baby does.

crea•ture (krē′chər) *n.* **1.** animal; a living being. **2.** a strange being: *The movie was about a creature from outer space.*

crept (krept) past and past participle of **creep.** moved along close to the ground.

cro•chet (krō shā′) *n.* needlework consisting of looped stitches made with a hooked needle. —*v.t.* to make by crocheting. [From French *crochet,* meaning "little hook."]

cross-coun•try (krôs′kun′trē) *adj.* **1.** stretching or moving across a country: *Russ traveled on a cross-country railroad.* **2.** going across the countryside rather than on roads or tracks: *cross-country skiing.*

cruise (krüz) *n.* a journey or vacation, usually on a ship that stops at a number of places. —*v.i.* **cruised, cruis•ing. 1.** to sail about, stopping at a number of places. **2.** to travel for enjoyment. **3.** to travel at the best operating speed: *The airplane cruises at a speed of about 600 miles per hour.*

crust (krust) *n.* **1.** the hard outer surface of a loaf or a slice of bread. **2.** a piece of dry bread. **3.** the pastry portion of a pie. **4.** the outer part of the earth.

cue[1] (kū) *n.* a hint or signal that tells what to do or when to act. —*v.t.* **cued, cu•ing.** to give a hint or a signal.

cue[2] (kū) *n.* a stick used to hit the ball in a game of pool.

curb (kûrb) *n.* **1.** check, restraint: *A price curb has been placed on all foreign cars.* **2.** an edging built along a street or sidewalk. —*v.t.* check; to hold back or control: *Curb your anger.*

cy•cle (sī′kəl) *n.* **1.** a period of time during which actions or events repeat themselves regularly and in the same order: *We have reached the busiest time in the yearly cycle of holidays.* **2.** bicycle. **3.** motorcycle. —*v.i.* **cy•cled, cy•cling.** to ride a bicycle or motorcycle. —**cy′clist,** *n.*

dai•ly (dā′lē) *adj.* happening, used, or produced every day or every weekday: *I bought the daily paper.*

dawn (dôn) *n.* **1.** the first light in the morning. **2.** the beginning. —*v.i.* **1.** to begin to grow light as the sun rises: *Joan waited for the day to dawn.* **2.** to begin to appear or develop: *When did the space age dawn?*

day•dream (dā′drēm′) *n.* happy or pleasant imaginings about oneself or one's future. —*v.i.* to have a daydream: *There was time to daydream all we wanted.*

de- (dē, di) *prefix.* **1.** To do the opposite of. **2.** To remove from. **3.** To reduce or make smaller.

at, āpe, fär, câre; end, mē; it, īce, pîerce; hot, ōld, sông, fôrk, oil, out; up, ūse, rüle, pùll, tûrn; chin, sing, shop; thin, this; hw in **white; zh** in **treasure.** The symbol ə stands for the unstressed vowel sound in about, taken, pencil, lemon, and circus.

Spelling Dictionary

de•cent (dē′sənt) *adj.* **1.** in accordance with the standards of society, as in morality or social conduct; respectable: *It is not decent to pry into other people's business.* **2.** kind; generous: *It was very decent of you to help me.* **3.** fairly good; passable; satisfactory: *She makes a decent salary.* —**de′cent•ly,** *adv.*

dec•i•mal (des′ə məl) *adj.* relating to or based on the number 10; proceeding by tens. —*n.* **1.** a number based on multiples of tens, such as 10 x 10, 10 x 100, 10 x 1,000. **2.** a number containing a decimal point; decimal fraction.

dec•o•rate (dek′ə rāt′) *v.t.,* **dec•o•rat•ed, dec•o•rat•ing. 1.** to make more beautiful; ornament; adorn. **2.** to plan and execute the style and design of a room or rooms, as by selecting and arranging furniture, choosing fabrics, paint, or wallpaper. **3.** to honor, as with a medal: *The army decorated the soldier for bravery.*

de•coy (*n.,* di koi′, dē′koi; *v.,* di koi′) *n.* something, especially a wooden bird, intended to lead a person or animal into a trap. —*v.t.* to lure by a decoy.

decoy

de•crease (*v.,* di krēs′; *n.,* dē′crēs, di krēs′) *v.,* **de•creased, de•creas•ing.** to become less; to make less. —*n.* **1.** lessening; the state or process of decreasing. **2.** The amount by which something decreases: *There was a 10 percent decrease in sales.*

de•lay (di lā′) *n.* **1.** the act or state of being postponed: *Rain caused a delay in our trip.* **2.** the time during which something is postponed: *The delay lasted only a half hour.* —*v.t* **1.** postpone; to put off. **2.** to stop or hold back for a while: *The storm may delay our plans.* —*v.i.* to move or act slowly: *We haven't much time left, so don't delay.*

de•li•cious (di lish′əs) *adj.* highly pleasing or delightful, especially to the taste or smell. —**de•li′cious•ly,** *adv.* [From Latin *delicere,* meaning "to attract."]

de•liv•er•y (di liv′ə rē) *n., pl.* **de•liv•er•ies. 1.** the act of handing over. **2.** something handed over.

de•nom•i•na•tor (di nom′ə nā′tər) *n.* a number below or to the right of the line in a fraction, indicating the number of equal parts into which the whole is divided; divisor. In the fraction 1/2, 2 is the denominator. [From Latin *nominare,* meaning "to name."]

de•ny (di nī′) *v.,* **de•nied, denying. 1.** to declare not to be true. **2.** to refuse to grant.

de•par•ture (di pär′chər) *n.* **1.** the act of departing or leaving: *The departure of the plane was on time.* **2.** a change, as from a standard or usual course of action: *a departure from habit.*

de•pen•dent (di pen′dənt) *n.* one who is supported by another. —*adj.* relying on someone or something else for support: *Babies are dependent on their parents.* —**de•pen′dent•ly,** *adv.*

de•pres•sion (di presh′ən) *n.* **1.** a sunken place or surface; hollow: *The car bumped over the depression in the road.* **2.** lowness of spirits; sadness; dejection: *The win erased the team's depression.* **3.** a period marked by a severe reduction in business activity, a rise in unemployment, and falling wages and prices.

de•scen•dant (di sen′dənt) *n.* one who comes from an ancestor or family: *Two American Presidents have had descendants who also became Presidents.*

de•scent (di sent′) *n.* **1.** movement from a higher place to a lower one: *the descent of an elevator.* **2.** downward slope or inclination: *a hill with a steep descent.*

de•scribe (di skrīb′) *v.t.,* **de•scribed, de•scrib•ing.** to tell about or give an account of: *This essay describes our trip to Michigan.*

de•scrip•tion (di skrip′shən) *n.* **1.** an account of something that presents a picture to the person who reads or hears it. **2.** sort; kind: *People of every description attended the fair.*

de•serve (di zûrv′) *v.t.,* **de•served, de•serv•ing.** to be worthy of; merit: *You don't deserve another chance.* —**de•serv′ed•ly,** *adv.*

de•sign (di zīn′) *n.* **1.** a sketch or plan showing the main features of something to be made or done. **2.** the arrangement of elements that make up a structure or work of art: *The design of the furniture makes it unique.* **3.** a decorative pattern. —*v.t.* **1.** to plan for a specific purpose. **2.** to conceive and make a sketch of or plans for. —**de•sign′er,** *n.*

de•sire (di zīr′) *v.t.,* **de•sired, de•sir•ing. 1.** to have a strong wish for; long for; crave: *to desire success.* **2.** to express a wish for; request: *We desire information about vacationing in the mountains.* —*n.* **1.** a longing; wish: *a desire for wealth.* **2.** something desired.

de•spair (di spâr′) *n.* complete loss of hope; a feeling of complete hopelessness. —*v.i.* to lose all hope.

de•spite (di spīt′) *prep.* in spite of: *He swam a mile despite his illness.*

de•tail (di tāl′, dē′tāl) *n.* **1.** item; a small part. **2.** a group of soldiers chosen for a special duty. —*v.t.* **1.** to tell or describe item by item. **2.** to assign to a task.

de•ter•mine (di tûr′min) *v.t.* **1.** to decide or settle on something: *The members of the committee determined the date for the next meeting.* **2.** to find out for oneself: *to determine the cause.* **3.** to be the cause of or reason for: *The number of votes each candidate receives will determine the result of the election.*

de•vote (di vōt′) *v.t.,* **de•vot•ed, de•vot•ing. 1.** dedicate; to set apart for a special purpose: *I devote an hour a day to exercise.* **2.** to give up to completely: *My sister has chosen to devote her life to her career.*

di•ag•o•nal (dī ag′ə nəl) *adj.* **1.** *Geometry.* **a.** connecting two nonadjacent angles of a figure. **b.** connecting two nonadjacent edges of a solid figure. **2.** having a slanting direction: *The fabric has a diagonal pattern.* —*n.* **1.** a diagonal straight line or plane. **2.** anything slanting.

dic•ta•tion (dik tā′shən) *n.* **1.** the act of dictating something to be written down or recorded by another: *The students listened carefully to the teacher's dictation.* **2.** material that is dictated or recorded: *Part of the French exam was a dictation.*

dic•ta•tor (dik′tā tər, dik tā′tər) *n.* a ruler who has absolute power; tyrant.

at, āpe, fär, câre; end, mē; it, īce, pîerce; hot, ōld, sông, fôrk, oil, out; up, ūse, rüle, pu̇ll, tûrn; chin, sing, shop; thin, this; hw in white; zh in treasure. The symbol ə stands for the unstressed vowel sound in about, taken, pencil, lemon, and circus.

dif•fer•ent (dif′ər ənt, dif′rənt) *adj.* **1.** partly or totally unlike another. **2.** other, separate: *They all arrived at different times.* —**dif′fer•ent•ly,** *adv.* —**dif′fer•ence,** *n.*

dine (dīn) *v.,* **dined, din•ing.** —*v.i.* **1.** to eat dinner: *The family always dines at six o'clock.* **2.** to eat (with *on* or *upon*): *to dine on roast beef.*

dis- (dis) *prefix.* **1.** opposite of. **2.** not.

dis•a•gree (dis′ə grē′) *v.i.,* **dis•a•greed, dis•a•gree•ing. 1.** to fail to match or correspond to: *Your answers disagree with the ones in the book.* **2.** to have different opinions.

dis•ap•prove (dis′ə prüv′) *v.,* **dis•ap•proved, dis•ap•prov•ing.** —*v.t.* to refuse to approve; reject: *The boss disapproved your request for a vacation.* —*v.i.* to have or express an unfavorable opinion: *I disapprove of practical jokes that hurt people's feelings.* —**dis′ap•prov′ing•ly,** *adv.*

dis•count (*n.,* dis′kount′; *v.,* dis′kount′, dis kount′) *n.* a deduction of a specified amount or percentage, as from a price or other amount: *to sell a radio at a 25% discount.* —*v.t.* **1.** to offer for sale at a reduced rate: *That store discounts its merchandise.* **2.** to take off or deduct (a specified amount or percentage) from the total amount charged or owed: *The seller discounted 15% from the price.* **3.** to view as exaggerated or not entirely true: *Discount most of the stories about that athlete's ability.*

dis•cov•er (dis kuv′ər) *v.t.* to locate or find out for the first time: *Did Marie Curie discover radium?* —**dis•cov′er•er,** *n.*

dis•grace (dis grās′) *n.* **1.** loss of honor, respect, or favor; shame: *to bring disgrace upon one's good name.* **2.** the state of being dishonored or out of favor: *The noisy children were sent from the dining room in disgrace.* **3.** a person or thing that brings about shame, dishonor, or reproach: *This messy bedroom is a disgrace.* —*v.t.,* **dis•graced, dis•grac•ing.** to bring shame, dishonor, or reproach to or upon: *to disgrace one's family.*

dis•miss (dis mis′) *v.t.* **1.** to send away; to allow to go. **2.** to remove from office or employment. **3.** to put out of one's mind: *I can't dismiss her rudeness.* —**dis•miss′al,** *n.*

dis•o•bey (dis′ə bā′) *v.t.* to refuse or fail to obey (someone or something): *to disobey orders.* —*v.i.* to refuse or fail to obey: *That naughty dog always disobeys.*

dis•pose (di spōz′) *v.t.,* **dis•posed, dis•pos•ing.** to arrange; to put in place: *The farmer disposed the plants in rows.* •**to dispose of** to get rid of; throw away: *to dispose of garbage.*

dis•tance (dis′təns) *n.* **1.** the amount of space between two points: *What is the distance from San Francisco to Los Angeles?* **2.** a far-off place or region: *They saw a house in the distance.*

dis•trib•u•tive (di strib′yə tiv) *adj.* **1.** of or relating to distribution. **2.** *Grammar.* referring to each member of a group considered individually. *Each* and *every* are distributive words. **3.** *Mathematics.* relating to a law or principle stating that the product of multiplication is the same when the operation is performed on a whole set as when it is performed on the individual members of the set. For example: $4 \times (2 + 5) = 4 \times 2 + 4 \times 5$. —*n. Grammar.* a distributive word or expression.

dis•turb•ance (di stûr′bəns) *n.* **1.** trouble; the act of disturbing. **2.** public disorder.

di•vi•sion (di vizh′ən) *n.* **1.** the act of dividing or the state of being divided. **2.** one of the parts into which something is divided. **3.** *Mathematics.* the process of dividing two numbers to show how many times one number contains the other. **4.** something that divides: *The fence acted as a division between the two yards.* **5.** lack of agreement.

dodge (doj) *n.* **1.** a sudden move aside. **2.** a way to avoid something. —*v.,* **dodged, dodg•ing.** —*v.t.* **1.** to keep away from or avoid by moving aside quickly or suddenly: *to dodge a blow.* **2.** to get out of or evade by cunning: *Lee dodged my question about the surprise party.* —*v.i.* to move quickly or suddenly: *We dodged in and out of the crowd.*

dom•i•no (dom′ə nō′) *n., pl.* **dom•i•noes. 1.** a flat, oblong block, one side of which is divided in half, with each half either blank or marked with from one to six dots. **2.** *plural* a game played with dominoes.

dough•nut (dō′nut′) *n.* **1.** a small, usually ring-shaped cake fried in fat. **2.** something shaped like a doughnut.

dove[1] (duv) *n.* any of various small birds related to pigeons.

dove[2] (dōv) *v.i.* a past tense of **dive. 1.** plunged headfirst, as into water. **2.** fell quickly. **3.** plunged into an activity.

dove

Dr. *abbr.* **1.** Doctor. **2.** Drive (in an address): *103 Evergreen Dr.*

dra•ma (dräm′ə, dram′ə) *n.* **1.** play; a composition that tells a story and is designed for theatrical performance. **2.** a series of events involving interesting or intense conflict of forces: *The drama of the game kept everyone on edge.* [From Greek *drama*, meaning "action" or "deed."] —**dra•mat′ic,** *adj.*

drawn (drôn) *v.* past participle of **draw. 1.** made a picture by hand. **2.** attracted: *We hope the concert has drawn a crowd.* **3.** removed or brought out, as from a holder: *He drew his credit card out of its case.*

drive-in (drīv′in′) *n.* any place of business such as a theater, restaurant, or bank designed to serve customers while they remain in their cars; drive-through.

drive•way (drīv′wā′) *n.* a path wide enough for a car, leading from the street to a building.

drought (drout) *n.* **1.** the lack of rain or water. **2.** a long period of dry weather.

du•al (dü′el, dū′əl) *adj.* having two parts; twofold. —**du•al′i•ty,** *n.*

du•el (dü′el, dū′əl) *n.* **1.** a struggle or contest between two parties. **2.** formal fight between two persons using swords or pistols. —*v.,* **du•eled, du•el•ing.** —*v.i.* to fight in a duel. —*v.t.* to fight a duel with (someone).

dun•geon (dun′jən) *n.* a dark cell or prison, especially one underground.

at, āpe, fär, câre; end, mē; it, īce, pîerce; hot, ōld, sông, fôrk, oil, out; up, ūse, rüle, pùll, tûrn; chin, sing, shop; thin, this; hw in white; zh in treasure. The symbol ə stands for the unstressed vowel sound in about, taken, pencil, lemon, and circus.

eas•i•ly (ē′zə lē) *adv.* **1.** in an easy way; without difficulty: *Jill finished the test easily.* **2.** without doubt; certainly: *This is easily the best book I've read this month.*

ech•o (ek′ō) *n., pl.* **ech•oes. 1.** a repeated sound; a sounding again. **2.** a repetition or imitation of something. —*v.t.* **1.** to send back an echo: *The corridor of the school echoed our cries.* **2.** to repeat or closely imitate: *The students echoed the thoughts of their teacher.* —*v.i.* **1.** to send back an echo: *The corridor of the school echoed with voices and footsteps.* **2.** to be repeated by an echo: *Joyous laughter echoed through the house.*

ed•u•ca•tion (ej′ə kā′shən) *n.* **1.** the process of acquiring knowledge: *We go to school to get an education.* **2.** the field of study that deals with teaching methods and problems: *I took courses in elementary education.*

ef•fect (i fekt′) *n.* **1.** something brought about by a cause or agent; result: *The cooler air was an effect of the rainstorm.* **2.** the state or fact of being in force: *The club members wanted to put their plan into effect.* **3.** something used to make an impression: *The movie had great special effects.* —*v.t.* to bring about; produce as a result; cause: *Congress effected a program to provide health care for elderly people.*

el•der[1] (el′dər) *n.* **1.** someone born earlier; one who is of greater age. **2.** one with authority because of age and experience. —*adj.* senior; of greater age: *Their elder brother was shy.*

el•der[2] (el′dər) *n.* any of a group of shrubs and small trees bearing edible berries. Also, **elderberry.**

e•lec•tri•cal (i lek′tri kəl) *adj.* **1.** another word for **electric. 2.** dealing with electricity: *electrical engineering.* —**e•lec′tri•cal•ly,** *adv.*

e•lec•tric•i•ty (i lek tris′i tē) *n.* **1.** a source of energy found in nature but which can be artificially produced. **2.** an electric current. **3.** a strong feeling of excitement.

electricity

em•i•grate (em′i grāt′) *v.i.,* **em•i•grat•ed, em•i•grat•ing.** to leave one place or country to live in another: *to emigrate from Europe to the United States.*

em•ploy•er (em ploi′ər) *n.* a person or company that hires one or more persons for pay.

-ence (əns) *suffix.* **1.** the action, quality, state, or condition of being.

en•chi•la•da (en′chə lä′də) *n.* a tortilla (a flat, round bread) on which a meat or cheese filling is spread and which is rolled up and covered with a spicy tomato or chili sauce. [From Spanish *enchilar,* meaning "to season with chili."]

en•cir•cle (en sûr′kəl) *v.t.,* **en•cir•cled, en•cir•cling. 1.** to form a circle around; surround: *The campers encircled the bonfire.* **2.** to move in a circle around: *Many satellites encircle the earth today.*

en•close (en klōz′) *v.t.,* **en•closed, en•clos•ing. 1.** to close in on all sides; surround: *Trees enclosed the field.* **2.** to include with a letter or parcel: *to enclose a picture with a letter.*

Spelling Dictionary

en•e•my (en′ə mē) *n., pl.* **en•e•mies.** a person, group, or nation that has hatred for, or wishes to cause harm to, another.

en•joy•a•ble (en joi′ə bəl) *adj.* pleasurable; giving pleasure or satisfaction. —**en•joy′a•bly,** *adv.* —**en•joy′•ment,** *n.*

en•sure (en shùr′) *v.t.,* **en•sured, en•sur•ing.** guarantee; to make certain or safe: *Money does not ensure happiness.* Also, **insure.** ▲ **Ensure** and **insure** are both used in the same sense given here. **Insure** is also used in an additional sense, meaning to protect against loss by means of financial insurance.

-ent (ənt) *suffix.* **1.** a person or thing that does: *superintendent.* **2.** doing or being: *independent.*

en•trance¹ (en′trəns) *n.* **1.** the act of entering: *Everyone rose at the judge's entrance.* **2.** a place or means for entering: *an entrance to a building.*

en•trance² (en trans′) *v.t.,* **en•tranced, en•tranc•ing.** to fill with delight or wonder; to charm: *The jugglers entranced the audience.*

en•vy (en′vē) *n.* a feeling of resentment, jealousy, or desire brought on by another person's abilities, possessions, or good fortune.—*v.t.,* **en•vied, en•vy•ing. 1.** to feel envy toward (someone); regard with envy. **2.** to feel envy because of: *My friends envy my good grades.*

e•quip•ment (i kwip′mənt) *n.* **1.** anything needed for a particular purpose; supplies or gear: *sports equipment.* **2.** the act of fitting out: *The equipment of the team with new uniforms will be expensive.*

-er (ər) *suffix.* **1.** someone who is or does: *teacher.* **2.** more: *taller, faster.*

e•ras•er (i rā′sər) *n.* a device like a piece of rubber or cloth that wipes off or removes marks from a surface.

es•pe•cial•ly (e spesh′ə lē) *adv.* **1.** particularly: *I made this dessert especially for you.* **2.** to a special degree.

es•tab•lish (e stab′lish) *v.t.* **1.** to set up permanently; found: *to establish a university.* **2.** to settle securely or permanently, as in a place, position, or occupation: *I established myself in the clothing business.*

etc. *abbr.* et cetera; and so forth; and the rest. [From the Latin phrase *et cetera,* meaning "and all the rest."]

ex- *prefix.* **1.** former **2.** outside; outer.

ex•act (eg zakt′) *adj.* **1.** very accurate; precise; correct: *The clock gives the exact time.* **2.** being the same in every way: *an exact copy.* —*v.t.* to demand and get by force or authority: *to exact the payment of a debt on time.*

ex•cel•lent (ek′sə lənt) *adj.* very good. —**ex′cel•lent•ly,** *adv.*

ex•change (eks chānj′) *n.* **1.** trade; the giving or taking of one thing in return for something else. **2.** a place where things are bought, sold, or traded: *the Stock Exchange.* —*v.t.,* **ex•changed, ex•chang•ing.** to trade; to give in return.

ex•cite (ek sīt′) *v.t.,* **ex•cit•ed, ex•cit•ing.** to rouse; to stir the activity or feelings of. —**ex•cite′ment,** *n.*

at, āpe, fär, câre; end, mē; it, īce, pîerce; hot, ōld, sông, fôrk, oil, out; up, ūse, rüle, pùll, tûrn; chin, sing, shop; thin, **th**is; **hw** in **wh**ite; **zh** in treasure. The symbol ə stands for the unstressed vowel sound in about, taken, pencil, lemon, and circus.

Spelling Dictionary

excuse (*v.*, ek skūz′; *n.*, ek skūs′) *v.t.*, **ex•cused, ex•cus•ing. 1.** to make an apology for; to remove blame from: *Larry tried to excuse himself for being late.* **2.** to accept an excuse for. **3.** to free or let off from doing something: *The coach excused him from practices while his arm healed.* —*n.* **1.** a reason given in explanation; justification: *Oversleeping is not a good excuse for being late.* **2.** the act of excusing. **ex•cus′a•ble,** *adj.*

ex•pect (ek spekt′) *v.t.* **1.** to look forward to as certain: *He expects a large number of people to attend.* **2.** to look forward to as necessary or right: *I expect an explanation from you.*

ex•pe•di•tion (ek′spi dish′ən) *n.* a journey made for a specific purpose: *The explorers made an expedition to the North Pole.*

ex•pe•ri•ence (ek spîr′ē əns) *n.* **1.** something one has seen, done, or lived through: *My aunt's first experience with skydiving was a great success.* **2.** skill or knowledge gained by doing something: *Will had experience as a cook.* —*v.t.,* **ex•pe•ri•enced, ex•pe•ri•enc•ing.** to live through something; to undergo: *We experienced real fear when the plane developed engine trouble.*

ex•per•i•ment (ek sper′ə mənt) *n.* test; trial; an operation done under controlled conditions. —*v.i.* to make experiments; to test.

ex•plode (ek splōd′) *v.,* **ex•plod•ed, ex•plod•ing.** —*v.i.* **1.** to burst suddenly and violently with a loud noise; blow up: *The sealed bottle exploded in the fire.* **2.** to break forth violently or noisily: *to explode with*

experiment

rage. **3.** to increase rapidly: *That country's population has exploded in the last few years.* —*v.t.* **1.** to cause (something) to burst suddenly and violently with a loud noise. **2.** to prove wrong: *The theory that the earth was flat was exploded long ago.*

ex•plore (ek splôr′) *v.t.,* **ex•plored, ex•plor•ing. 1.** to travel over and investigate little-known places: *to explore the planets.* **2.** to look into closely: *to explore the causes of the Civil War.*

ex•plo•sion (ek splō′zhən) *n.* **1.** an instance of bursting violently and noisily. **2.** a large, fast, and spectacular expansion, outbreak, or upheaval: *Nearly all jobs have been affected by the recent explosion in computer technology.* —**ex•plo′sive,** *adj.*

export (*v.*, ek spôrt′, ek′spôrt′; *n.*, ek′spôrt′) *v.t.* to carry or send (goods or products) to other countries for sale or trade: *Spain exports olives to the United States.* —*n.* something that is exported: *Wool is an important Australian export.* —**ex′por•ta′tion,** *n.;* **ex•port′er,** *n.*

ex•press (ek spres′) *v.t.* **1.** state; to put into words: *to express an opinion.* **2.** to show or reveal outwardly; indicate: *to express happiness by smiling.* **3.** to make known; communicate: *Those paintings express the artist's love of nature.* —*adj.* **1.** particular or sole; special: *to call a friend for the express purpose of inviting her to the party.* **2.** clear and unmistakable: *to give express orders.* **3.** of or relating to a system of rapid transportation or delivery: *an express bus.* —*n., pl.* **ex•press•es. 1.** a system for the rapid and direct transportation or delivery of goods or money. **2.** a company engaged in such transportation or delivery. **3.** a train, bus, or elevator that is quick and direct and makes few or no stops.

fa•cial (fā′shəl) *adj.* of, for, or relating to the face. —*n.* a massage or other treatment for the face. —**fa′cial•ly,** *adv.*

fal•low (fal′ō) *adj.* (of land) tilled and left without being planted for one or more growing seasons. —*n.* fallow land.

fare•well (fâr′wel′) *interj.* good-bye and good luck. —*n.* the act of parting; departure; leave-taking. —*adj.* of or relating to a farewell; last: *a farewell dinner.*

fash•ion (fash′ən) *n.* **1.** manner; a way of doing something: *Tad did his work in a careless fashion.* **2.** a style of clothing: *the latest fashion.* —*v.t.* to make; to give form to: *I like to fashion flowers out of tissue paper.*

fa•tal (fā′təl) *adj.* **1.** causing death: *a fatal accident.* **2.** causing destruction or ruin; disastrous: *a fatal mistake.*

fau•cet (fô′sit) *n.* a fixture for drawing a liquid from a pipe or tank.

fau•na (fô′nə) *n., pl.* **fau•nas** or **fau•nae** (fô′nē). the animals characteristic of a particular region, time, or environment: *the fauna of the African plains.*

fa•vor•ite (fā′vər it) *n.* **1.** a person or thing liked best. **2.** a contestant who is expected to win. —*adj.* favored or best-liked.

fax (faks) *n., pl.* **fax•es. 1.** a method of electronically transmitting pictures or texts, as by telephone lines or radio. **2.** an image or document transmitted by fax. —*v.t.* to transmit by fax. [Short for *facsimile,* meaning "an exact copy."]

feath•er (feth′ər) *n. pl.,* **feath•ers.** a light, thin growth that forms the natural covering of a bird. —**feath′er•y,** *adj.*

fea•ture (fē′chər) *n.* **1.** a part of the face: *Tracy's eyes are her best feature.* **2.** the main attraction, as a film or a newspaper column. —*v.,* **fea•tured, fea•tur•ing.** —*v.t.* to give an important place to: *The concert features a guitarist.* —*v.i.* to play an important part: *School issues featured prominently in the campaign.*

fel•low (fel′ō) *n.* man; boy. —*adj.* belonging to the same class, group, or condition: *fellow students.*

fer•tile (fûr′təl) *adj.* **1.** producing or able to produce crops or vegetation abundantly: *fertile soil.* **2.** able to produce eggs, seeds, pollen, or the like.

file[1] (fīl) *n.* **1.** any device, such as a folder, drawer, or cabinet, in which papers or other documents are arranged in order for easy reference. **2.** a collection of records: *We had a file of all our receipts.* **3.** *Computers.* a collection of data created on a computer and stored on a disk or in memory. —*v.t.,* **filed, fil•ing. 1.** to keep documents arranged in order. **2.** to make an application: *to file for a permit.*

file[2] (fīl) *n.* a line of persons, animals, or things placed one behind another: *a file of marchers in a parade.* —*v.i,* **filed, fil•ing.** to march in a row: *The students filed out of the building.*

at, āpe, fär, câre; end, mē; it, īce, pîerce; hot, ōld, sông, fôrk, oil, out; up, ūse, rüle, pùll, tûrn; chin, sing, shop; thin, this; hw in white; zh in treasure. The symbol ə stands for the unstressed vowel sound in about, taken, pencil, lemon, and circus.

Spelling Dictionary

file³ (fīl) *n.* a steel tool used for smoothing down a rough surface —*v.t.,* **filed, fil•ing.** to rub or make smooth with a file.

fi•nal•ly (fī′nə lē) *adv.* ultimately; at the end or conclusion: *She finally achieved her goal.* —**fi′nal,** *adj.* —**fi•nal′i•ty,** *n.*

first aid (fûrst ād) *n.* emergency treatment given to a sick or injured person. —**first-aid,** *adj.: a first-aid kit.*

flare (flâr) *n.* **1.** a sudden, very bright light. **2.** a fire or bright light used to signal or to attract attention. **3.** An outburst of sudden anger or emotion. —*v.i.* **flared, flar•ing. 1.** to burn with a sudden, bright light, especially one lasting for only a short time. **2.** to become suddenly angry.

fla•vor (flā′vər) *n.* **1.** a particular or characteristic taste: *Pepper will give the stew a spicy flavor.* **2.** flavoring; seasoning: *Ice cream is made with chocolate, vanilla, and other flavors.* —*v.t.* to give flavor to: *to flavor apple pie with cinnamon.* —**fla′vor•ful,** *adj.*

flaw (flô) *n.* blemish; an imperfect feature. —*v.t.* to make imperfect.

fled (fled) *v.* past tense and past participle of **flee. 1.** Ran away from danger or evil. **2.** Went away swiftly; vanished.

fledg•ling (flej′ling) *also,* **fledge•ling.** *n.* **1.** a young bird just fledged (whose feathers have matured enough to support it in flight). **2.** a young or inexperienced person.

flight (flīt) *n.* **1.** the act of passing through the air: *I watched the flight of the ducks.* **2.** a trip made by or in an aircraft. **3.** a set of stairs from one floor to another.

floun•der¹ (floun′dər) *v.i.* **1.** to move or struggle with stumbling or plunging motions: *to flounder about in the mud.*

2. to struggle or move in an awkward or confused way: *They floundered through their first dance class.*

floun•der² (floun′dər) *n. sing.* or *pl.* any of various saltwater flatfishes used for food.

flour•ish (flûr′ish) *v.i.* **1.** to grow or develop strongly or prosperously; thrive: *Crops flourish in rich soil.* **2.** to reach or be at the highest point of development or achievement: *Aztec civilization flourished centuries ago.* —*v.t.* to wave about with bold or sweeping gestures; brandish: *to flourish a flag.* —*n., pl.* **flour•ish•es.** a fancy or showy action or display.

fol•low (fol′ō) *v.t.* **1.** to come after. **2.** obey: *You must follow the*

follow

doctor's orders. **3.** to go along: *Follow this road until it ends.* **4.** to keep one's eyes or attention on: *I couldn't follow the story after the third surprise plot twist.*

fool•ish (fü′lish) *adj.* Silly; showing no sense. —**fool′ish•ly,** *adv.*

fool•proof (fül′prüf) *adj.* not capable of going wrong.

fore•arm¹ (fôr′ärm′) *n.* the part of the arm between the elbow and wrist.

fore•arm² (fôr′ärm′) *v.t.* to prepare beforehand for something, especially for trouble.

for•eign (fôr′ən, for′ən) *adj.* **1.** Belonging to another place or country: *They spoke a foreign language.* **2.** Related to other nations: *Most presidential candidates have some experience with foreign affairs.*

forge¹ (fôrj) *n.* a furnace or a shop with a furnace where metal is heated and formed. —*v.t.,* **forged, forg•ing. 1.** to form metal by heating and hammering. **2.** fashion; to form or shape: *The two sides will forge an agreement.* **3.** to counterfeit; falsify.

forge² (fôrj) *v.i.,* **forged, forg•ing.** to move forward slowly but steadily: *We forged ahead on the project.*

for•mal (fôr′məl) *adj.* **1.** according to rules or customs. **2.** suitable for a special occasion: *John wore formal clothing to the dance.* —**for′mal•ly,** *adv.*

for•mer (fôr′mər) *adj.* coming before in time; happening in the past. —**for′mer•ly,** *adv.*

for•tune (fôr′chən) *n.* **1.** chance, luck. **2.** what happens to a person; good or bad luck: *Angela had the good fortune to win.* **3.** wealth.

foul (foul) *n.* in a sport, something done against the rules: *Our team made one foul after another.* —*v.t.* **1.** to make an unfair play: *Don't let another player foul you.* **2.** to clog: *Grease will foul your kitchen drain.* **3.** *Sports.* to commit a foul (an unfair play) against. *adj.* **1.** dirty or smelly. **2.** wicked: *a foul deed.* —**foul′ly,** *adv.*

fowl (foul) *n., pl.* **fowl** or **fowls. 1.** a hen or rooster; chicken. **2.** the flesh of a fowl used as food.

frac•tion (frak′shən) *n.* **1.** a part of a whole; small part: *Only a fraction of the crowd attending the game left before the game was over.* **2.** *Mathematics.* a quantity expressing the division of one number by a second number, written as two numerals separated by a line, such as 2/3, 3/4, or 12/16.

fra•grant (frā′grənt) *adj.* sweet or pleasant in smell: *A rose is a fragrant flower.* —**fra′grant•ly,** *adv.*

fre•quent (frē′kwənt) *adj.* happening often: *They made frequent trips to visit their grandparents.* —**fre′quent•ly,** *adv.*

fright•en (frī′tən) *v.t.* **1.** scare; to make afraid. **2.** to drive away by scaring: *The noise of the engine will frighten the animals away.* —*v.i.* to become scared: *Deer frighten easily.*

fron•tier (frun tîr′) *n.* **1.** a border between two countries: *The French defended their frontier.* **2.** the outer limits of knowledge: *The frontier of science is always expanding.*

froze (frōz) *v.* past tense of **freeze. 1.** hardened into ice through loss of heat. **2.** became chilled with cold. **3.** became affected by cold in a harmful way: *The weather this spring froze my tomato plants.* **4.** became motionless: *Walt froze at the sight of the spider.*

frus•trate (frus′trāt) *v.t.,* **frus•trat•ed, frus•trat•ing. 1.** to keep from doing or achieving something; disappoint or thwart. **2.** to prevent (something) from being fulfilled; defeat: *The storm frustrated our plans.*

fun•nel (fun′əl) *n.* a narrow tube attached to a cone designed to catch and direct a downward flow of liquid. —*v.i.* to pass through or as if through a funnel. —*v.t.* to move or cause to move to a central point or into a central channel.

at, āpe, fär, câre; end, mē; it, īce, pîerce; hot, ōld, sông, fôrk, oil, out; up, ūse, rüle, pùll, tûrn; chin, sing, shop; thin, <u>th</u>is; hw in white; zh in treasure. The symbol ə stands for the unstressed vowel sound in about, taken, pencil, lemon, and circus.

Spelling Dictionary

fur•nace (fûr′nis) *n.* an enclosed structure in which heat is produced.

fur•nish (fûr′nish) *v.t.* **1.** to equip with furniture. **2.** to supply what is needed: *He furnished us with pencils and paper.* —**fur′nish•er,** *n.*

fu•sion (fū′zhən) *n.* **1.** the act or process of fusing; melting together: *the fusion of metals.* **2.** the union or blending together of different things, as of political parties. **3.** *Physics.* the combining of two light nuclei (of atoms) to form a heavier nucleus. Fusion releases huge amounts of energy, as in the explosion of a hydrogen bomb.

gain (gān) *v.t.* **1.** to get by effort; obtain. **2.** to increase. **3.** win—*n.* something that is gained.

gar•lic (gär′lik) *n.* an onionlike bulb used as a seasoning. — **gar′lick•y,** *adj.*

garlic

ge•om•e•try (jē om′i trē) *n., pl.* **ge•om•e•tries.** **1.** the branch of mathematics that deals with the properties, measurements, and relations of points, lines, angles, plane figures, and solids. **2.** shape or design: *the geometry of a building.*

gi•gan•tic (jī gan′tik) *adj.* like or resembling a giant, especially in size; huge; enormous.

giv•en (giv′ən) *v.* the past participle of **give.** —*adj.* **1.** inclined; disposed; prone: *a person given to exaggerating.* **2.** stated; specified: *to do something at a given time.*

gold•fish (gōld′fish′) *n., pl.* **gold•fish** or **gold•fishes.** a small yellow or orange fish usually kept in aquariums.

go•pher (gō′fər) *n.* any of several burrowing American rodents with large cheek pouches.

grape•fruit (grāp′früt′) *n.* a large citrus fruit with a bitter, yellow rind and flavorful, juicy pulp.

grav•i•ty (grav′i tē) *n., pl.,* **grav•i•ties.** the earth's pull on things at or near its surface toward its center.

grief (grēf) *n.* sorrow; sadness; distress.

grown-up (grōn′up′) *n.* an adult; an older person. —*adj.* like an adult; mature.

guard (gärd) *n.* **1.** a person or group that defends or protects. **2.** careful watch or supervision: *A sentry kept guard at the door.* —*v.t.* **1.** to defend; to protect from danger. **2.** to watch over so as to control or to prevent escape: *The sheriff will guard the prisoner.* **3.** *Sports.* to try to prevent an opponent from scoring. —*v.i.* to be on guard; to take precautions: *to guard against illness.*

guer•ril•la (gə ril′ə) *n.* a member of a band of fighters, usually not part of a regular army, who combat the enemy with such acts as sabotage, ambushes, and sudden raids. —*adj.* of, relating to, or involving guerrillas: *guerrilla warfare.*

gui•tar (gi tär′) *n.* a musical instrument with a flat, pear-shaped body and a long neck, usually with six strings. It is plucked or strummed with the fingers or with a small piece of metal or plastic. [From Spanish *guitarra,* meaning "guitar."] —**gui•tar′ist,** *n.*

hai•ku (hī′kü) *n., pl.* **hai•ku.** an unrhymed Japanese verse form of three lines containing five, seven, and five syllables respectively. [This word comes from Japanese, where it has the same meaning.]

half (haf) *n., pl.* **halves** (havz). Either of two equal parts into which anything is or may be divided. —*adj.* being one of two equal parts; forming a half: *a half gallon of milk.*

ham•per¹ (ham′pər) *v.t .,* **hampered, hampering.** to interfere with the action or progress of: *Stalled cars hampered efforts to remove the snow.*

ham•per² (ham′pər) *n.* a large basket or other container, usually with a cover: *Please put your dirty laundry in the clothes hamper.*

hand•ker•chief (hang′kər chif, hang′kər chēf′) *n., pl.* **hand•ker•chiefs** or **hand•ker•chieves.** a small piece of cloth used for wiping the face, nose, or eyes.

han•gar (hang′ər) *n.* a building for housing and repairing aircraft.

hap•pi•ly (hap′ə lē) *adv.* in a joyful manner: *Melissa smiled happily.*

has•n't (haz′ənt) *contr.* has not.

head•ache (hed′āk′) *n.* a pain in the head. —**head′achy,** *adj.*

head•quar•ters (hed′kwôr′tərz) *n.* **1.** the center of operations from which a commanding officer, chief, or other leader issues orders. **2.** any center of operations, as of a business; main office: *The firm's headquarters are in New York.*

heap (hēp) *n.* **1.** pile; a collection of things

piled one on top of the other. **2.** a great number or large quantity. —*v.t.* **1.** to throw or gather into a large pile. **2.** to give in large amounts. **3.** to fill a container more than full.

heat ex•haus•tion, (hēt eg zôs′chən) a condition in which the body loses excessive amounts of fluids due to long exposure to high temperatures.

hel•met (hel′mit) *n.* **1.** a protective covering for the head, usually made of a hard material. **2.** a piece of armor that covers the head. —**hel•met•like,** *adj.* [From Old French *helme,* a word with the same meaning.]

he•red•i•ty (hə red′i tē) *n.* **1.** the process by which characteristics are passed on genetically from an animal or plant to its offspring. **2.** all the characteristics passed on in this way.

he•ro (hîr′ō) *n., pl.* **he•roes. 1.** a person admired for great deeds, noble qualities, or bravery. **2.** a person who shows great courage. **3.** the main male character in a book, play, or film.

hes•i•tate (hez′i tāt′) *v.i.,* **hes•i•tat•ed, hes•i•tat•ing. 1.** to wait or stop a moment; pause briefly: *We hesitated and then rang the doorbell again.* **2.** to be unwilling: *I hesitate to ask because I know you will refuse.* **3.** to fail to take action or to delay an action because of fear, uncertainty, or doubt.

hi•ber•nate (hī′bər nāt′) *v.i.,* **hi•ber•nat•ed, hi•ber•nat•ing.** to spend the winter in a dormant or inactive state, as do many animals, such as squirrels, snakes, most

at, āpe, fär, câre; end, mē; it, īce, pîerce; hot, ōld, sông, fôrk, oil, out; up, ūse, rüle, p**ů**ll, tûrn; **ch**in, sin**g**, **sh**op; **th**in, **th**is; **hw** in **wh**ite; **zh** in treasure. The symbol **ə** stands for the unstressed vowel sound in about, tak**e**n, penc**i**l, lem**o**n, and circ**u**s.

Spelling Dictionary

amphibians, a few fish and birds, and certain insects. —**hi′ber•na′tion,** *n.*

high•er (hī′ər) *adj.* comparative of **high** **1.** taller. **2.** more noble: *Jay has set higher goals than many of his classmates.* **3.** more costly: *Prices are higher this year.*

high school *n.* a school for students in grades nine through twelve or ten through twelve.

hire (hī′ər) *v.t.,* **hired, hir•ing.** to give a job to: *The employer will hire three women.*

hoard (hôrd) *n.* a hidden supply; something stored away. —*v.t.* to store away supplies. —**hoard′er,** *n.*

hoe (hō) *n.* a tool with a thin, flat blade attached to a long handle, used for weeding and loosening earth. —*v.t.,* **hoed, hoe•ing.** to remove weeds or loosen dirt with a hoe.

hoist (hoist) *n.* **1.** lift; the act of lifting: *We'll need a stronger cable to give this a hoist.* **2.** an apparatus used in hoisting. —*v.t.* to lift or pull up, especially by ropes, cables, or a crane.

hoop (hüp, hùp) *n.* **1.** a circular strip used to hold a barrel together. **2.** a circular toy that can be rolled on the ground or spun around the body. **3.** a basketball goal.

horde (hôrd) *n.* swarm; a great crowd.

hor•ri•ble (hor′ə bəl, hôr′ə bəl) *adj.* **1.** causing horror. **2.** very unpleasant or disagreeable. —**hor′ri•bly,** *adv.*

howl (houl) *n.* a loud, long, sad sound. —*v.i.* to make a loud, long, sad or angry sound.

hur•dle (hûr′dəl) *n.* **1.** a barrier to be jumped in a race. **2.** a difficulty to be overcome. —*v.t.,* **hur•dled, hur•dling. 1.** to jump over while running. **2.** to overcome a difficulty. —**hur′dler,** *n.*

husk•y[1] (hus′kē) *adj.,* **husk•i•er, husk•i•est. 1.** strong; muscular: *The man has a husky build.* **2.** hoarse and deep in tone: *a husky voice.* **husk′i•ly,** *adv.*

husk•y[2] (hus′kē) *n., pl.* **husk•ies.** also **Si•be•ri•an husk•y.** a heavy-coated working dog of the Arctic region.

ice-skat•ing (īs′skāt′ing) *n.* the act of skating on ice.

i•ci•cle (ī′si kəl) *n.* a hanging piece of ice formed by water that freezes as it drips.

icicle

i•den•ti•fy (ī den′tə fī′) *v.,* **i•den•ti•fied, i•den•ti•fy•ing.** —*v.t.* **1.** to prove that (someone or something) is a particular person or thing: *I identified my photos in the display.* **2.** to connect closely; associate: *to identify money with success.* —*v.i.* to become as one with another or others: *to identify with a character in a movie or novel.* —**i•den′ti•fi′a•ble,** *adj.*

i•den•ti•ty (ī den′ti tē) *n., pl.* **i•den•ti•ties. 1.** a person's sense of being different from other persons; individuality. **2.** a person's sense of being part of a sociological group or category: *ethnic identity.* **3.** *Mathematics.* a statement of equality that is true for all values of a variable. The equation $3x + 2x = 5x$ is true for all values of x and is therefore an identity.

i•dle (ī′dəl) *v.i.,* **i•dled, i•dling. 1.** to spend time doing nothing. **2.** to run, as with an engine or machine, without being connected. —*adj.,* **i•dler, i•dlest. 1.** not working, in use, or busy: *an idle machine.* **2.** not employed —**i′dle•ness,** *n.* —**i′dly,** *adv.*

ig•loo (ig′lü) *n., pl.* **igloos.** a house, often dome-shaped, made of blocks of snow. [From Inuit *iglu,* meaning "snow house."]

ig•no•rant (ig′nər ənt) *adj.* **1.** having little knowledge. **2.** not informed or aware: *Since Jane missed the meeting, she was ignorant about the plans for the fair.* —**ig′no•rance,** *n.* —**ig′no•rant•ly,** *adv.*

ig•nore (ig nôr′) *v.,* **ig•nored, ig•nor•ing.** to refuse to take notice of; pay no attention: *Why did you ignore me when I was speaking?*

il- (il) *prefix.* see **in-.**

im- (im) *prefix.* see **in-.**

i•mag•i•na•tion (i maj′ə nā′shən) *n.* **1.** the power of forming a mental picture of something not present to the senses. **2.** creative ability.

im•me•di•ate•ly (i mē′dē it lē) *adv.* at once; without delay.

im•mense (i mens′) *adj.* of great size, extent, or degree; very large; huge: *An immense building is under construction.* —**im•mense′ly,** *adv.*

im•mi•grant (im′i grənt) *n.* a person who comes to a new country to live.

im•pa•tient (im pā′shənt) *adj.* **1.** not patient; unwilling to wait; restless. **2.** irritable; angry. —**im•pa′tience,** *n.* —**im•pa′tient•ly,** *adv.*

im•po•lite (im′pə līt′) *adj.* rude; not polite. —**im′po•lite′ly,** *adv.*

im•port (*v.,* im pôrt′, *n.,* im′pôrt′) *v.t.* to bring goods into the country for sale or use: *to import chocolates from Belgium.* —*n.* **1.** something imported. **2.** meaning; importance: *What is the import of your remark?* —**im•port′er,** *n.*

im•por•tance (im pôr′təns) *n.* **1.** the state of being important. **2.** power or authority: *a person of importance.*

im•pos•si•ble (im pos′ə bəl) *adj.* **1.** not able to be: *Once we thought it was impossible to fly.* **2.** hopeless: *Our situation was impossible.* —**im•pos′si•bly,** *adv.*

im•prac•ti•cal (im prak′ti kəl) *adj.* **1.** not practical; not useful. **2.** not sensible.

im•prop•er (im prop′ər) *adj.* **1.** not suitable. **2.** showing poor taste or bad manners. —**im•prop′er•ly,** *adv.*

im•prove (im prüv′) *v.,* **im•proved, im•prov•ing.** —*v.t.* to make better: *Otis should try to improve his skills.* —*v.i.* to become better: *The weather should improve next week.*

in. *abbr.* inch or inches.

in- (in) or **il-** or **im-** or **ir-** *prefix.* **1.** not. **2.** within; in; into; toward.

in•ac•tive (in ak′tiv) *adj.* **1.** not doing something; idle. **2.** out of action: *Our baseball team was inactive during the winter months.* —**in′ac•tiv′i•ty,** *n.*

at, āpe, fär, câre; end, mē; it, īce, pîerce; hot, ōld, sông, fôrk, oil, out; up, ūse, rüle, pùll, tûrn; chin, sing, shop; thin, <u>th</u>is; hw in white; zh in treasure. The symbol ə stands for the unstressed vowel sound in about, taken, pencil, lemon, and circus.

Spelling Dictionary

inc. *abbr.* incorporated.

in•cense[1] (in'sens') *n.* gums and spices that make a fragrant aroma when burned.

in•cense[2] (in sens') *v.t.*, **in•censed, in•cens•ing.** to make angry: *Rudeness and disrespect can incense anyone.*

in•cor•rect (in'kə rekt') *adj.* wrong; not correct. —**in'cor•rect'ly,** *adv.* —**in'cor•rect'ness,** *n.*

in•de•pend•ence (in'di pen'dəns) *n.* the quality or state of being independent or on one's own; freedom from control.

in•di•rect (in'di rekt', in'dī rekt') *adj.* **1.** not straight; not the shortest: *Anita traveled by an indirect route.* **2.** not closely connected: *The indirect cause of the breakdown was the car's age.* —**in'di•rect'ly,** *adv.* —**in'di•rect'ness,** *n.*

in•fi•nite (in'fə nit) *adj.* **1.** having no limits or end; boundless: *Space seems to be infinite.* **2.** very great; immense: *to take infinite pains with one's work.* **3.** *Mathematics.* of or designating a quantity larger than any assigned number. —*n.* something that is infinite. **in'fi•nite•ly,** *adv.*

in•flu•ence (in'flü əns) *n.* **1.** the act or power of making something happen. **2.** a person or thing that uses influence: *Cheng was a good influence on his friends.* —*v.t.,* **in•flu•enced, in•flu•enc•ing.** to have an influence on; to affect.

in•for•mal (in fôr'məl) *adj.* **1.** casual: *We wore informal clothes to the party.* **2.** without ceremony: *The proceedings were conducted in an informal way* —**in•for'mal•ly,** *adv.*

in•for•ma•tion (in'fər mā'shən) *n.* **1.** knowledge or facts about something: *We asked for information about the train schedule.* **2.** a service that answers questions and gives facts: *Information gave me the store's phone number.*

in•no•cent (in'ə sənt) *adj.* **1.** not guilty of wrongdoing. **2.** harmless: *It was just an innocent game.* —**in'no•cence,** *n.* —**in'no•cent•ly,** *adv.*

in•sect (in'sekt') *n.* any of a group of small animals without a backbone, having six legs and a body divided into three parts: *Ants and flies are insects.*

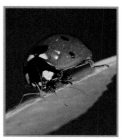

insect

in•stall (in stôl') *v.t.* **1.** to set up for use or service: *They will install the dishwasher tomorrow.* **2.** to put into office: *The company will install its new president.* —**in•stall'er,** *n.*

in•stance (in'stəns) *n.* example: *The rescue attempt was an instance of true courage.*

•**for instance**. as an example: *I like sports: for instance, baseball and judo.*

in•stru•ment (in'strə mənt) *n.* **1.** a device with which something is done: *A stethoscope is an instrument for listening to the heart and lungs.* **2.** a device that makes music: *The harp is my favorite musical instrument.*

in•sur•ance (in shùr'əns) *n.* **1.** an agreement for protection against risk or loss by means of a contract between two parties, usually a company and an individual. **2.** the business of insuring persons or property. **3.** any protection against risk, harm, or loss.

in•sure (in shùr') *v.t.,* **in•sured, in•sur•ing.** **1.** to protect against risk or loss by means of insurance; cover with insurance: *to insure a car.* **2.** another word for **ensure.** (See **ensure** for usage note.)

in•te•gra•tion (in′ti grā′shən) *n.* **1.** the elimination of racial segregation, as in schools or housing. **2.** the act of integrating parts into a whole.

in•tel•li•gence (in tel′i jəns) *n.* **1.** the ability to learn, understand, and reason. **2.** secret information, especially about an enemy: *After receiving the intelligence, the President relaxed the state of alert.*

inter- (in′tər) *prefix.* between; among.

in•ter•fere (in′tər fir′) *v.i.* **in•ter•fered, in•ter•fer•ing. 1.** clash; to get in the way of: *Does your job interfere with your studying?* **2.** to meddle in the affairs of others.

in•ter•na•tion•al (in′tər nash′ə nəl) *adj.* Having to do with two or more nations: *Marsha worked for an international company.*

In•ter•net (in′tər net′) *n.* a network of computers, interconnected through the telephone, that enables interactive communications and information retrieval on a global scale.

in•ter•pre•ta•tion (in tûr′pri tā′shən) *n.* **1.** the act of interpreting, or of making clear or understandable. **2.** the meaning that results from interpreting: *The students developed an imaginative interpretation of the poem.*

in•ter•sec•tion (in′tər sek′shən) *n.* the place where two or more things, especially streets, cross each other: *This intersection needs a traffic light.*

in•ter•state (in′tər stāt′) *adj.* having to do with two or more states: *We drove along the interstate highway.*

in•ter•val (in′tər vəl) *n.* **1.** time or space between: *An interval of a year passed before we were able to return.* **2.** *Music.* a difference in pitch between any two notes.

in•ter•view (in′tər vū′) *n.* a meeting to talk or consult with another person or people, especially about a job. —*v.t.* to meet with someone for a talk or consultation, especially about a job. —**in′ter′view•er,** *n.*

in•vent (in vent′) *v.* **1.** to think up or make up: *Did you invent that excuse?* **2.** To create for the first time. —**in•ven′tion, in•ven′tor,** *n.* —**in•ven′tive,** *adj.*

in•ver•sion (in vûr′zhən) *n.* **1.** the act of putting in reverse, as in order, position, direction, or effect. **2.** something that is in reverse. **3.** *Music.* the process of changing or reversing the positions of the notes of a musical chord or phrase.

in•vis•i•ble (in viz′ə bəl) *adj.* not able to be seen. —**in•vis′i•bly,** *adv.*

in•vite (in vīt′) *v.t.,* **in•vit•ed, in•vit•ing. 1.** to ask to be present. *Did Kim invite you to the party?* **2.** to attract. *Picnics invite ants.*

in•voice (in′vois′) *n.* an itemized list of goods sent to a buyer, indicating the quantities shipped, prices, and shipping charges. —*v.t.,* **in•voiced, in•voic•ing.** to make an invoice: *to invoice a shipment of goods.*

-ion *suffix.* **1.** the act of. **2.** the result of an act or process. **3.** the state or condition.

ir- (ir) *prefix.* See **in-**.

is•sue (ish′ü) **1.** a point of discussion: *What is the main issue in this campaign?* **2.** a copy of a publication: *Please buy me the latest issue of that magazine.* **3.** the action of going or coming out. —*v.t.,* **is•sued,**

at, āpe, fär, câre; end, mē; it, īce, pîerce; hot, ōld, sông, fôrk, oil, out; up, ūse, rüle, pùll, tûrn; chin, sing, shop; thin, this; hw in white; zh in treasure. The symbol ə stands for the unstressed vowel sound in about, taken, pencil, lemon, and circus.

is•su•ing. to bring out a publication or something for sale. *The post office will issue a new stamp this week.* —*v.i.* to go or come out. *Smoke issued from the chimney.*

-ity *suffix (used to form nouns).* quality, state, or degree.

jag•uar (jag′wär) *n., pl.* **jag•uars.** a large, wild member of the cat family with spotted fur, native to the southwestern United States and Central and South America. [From the Tupi (native Brazilian) word *jaguara,* with the same meaning.]

jour•nal (jûr′nəl) *n.* **1.** diary; a brief account of daily events. **2.** a daily newspaper. **3.** a news magazine.

jour•ney (jûr′nē) *n., pl.* **jour•neys. 1.** a trip, especially one over a long distance or taking a long time. **2.** the distance that is traveled, or that can be traveled, in a specified time: *four days' journey from here.* —*v.i.,* **jour•neyed, jour•ney•ing.** to make a trip; travel: *to journey through Europe.*

Jr. *abbr.* Junior: *James Valdez, Jr.* Also **jr.**

jump•er[1] (jum′pər) *n.* **1.** leaper; a person or thing that springs into the air. **2.** a cable, wire, or other conductor used to complete or bypass a circuit: *She used jumper cables to start the stalled car engine.*

jump•er[2] (jum′pər) *n.* a sleeveless dress usually worn with a blouse.

ka•ra•te (kə rät′ē) *n.* a Japanese system of unarmed self-defense using the hands, elbows, knees, and feet as weapons. [From Japanese *kara,* meaning "empty," and *te,* meaning "hand," because this method of self-defense does not require someone to hold a weapon.]

keen (kēn) *adj.* **1.** sharp: *Her keen knife cut the rope with ease.* **2.** sharply sensitive: *a keen sense of smell.* —**keen′ly,** *adv.* —**keen′ness,** *n.*

ker•nel (kûr′nəl) *n.* **1.** the inside of a seed or nut or the stone of a fruit. **2.** the grain or seed of various plants, such as wheat or corn.

kil•o- (kil′ō, kē′lō) *combining form.* thousand.

ki•mo•no (ki mō′nə, ki mō′nō) *n., pl.* **ki•mo•nos. 1.** a gown worn in Japan, having loose sleeves and tied with a sash. **2.** a loose dressing gown similar to this. [A Japanese word, meaning "clothing, garb."]

knack (nak) *n.* a special skill, ability, or method for doing something easily: *a knack for repairing things.*

knap•sack (nap′sak′) *n.* a bag worn on the back to carry clothes or supplies.

knapsack

knave (nāv) *n.* a deceitful or dishonest, disloyal person; scoundrel.

knowl•edge (nol′ij) *n.* **1.** something learned and kept in the mind. **2.** understanding: *Chang had a good knowledge of history.*

known (nōn) *v.t.* past participle of **know**.
1. had direct awareness of. **2.** had an understanding of: *Kim has always known what she wants to be when she grows up.*

late•ly (lāt′lē) *adv.* recently.

laun•dry (lôn′drē) *n., pl.* **laun•dries.**
1. clothes or linens that have been or are to be washed. **2.** a place where clothes are washed.

lead•er (lē′dər) *n.* **1.** one who goes ahead and shows others the way. **2.** a person in charge or in control: *The leader of our troop planned a retreat for next weekend.*
—lead′er•ship′, *n.*

league[1] (lēg) *n.* **1.** an association of people or countries formed to promote their common interests. **2.** an association of sports teams that compete regularly with one another: *a basketball league.*

league[2] (lēg) *n.* a measure of distance equal to 3 miles (4.8 kilometers).

leap year (lēp′yîr) *n.* a year containing an extra day, February 29. A leap year occurs when the number of the year can be divided evenly by 4, except in the last year of a century, when the number must be divided evenly by 400.

lec•ture (lek′chər) *n.,* **lec•tur•er.** a speech or talk given to teach or instruct. —*v.t.*
lec•tured, lec•tur•ing. to teach or instruct by means of a speech or talk.

lem•on•ade (lem′ə nād′) *n.* a drink made of lemon juice, water, and a sweetener such as sugar.

-less *suffix.* without.

lib•er•ty (lib′ər tē) *n., pl.* **lib•er•ties.**
1. freedom; the state of being free and independent. **2.** the power to do what one pleases: *The teacher gave the students the liberty to choose their own tasks.*

li•cense (lī′səns) also **li•cence.** *n.*
1. permission to do something. **2.** a document, plate, or tag showing that something is permitted. —*v.t.,* **li•censed, li•cens•ing.** to permit something to be done. [From Latin *licens,* meaning "to be permitted."]

light•ing (lī′ting) *n.* **1.** the act of putting on a light or the state of being lighted. **2.** an arrangement or system of lights; *stage lighting.*

like•ly (līk′lē) *adj.,* **like•li•er, like•li•est.**
with a good chance of happening: *It is likely to rain tomorrow.*

lime[1] (līm) *n.* a white, powdery compound of calcium and oxygen, made from limestone or seashells, used in mortar and plaster and in farming. —*v.t.,* **limed; lim•ing.** to treat or cover with lime.

lime[2] (līm) *n.* a greenish yellow citrus fruit similar to the lemon but smaller.

li•mit (lim′it) *n.* **1.** the highest or lowest possible amount. **2.** boundary. —*v.t.,* **limited, limiting.** to keep within bounds; restrict; confine: *to limit spending.*

lin•en (lin′ən) *n.* **1.** a cloth, thread, or yarn made from flax. **2. linens.** household

at, āpe, fär, câre; end, mē; it, īce, pîerce; hot, ōld, sông, fôrk, oil, out; up, ūse, rüle, pùll, tûrn; chin, sing, shop; thin, **this**; hw in white; zh in treasure. The symbol ə stands for the unstressed vowel sound in about, taken, pencil, lemon, and circus.

articles such as sheets, tablecloths, and other items made of linen or similar cloth. —*adj.* made of linen.

living room (liv′ing rüm, liv′ing rủm) *n.* a room in a house where people sit and talk.

loaf¹ (lōf) *n., pl.* **loaves. 1.** bread molded and baked as one mass. **2.** a shaped mass of other substances, such as food: *meat loaf.*

loaf² (lōf) *v.i.* to spend time doing little or nothing; to be idle: *This morning I loafed around, but this afternoon, I'm working hard.*

lo•cal (lō′kəl) *adj.* **1.** relating to or occupying a particular place: *This is the local news.* **2.** mainly serving the needs of a particular district. —**lo′cal•ly,** *adv.*

lo•cate (lō′kāt) *v.t.* **1.** settle; to set or establish in a certain spot. **2.** to find the place of something. —*v.i.,* to establish oneself in a particular place.

lo•ca•tion (lō kā′shən) *n.* **1.** a place or site. **2.** a setting where a movie is filmed away from a studio: *That part of the film was shot on location.*

loi•ter (loi′tər) *v.i.* **1.** to delay or interrupt a task or journey with many short stops. **2.** to hang around doing nothing. **3.** to lag behind.

lone•ly (lōn′lē) *adj.,* **lone•li•er, lone•li•est. 1.** lonesome; missing friends: *Lisa felt lonely after we left.* **2.** desolate; unvisited: *The house stood on a lonely hill.*

long dis•tance (lông dis′təns) *n.* **1.** communication by a telephone from a distant point. **2.** a telephone operator who gives connections to distant places: *Call long distance if you want to reach someone in Australia.*

loom¹ (lüm) *n.* a frame for weaving threads or yarns into cloth.

loom² (lüm) *v.i.* **1.** to appear in a large, unclear, or twisted form: *We watched the figure loom briefly above the trees.* **2.** to be about to happen: *We could feel danger loom as we rounded the corner.*

lose (lüz) *v.,* **lost, los•ing.** *v.t.* **1.** to be unable to find: *Did you lose your gloves?* **2.** to become deprived of by accident or death. **3.** waste: *I hate to lose a day of shopping.* **4.** to fail to win or obtain. —*v.i.* to suffer loss: *to lose heavily on the stock market.*

loss (lôs) *n., pl.* **loss•es. 1.** the act or instance of losing: *I felt chilly after the loss of my scarf.* **2.** the harm resulting from losing: *Her death was a loss to the community.* **3.** a person, thing, or amount lost: *His loss amounted to a hundred dollars.* **4.** a failure to win.

loy•al•ty (loi′əl tē) *n., pl.* **loy•al•ties.** allegiance; the quality or state of being faithful to a person, government, cause, or ideal.

lu•nar (lü′nər) *adj.* of or relating to the moon: *a lunar eclipse.*

-ly (lē) *suffix.* in a particular manner.

mac•a•ro•ni (mak′ə rō′nē) *n., pl.* **mac•a•ro•nis** or **mac•a•ro•nies.** a food made from wheat flour paste in the shape of curved tubes. [From Italian *maccaroni,* a word with the same meaning.]

mag•net (mag′nit) *n.* a piece of metal that has the property of attracting iron.

maid (mād) *n.* **1.** a female servant. **2.** a girl.

mail¹ (māl) *n.* **1.** letters, packages, or messages

sent from one person to another through the post office **2.** communication sent through a computer network. **3.** the system used in the sending and delivery of letters and packages. —*v.t.;* **mailed, mailing.** to send something through the post office system or a computer network.

mail² (māl) *n.* a flexible network of small metal rings linked together to use as armor: *The Knights of the Round Table wore coats of mail during battle.*

mail•box (māl′boks′) *n.* a box into which mail is deposited for collection by the post office.

mailbox

main•land (mān′land′, mān′lənd) *n.* the main part of a continent or a country as distinguished from a peninsula or an island.

ma•jor (mā′jər) *n.* an officer ranking just below a lieutenant colonel. —*adj.* **1.** most important. **2.** greater. —*v.i.* to study or specialize in a college subject: *to major in English.*

male (māl) *n.* **1.** a man or boy. **2.** an animal that can father young. —*adj.* of, relating to, or characteristic of males.

ma•neu•ver (mə nü′vər), *n.* **1.** a planned movement of ships or troops. **2.** a skillful plan or move. —*v.t.* **1.** to move (ships or troops). **2.** to manage or move skillfully. [From French *manoeuvre,* meaning "hand labor."]

man•ner (man′ər) *n.* **1.** a way of acting: *Anna finished it in her usual manner.* **2. manners.** behavior; especially social behavior: *The child had good manners.*

man•u•fac•ture (man′yə fak′chər) *v.t.,* **man•u•fac•tured, man•u•fac•tur•ing. 1.** to make or produce (a product), especially on a large scale by means of machinery. **2.** to make or process (a raw material) into a form or product suitable for use: *to manufacture wool into cloth.* **3.** to make up; invent: *to manufacture an excuse.* —*n.* the act or process of manufacturing: *The manufacture of cars is an important industry.*

mare (mâr) *n.* the full-grown female of certain animals, such as the horse, donkey, or zebra.

mar•ga•rine (mär′jər in, mär′jə rēn) *n.* a food product usually made from vegetable oil with milk or water and salt, used as a substitute for butter.

ma•roon¹ (mə rün′) *n.* a dark brownish red color. —*adj.* having the color maroon.

ma•roon² (mə rün′) *v.t.* **1.** to put ashore and leave on a desolate island or coast. **2.** to leave helpless and alone.

mar•shal (mär′shəl) *n.* **1.** an officer of a federal court who is appointed to a judicial district to perform duties similar to those of a sheriff. **2.** in some states, a law officer of a city or borough having powers similar to those of a sheriff. **3.** the head of a city police or fire department.

ma•te•ri•al (mə tîr′ē əl) *n.* **1.** the substance of which something is made: *The material in this dress is cotton.* **2.** apparatus and supplies for doing or making something. —*adj.* **1.** relating to or consisting of matter. **2.** important: *material witness.*

at, āpe, fär, câre; end, mē; it, īce, pîerce; hot, ōld, sông, fôrk, oil, out; up, ūse, rüle, pull, tûrn; chin, sing, shop; thin, <u>th</u>is; hw in white; zh in treasure. The symbol ə stands for the unstressed vowel sound in about, taken, pencil, lemon, and circus.

Spelling Dictionary

meg•a•byte (meg′ə bīt′) *n.* 1,024 kilobytes, or 1,048,576 bytes. [From the Greek word *mega* meaning "*large*" or "*great*," combined with the computer term *byte.*]

mel•o•dy (mel′ə dē) *n. pl.* **mel•o•dies. 1.** a pleasing arrangement of sounds. **2.** a tune; the main part in a musical composition.

mel•on (mel′ən) *n.* a large, juicy fruit, such as a watermelon, that has a firm rind and a sweet pulp.

men•tion (men′shən) *v. t.* to refer to or talk about briefly: *I mentioned them in my last letter.*

mere (mīr) *adj. superlative,* **mer•est.** being only this and nothing more; nothing more than: *Kirk was a mere child.* —**mere′ly,** *adv.* [From the Latin *merus,* meaning "clear, pure, or unmixed."]

meth•od (meth′əd) *n.* **1.** a way or means of doing something, especially an orderly way. **2.** orderliness and regularity in thought or activity: *His preparation for the test lacked method.*

mi•crobe (mī′krōb) *n.* a microscopic living thing, especially one that causes disease.

mid•night (mid′nīt′) *n.* twelve o'clock at night; the middle of the night. —*adj.* of, relating to, or occuring at midnight: *a midnight train.*

might•y (mī′tē) *adj.,* **might•i•er, might•i•est. 1.** powerful, strong: *She led a mighty army.* **2.** done by might; showing great power: *mighty deeds.*

min•er (mī′nər) *n.* a person who works in an underground tunnel from which coal or other natural substances are taken.

miner

mi•nor (mī′nər) *n.* a person under the legal age of 18 or 21: *A minor may not legally vote.* —*adj.* **1.** less important: *There were a few minor errors in your paper.* **2.** *Music.* based on a minor scale: *That song sounds sad because it is in a minor key.*

mi•nor•i•ty (mə nôr′i tē, mə nor′i tē) *n. pl.* **mi•nor•i•ties. 1.** the smaller part of a group or whole: *Only a minority of the students voted.* **2.** an ethnic, religious, political, or other group that is different from the majority of the group of which it is a part.

misc. *abbr.* miscellaneous.

mis•cal•cu•late (mis kal′kyə lāt′) *v.t., v.i.,* **mis•cal•cu•lat•ed, mis•cal•cu•lat•ing.** to figure, plan, or judge incorrectly: *The plumber apologized for miscalculating our bill.* —**mis′cal•cu•la′tion,** *n.*

mis•for•tune (mis fôr′chən) *n.* **1.** bad luck **2.** disaster; a bad state.

mis•spell (mis spel′) *v.t.,* **mis•spelled** or **mis•spelt** (mis spelt′), **mis•spell•ing.** to spell incorrectly.

mist (mist) *n.* **1.** water in the air in the form of floating particles or fine rain. **2.** haze; something that blurs the vision. —*v.i.* **1.** to become misted. **2.** to become blurred or dim.

mis•take (mis tāk′) *n.* **1.** a misunderstanding: *I ate your dessert by mistake.* **2.** an error or wrong action: *It was my mistake that the door wasn't locked.* —*v.t.,* **mis•took, mis•tak•en, mis•tak•ing.** to identify incorrectly: *You might mistake me for my twin sister.*

mis•tak•en [mis tā′kən] *v.* past participle of **mis•take.** —*adj.* based on error; wrong: *a mistaken belief.* —**mis•tak′en•ly,** *adv.*

mis•un•der•stand (mis′un dər stand′) *v.t.*, **mis•un•der•stood, mis•un•der•stand•ing. 1.** to fail to understand. **2.** to get the wrong meaning or message.

mix•ture (miks′chər) *n.* **1.** a product or result of mixing; combination; blend: *This batter is a mixture of milk, eggs, and flour.* **2.** *Chemistry.* two or more substances that, when put together, keep their individual properties, and are not chemically combined.

ml *abbr.* milliliter; milliliters.

mo•dem (mō′dəm) *n. Computers.* an electronic device, either built into a control unit or separate from it, that makes possible the transmission of data to or from a computer via telephone or other communication lines.

mod•est (mod′ist) *adj.* **1.** not boastful: *He is modest about his good looks.* **2.** not excessive: *The Allens live in a modest home.* —**mod′est•ly,** *adv.*

mois•ture (mois′chər) *n.* dampness; a small amount of liquid that causes wetness.

mold[1] (mōld) *n.* **1.** a hollow form for giving a particular shape to something: *The liquid plaster hardened in the mold.* **2.** something formed or made in a mold: *I made a mold of the leaf.* —*v.t.* **1.** to shape: *George can mold the clay.* **2.** to form or make in a mold.

mold[2] (mōld) *n.* a fungus that grows on food or other decaying matter.

moon•light (mün′līt′) *n.* the light of the moon. —*adj.* happening or done by the light of the moon: *to take a moonlight ride.* —*v.i.* to work at a second job, especially at night, in addition to one's regular job.

mo•tion (mō′shən) *n.* **1.** movement: *The motion of the cradle helped the baby fall asleep.* **2.** a proposed action suggested at a meeting: *Connie made a motion to change the club rules.* —*v.i.* to make a movement: *Did she motion for me to approach?* —*v.t.* to direct with a movement or gesture: *The usher motioned me to a seat.*

mourn (môrn) *v. i.* **1.** to feel or show grief or sorrow, especially over a death. —*v.t.* **2.** to feel or express sorrow or grief over: *The people mourned their misfortunes.* —**mourn′er,** *n.*

mph *abbr.* miles per hour.

Mr. (mis′tər) *pl.* **Messrs.** form of address used before a man's name or title: *We welcome you, Mr. President.*

Mrs. (mis′iz, mis′is) *pl.* **Mmes.** a form of address used before a married woman's name: *Do you know Mrs. Gonzalez?*

Ms. (miz) *pl.* **Mses.** a form of address used before a married or unmarried woman's name. [This form of address probably came from a blend of **Miss** and **Mrs.**]

muf•fin (muf′in) *n.* a small, cup-shaped bread product, usually eaten with butter.

mul•ti•ple (mul′tə pəl) *adj.* made up of or involving many or more than one: *Multiple prizes were awarded because all the artwork was so good.* —*n.* a number that is a product of a given number and an integer: *The numbers 8, 12, and 16 are multiples of four.*

mus•cu•lar (mus′kyə lər) *adj.* **1.** of, relating to, or involving muscles: *muscular coordination.* **2.** having well-developed muscles; strong: *a muscular athlete.* **3.** composed of or consisting of muscle.

at, āpe, fär, câre; end, mē; it, īce, pîerce; hot, ōld, sông, fôrk, oil, out; up, ūse, rüle, pu̇ll, tûrn; chin, sing, shop; thin, <u>th</u>is; hw in white; zh in treasure. The symbol ə stands for the unstressed vowel sound in about, taken, pencil, lemon, and circus.

must've *Contr.* must have: *They must've been in a real hurry.*

mys•ter•y (mis′tə rē) *n., pl.* **mys•ter•ies. 1.** a thing that cannot be explained. **2.** a deep secret: *No one could uncover the mysteries of the ancient tomb.* **3.** stories about mysterious crimes.

myth (mith) *n., pl.* **myths.** an imaginary tale, usually from long ago, that explains a natural event or the practices or beliefs of a people. [From Greek *mythos,* meaning first "speech" or "word" and then "story" or "tale."]

nat•u•ral (nach′ər əl) *adj.* **1.** existing or produced in nature:*We must use our natural resources carefully.* **2.** normal: *It is natural to like to eat.* **3.** relating to or agreeing with the laws of nature: *Gravity is a natural force.*

naugh•ty (nô′tē) *adj.,* **naugh•ti•er, naugh•ti•est.** behaving badly.

na•val (nā′vəl) *adj.* of or relating to a navy or ships.

na•vel (nā′vəl) *n.* a rounded scar in the middle of the abdomen; the belly button.

neat (nēt) *adj.* **1.** clean and orderly; tidy: *a neat room, a neat person, neat work.* **2.** *Informal.* wonderful; fine: *We had a neat time at the party.* —**neat′ly,** *adv.* —**neat′ness,** *n.*

ne•go•ti•a•tion (ni gō′shē ā′shən) *n.* **1.** the act of negotiating. **2.** a discussion for the purpose of bringing about an agreement or sale.

nerve (nûrv) *n.* **1.** a bundle of fibers carrying impulses between the brain and spinal cord and other parts of the body. **2.** boldness, daring. **3.** a sensitive point.

nervous system (nûr′vəs sis′təm) *n.* the system that includes the brain, spinal cord, and nerves: *The nervous system controls and coordinates all the activities of the body.*

new•born (nü′bôrn′) *adj.* recently born: *a newborn infant.*

niece (nēs) *n.* the daughter of one's sister or brother.

night•gown (nīt′goun′) *n.* a loose gown worn in bed by women or children.

no one (nō′wun) *pron.* nobody: *No one likes to be left out.*

nor (nôr) *conj.* and not, used especially between two words or phrases preceded by *neither.*

nos•tril (nos′trəl) *n.* either of the outer openings of the nose.

no•tion (nō′shən) *n.* **1.** idea: *I don't have any notion of the song's true meaning.* **2.** whim. *Sally had a sudden notion to walk out.*

nour•ish (nûr′ish, nur′ish) *v.t.* **1.** to help the growth or development of. **2.** feed; to provide with food: *Rain and good soil nourish the plants.*

Nov. *abbr.* November.

nov•el[1] (nov′əl) *n.* a fictional story written in prose, usually fairly long and having a detailed plot.

nov•el[2] (nov′əl) *adj.* new and unusual: *a novel idea.*

no•where (nō′hwâr′, nō′wâr′) *n.* no place: *There is nowhere I'd rather be.* —*adv.* **1.** not in or at any place. **2.** to no place.

nu•cle•ar (nū′klē ər, nū′klē ər) *adj.* **1.** of, relating to, or forming a nucleus, for example in a cell or an atom: *nuclear material.* **2.** of, relating to, or involving atomic nuclei or energy derived from atomic nuclei: *a nuclear chain reaction, a nuclear weapon.* **3.** of, relating to, or having atomic weapons: *The United States is a nuclear power.*

nu•cle•us (nū′klē əs, nū′klē əs) *n., pl.* **nu•cle•i** or **nu•cle•us•es. 1.** a central or necessary part around which other parts are collected; core: *The nucleus of the building is a large open court.* **2.** a small, dense body located near the center of a plant or animal cell. **3.** the central portion of an atom.

numb (num) *v.t.* to cause to have no sensation: *The dentist had to numb the patient's mouth.* —*adj.* **1.** having no sensation. **2.** having no emotion; unfeeling, unemotional. —**numb′ly,** *adv.* —**numb′ness,** *n.*

o•a•sis (ōā′sis) *n., pl.* **o•a•ses.** a fertile or green area in a desert. [From Greek *oasis,* meaning "fertile spot."]

oat (ōt) *n., pl.* **oats.** a grain with long clusters of seeds that is used for human and livestock food.

oat•meal (ōt′mēl′) *n.* **1.** oats ground into a coarse powder or flattened to make flakes. **2.** a cooked cereal made from oatmeal.

o•bey (ō bā′) *v.t.* to carry out the requests or orders of: *to obey one's parents; to obey the law.* —*v.i.* to be obedient.

o•dor (ō′dər) *n.* the quality of a thing or substance that affects the sense of smell; a scent. —**o′dor•less,** *adj.*

of•fi•cer (ô′fə sər) *n.* **1.** a member of the police or some other person charged with enforcement of the law. **2.** a person holding an office of trust or authority: *The president and the treasurer are club officers.* **3.** a person holding a position of command in the armed forces.

of•fi•cial (ə fish′əl) *n.* officer; one who holds an office. —*adj.* **1.** of or relating to an office or position of authority: *a president's official duties.* **2.** ordered or permitted by authority: *This is an official major-league baseball.* —**of•fi′cial•ly,** *adv.*

one-way (wun′wā′) *adj.* moving or permitting movement in one direction only: *The man bought a one-way ticket to London.*

o•pin•ion (ə pin′yən) *n.* **1.** what one believes or thinks about something: *In Carol's opinion, it was a good idea.* **2.** a judgment about a person or thing: *Kelly has a high opinion of her soccer coach.*

or•chard (ôr′chərd) *n.* **1.** an area where fruit or nut trees are grown. **2.** a group of such trees.

orchard

or•ches•tra (ôr′kə strə) *n.* **1.** a large group of musicians who perform together. **2.** the front section of seats on the main floor of a theater: *We selected seats in the orchestra.*

at, āpe, fär, câre; end, mē; it, īce, pîerce; hot, ōld, sông, fôrk, oil, out; up, ūse, rüle, pùll, tûrn; chin, sing, shop; thin, this; hw in white; zh in treasure. The symbol ə stands for the unstressed vowel sound in about, taken, pencil, lemon, and circus.

Spelling Dictionary

or•di•nal (ôr′də nəl) *adj.* of, relating to, or indicating order or position in a series. —*n.* **•ordinal number.** a number that shows sequence or position in a set or sequence of numbers, as first, second, and so on.

ore (ôr) *n.* a mineral containing a substance for which it is mined.

out•put (out′pu̇t′) *n.* **1.** the amount of something produced: *electrical output, work output.* **2.** the information made available by a computer.

o•ver•coat (ō′vər kōt′) *n.* a warm coat worn over indoor clothes.

oys•ter (oi′stər) *n.* a kind of shellfish.

pain (pān) *n.* **1.** a feeling of strong discomfort, usually in a particular part of the body; physical distress or suffering. **2.** emotional or mental distress or suffering; anxiety; grief: *the pain of loneliness.* **3. pains.** care or effort: *She took great pains to make sure her party was perfect.* —*v.t.,* to cause pain to; make suffer. *My knee pains me on rainy days.*

pa•ja•mas *also British,* **py•ja•mas.** (pə jä′məz, pə jam′əz) *n., pl.* a loose, lightweight shirt and trousers designed for sleeping. [From Hindi *pajama,* meaning "pair of lightweight trousers."]

palm[1] (päm) *n.* the inner surface of the hand between the wrist and the fingers: *Hal held out his palm to receive his change from the cashier.*

palm[2] (päm) *n.* **1.** a tropical tree with a long stem and a crown of large, fan-shaped leaves. **2.** a leaf from a palm tree, carried as a symbol of victory.

pan•el (pan′əl) *n.* **1.** a rectangular section of a door, wall, or ceiling. **2.** a surface on which instruments or controls are mounted. **3.** a group of persons who discuss a topic before an audience. —*v.t.,* **pan•eled, pan•el•ing.** to cover or decorate with panels.

pants (pants) *n., pl.* trousers.

par•a•chute (par′ə shüt′) *n.* a piece of equipment often shaped like an umbrella, made of a lightweight fabric, and used for descending through the air from an airplane. —*v.,* **par•a•chut•ed, par•a•chut•ing.** *v.i.* to descend by parachute: *The pilot parachuted from the plane.* —*v.t.* to drop (something, such as troops or supplies) by parachute: *They parachuted medical supplies.*

par•don (pär′dən) *v.t.* **1.** to free (a person) from punishment for an offense: *The governor pardoned the prisoner.* **2.** to pass over (an offense) without placing blame or requiring punishment; forgive. **3.** to excuse or overlook: *Please pardon my questions.* —*n.* **1.** a freeing from punishment for an offense, or a document granting this. **2.** polite excuse or toleration: *I beg your pardon if I bumped you.* —**par′don•a•ble,** *adj.*

par•tial (pär′shəl) *adj.* relating to or being only part of.

pas•ta (pä′stə) *n.* **1.** wheat paste in processed form or in the form of fresh dough. **2.** a dish of cooked pasta: *The meal consisted of pasta and vegetables.* [From Italian *pasta,* a word with the same meaning.]

pasta

Spelling Dictionary

paste (pāst) *n.* **1.** a mixture of starch and water used to stick things together. **2.** any soft, smooth, usually moist mixture: *tomato paste.* —*v.t.,* **past•ed, past•ing.** to fasten together with paste.

pa•tience (pā′shəns) *n.* the quality or fact of being patient: *The crowd showed great patience as they waited on the long line for tickets.*

pa•tient (pā′shənt) *n.,* a person under medical care: *Sarah was a patient in the hospital for two weeks.* —*adj.* willing to put up with pain, waiting, or trouble: *The teacher was very patient with the beginners.*

pa•ti•o (pat′ē ō′) *n.* **1.** a courtyard, especially an inner courtyard, open to the sky. **2.** an outdoor paved or tiled area next to a house. [From Spanish *patio,* meaning "courtyard."]

pave (pāv) *v.t.,* **paved, pa•ving.** to cover with asphalt or concrete to make a hard, level surface: *The town paved the road with asphalt.* —**pave′ment,** *n.*

pearl (pûrl) *n.* **1.** a nearly white gem that is formed within the shells of oysters and some other shellfish. **2.** something like a pearl in beauty or value: *pearls of wisdom.*—*adj.* made of or looking like a pearl or pearls: *a pearl necklace.*

ped•al (ped′əl) *n.* a device worked by the foot and found on pianos, bicycles, motor vehicles, and various types of machinery. —*v.t.* to work the pedal of something: *to pedal a bicycle.* —*v.i.* to ride a bicycle or tricycle: *to pedal slowly.*

pe•des•tri•an (pə des′trē ən) *n.* walker; a person who travels on foot. —*adj.* **1.** unimaginative, ordinary: *a pedestrian idea.* **2.** relating to people traveling on foot: *pedestrian traffic.*

pen•cil (pen′səl) *n.* a tool for writing made of a stick of dark material encased in wood, plastic, or metal. —*v.t.,* **pen′ciled, pen′cil•ing.** to draw or write with a pencil: *Pencil your name at the bottom of the list.*

per•form•ance (pər fôr′məns) *n.* **1.** the doing of an action: *Your performance of the swan dive was superb.* **2.** the action of playing a character in a play. **3.** a public presentation: *a performance of a school play.* **4.** the way something performs: *Your car's performance will improve with a better grade of gasoline.*

per•fume (*n.,* pûr′fūm, pər fūm′; *v.,* pər fūm′) *n.* **1.** a scent, usually pleasant. **2.** a substance that gives off a pleasant odor, especially a liquid used for scenting. —*v.t.* to fill with a pleasing odor: *The roses perfume the air.*

per•mis•sion (pər mish′ən) *n.* the act of permitting, allowing, or approving: *They had their parents' permission to go to the store.*

per•mit (*n.,* pûr′mit; *v.,* pər mit′) *n.* license; a written statement giving permission. —*v.t.,* **per•mit•ted, per•mit•ting. 1.** allow; to give permission. **2.** to make possible; to give an opportunity: *The window permitted a view of the mountains.*

pet•al (pet′əl) *n.* one of the parts, usually colored, of a flower. —**pet′aled,** *adj.*

pho•to (fō′tō) *n.* a photograph; a picture made by a camera.

phrase (frāz) *n.* a group of two or more words that make sense but do not form a complete sentence.

at, āpe, fär, câre; end, mē; it, īce, pîerce; hot, ōld, sông, fôrk, oil, out; up, ūse, rüle, pùll, tûrn; chin, sing, shop; thin, this; hw in white; zh in treasure. The symbol ə stands for the unstressed vowel sound in about, taken, pencil, lemon, and circus.

Spelling Dictionary

phys•i•cal fit•ness the state of being in good physical shape.

phys•i•cal•ly (fiz′i kə lē) *adv.* in a manner that relates to the body: *He has recovered from the accident both physically and emotionally.*

pierce (pîrs) *v.t.,* **pierced, pierc•ing. 1.** to make a hole through. **2.** to force or make a way into or through something.

pi•lot (pī′lət) *n.* **1.** a person who operates a plane, ship, or other vehicle. **2.** a television program made as a test for a proposed show or series of shows: *The pilot for the new series aired on June 12.* —*v.t.* to steer or control: *to pilot a helicopter.*

pi•o•neer (pī′ə nîr′) *n.* **1.** a person who goes first, opening up new ways. *Ben Franklin was a pioneer in science.* **2.** colonist; one of the first to settle in an area—*v.t.* to explore or settle.—*v.i.* to be a pioneer --*adj.* of or relating to a pioneer: *Her pioneer spirit made her a leader among women.*[From the Old French word *peonier,* meaning "foot soldier," which came from Latin *pes,* meaning "foot."]

pir•ou•ette (pîr′ü et′) *n.* a rapid turning about on the toes, especially in dancing. —*v.i.,* **pir•ou•et•ted, pir•ou•et•ting.** to perform a pirouette.

piz•za (pēt′sə) *n.* an open, baked pie of flat bread dough covered with tomato sauce and cheese and sometimes other foods. [From Italian *pizza,* with the same meaning.]

plaid (plad) *n.* **1.** a design of unevenly spaced stripes crossing each other at right angles. **2.** tartan; any plaid pattern designating a particular Scottish clan, or family. [From Gaelic (a language of Scotland) *plaide,* meaning "a blanket."]

plas•ma (plaz′mə) *n.* a clear liquid that forms the fluid portion of blood, and in which the blood cells are suspended.

pla•teau (pla tō′) *n., pl.* **pla•teaus** or **pla•teaux.** a high, flat plain. [From Old French *platel,* meaning "flat object" or "little plate."]

play•off (plā′ôf′) *n., pl.* **play•offs. 1.** a game played to break a tie. **2.** *usually plural.* one or more games played to decide a championship.

plum (plum) *n.* **1.** a round, juicy fruit. **2.** a dark bluish purple color.

plumb•er (plum′ər) *n.* one who installs or repairs water pipes.

p.m. *abbr.* the time between noon and midnight; afternoon and evening. [From Latin *post,* meaning "after," and *meridiem,* meaning "noon."]

poach[1] (pōch) *v.t.* to cook in simmering liquid: *to poach eggs.*

poach[2] (pōch) *v.i.* to hunt or fish unlawfully, usually on private property. —**poach′er,** *n.*

po•et (pō′it) *n.* a person who writes poetry.

poise (poiz) *n.,* quiet self-confidence.—*v.t.,* **poised, pois•ing. 1.** to balance; to hold or make steady by balancing: *The waiter poised the platter on his palm.* —*v.i.* to be held in balance.

pol•lut•ant (pə lü′tənt) *n.* something that pollutes, especially industrial waste or other material that harms air, water, or soil.

pork (pôrk) *n.* the meat of a pig or hog used as food.

por•poise (pôr ′pəs) *n.*, *pl.* **por•pois•es** or **por•poise.** a mammal that is closely related to the dolphin and is found in all oceans except those in polar regions.

porpoise

po•si•tion (pə zish′ən) *n.* **1.** the way something is placed or arranged. **2.** posture. **3.** a way of looking at things. **4.** the place occupied by an object or person: *Rita plays the forward position on our basketball team.* —*v.t.* to place something in a particular location: *She positioned the candles on the table.*

post of•fice (pōst ô′fis) *n.* **1.** a nation's postal service. **2.** a branch of the postal service that handles mail for a particular area.

pouch (pouch) *n.*, *pl.* **pouch•es. 1.** bag, sack; especially one that fastens: *The postal carrier's pouch was heavy.* **2.** a bag-like pocket on the abdomen of some animals for carrying their young.

prac•ti•cal (prak′ti kəl) *adj.* **1.** relating to or coming from action and practice rather than thoughts or ideas. **2.** useful; capable of being used.

prai•rie (prâr′ē) *n.*, *pl.* **prairies.** a large area of level or slightly hilly grassland. [From Old French *praerie,* meaning "meadowland."]

prawn (prôn) *n.* any of various shellfish resembling shrimp but larger, found in salt and fresh waters.

pre•fix (*n.*, prē′fiks′; *v.*, prē fiks′) *n.*, *pl.* **pre•fix•es.** a syllable or group of syllables added to the beginning of a word, root, or stem so as to change its meaning or to form a new word. In the word *postwar,* *post-* is a prefix.

pre•pare (pri pâr′) *v.*, **pre•pared, pre•par•ing.** —*v.t.* **1.** to make ready or fit, as for a particular purpose, event, or undertaking: *They prepared themselves for the marathon.* **2.** to put together by combining various ingredients or parts, or according to a plan: *to prepare a meal.* —*v.i.* to get ready: *to prepare for college.*

pres•ence (prez′əns) *n.* **1.** the state or fact of being in a specific place at a given time: *The big dog's presence made me feel safe.* **2.** the area immediately surrounding a person or thing: *to sign a contract in the presence of a witness.*

pre•vent (pri vent′) *v.* stop; to keep from happening: *Bad weather can prevent a plane from taking off.* —**pre•ven′tion,** *n.*

pride (prīd) *n.* **1.** the state of being proud: *My parents take great pride in their home.* **2.** proud behavior: *Jess held his head high with pride.* **3.** something that makes one proud: *Molly's car is her pride and joy.* **4.** a family or group of lions. —*v.t.,* **prid•ed, prid•ing.** to feel proud: *Does Brad pride himself on being the best bronco rider in the state?*

prin•ci•pal (prin′sə pəl) *n.* the head of a school. —*adj.* main, chief: *the principal cause.*

prin•ci•ple (prin′sə pəl) *n.* **1.** a basic truth, law, belief, or doctrine: *This government is based on the principle that all people are created equal.* **2.** a rule of personal conduct: *It is my principle to answer letters promptly.* **3.** a sense of right or honorable action; integrity: *to follow the rules as a matter of principle.*

at, āpe, fär, câre; end, mē; it, īce, pîerce; hot, ōld, sông, fôrk, oil, out; up, ūse, rüle, pùll, tûrn; chin, sing, shop; thin, **th**is; hw in white; zh in treasure. The symbol ə stands for the unstressed vowel sound in about, taken, pencil, lemon, and circus.

Spelling Dictionary

pris•on (priz′ən) *n.* **1.** a building or institution in which persons convicted or accused of crimes are confined. **2.** any place of confinement.

prob•a•bly (prob′ə blē) *adv.* **1.** likely to be true. **2.** likely to happen.

pro•fes•sion (prə fesh′ən) *n.* **1.** an occupation requiring special knowledge and education. **2.** a group of persons in a certain job: *They are members of the medical profession.* **3.** an open declaration: *a profession of loyalty.*

prof•it (prof′it) *n.* **1.** also, **profits.** the amount remaining after all the costs of a business or business transaction have been paid. **2.** *also,* **profits.** financial gain, especially return or income received from investment or property. **3.** a benefit or advantage; gain. —*v.i.* to get benefit or profit; gain: *to profit from an experience.* —*v.t.* to be of advantage, use or benefit to: *It will profit you to listen.*

prom•ise (prom′is) *n.* **1.** a statement that a person will or will not do something: *Lee made a promise to come to the meeting.* **2.** something promised: *I kept my promise.* —*v.t.* **prom•ised, prom•is•ing.** to agree to do or not to do something.

pro•noun (prō′noun′) *n.* a word used as a substitute for a noun. Pronouns include the words *I, me, you, he, him, she, her, it, we, this,* and *that.*

proof (prüf) *n., pl.* **proofs. 1.** evidence that something is so: *Audrey gave proof of her age.* **2.** a test photographic print made from a negative.

pro•ton (prō′ton) *n.* a particle found in the nucleus of all atoms, having a positive electrical charge.

pro•vi•sion (prə vizh′ən) *n.* **1.** the act of providing. **2.** preparation: *Be sure to make provision for emergencies.* **3.** a stock of supplies, especially food (usually used in the plural): *provisions for the hike.* **4.** condition: *A provision forbidding pets has been added to the rental contract.* —*v.t.* to supply with food and other necessary materials: *to provision oneself for a three-day hike.*

P.S. *abbr.* postscript (usually in a letter or note). [From Latin *post scriptum,* meaning "something written afterwards."]

pub•lish (pub′lish) *v.t.* **1.** to produce and issue printed material, such as a book for sale or distribution to the public. **2.** to print and sell the works of (a writer): *That company publishes Walt Whitman and Emily Dickinson.*

pun•ish•ment (pun′ish mənt) *n.* **1.** a penalty inflicted for a crime, offense, or fault. **2.** severe treatment; rough handling: *The car took a lot of punishment on the bumpy road.*

puz•zle (puz′əl) *n.* a hard problem. —*v.* **puz•zled, puz•zling.** —*v.t.* **1.** to confuse or bewilder: *This problem will puzzle you.* **2.** to solve with difficulty: *How long did you puzzle over that game?*

pyramid

pyr•a•mid (pir′ə mid′) *n.* **1. Pyramids.** the massive stone structures, having a square base and four triangular sides that slope upward to an apex, built as tombs by the ancient Egyptians. **2.** a solid figure having a polygon for a base and triangular sides intersecting at a point. **3.** anything resembling a pyramid in form or structure: *The acrobats have formed a human*

Spelling Dictionary

pyramid. —*v.i.* to rise or increase: *The cost of food has pyramided in recent years.* [From the Latin word *pyramid*, with the same meaning; originally from the Greek word *pyramís.*]

qual•i•ty (kwol′i tē) *n., pl.* **qual•i•ties.**
1. degree of excellence: *The actor's performance was of high quality.*
2. characteristic: *What is the main quality you look for in a friend?*

quan•ti•ty (kwon′ti tē) *n., pl.* **quan•ti•ties.**
1. an amount; a number. **2.** a large amount.

quar•rel (kwôr′əl, kwor′əl) *n.* an angry disagreement. —*v.i.* to argue, fight, or disagree actively. —**quar′rel•er,** *n.*

quar•tet (kwôr tet′) *n.* **1.** a musical composition for four voices or instruments. **2.** a musical group of four performers. **3.** any group or set of four.

ques•tion mark (kwes′chən märk) *n.* a punctuation mark used at the end of a direct question.

qui•et•ly (kwī′it lē) *adv.* in a quiet manner: *The class sat quietly.*

rack•et[1] (rak′it) *n.* a loud or confusing noise or clatter: *We couldn't sleep with all the racket.*

rack•et[2] (rak′it) *n.* a round or oval frame strung with a network of nylon or other material and having a handle, used to strike a ball: *a tennis racket.*

ra•dar (rā′där) *n.* an electronic detector that sends out a powerful beam that reflects off a distant object to show its position and direction of movement. [From the beginning letters of *ra*(dio) *d*(etecting) *a*(nd) *r*(anging).]

RAM (ram) *n.* a type of computer memory that stores data temporarily. The time required to store or retrieve data in RAM does not depend on the position of the data in the memory. [Short for *R*(andom)-*A*(ccess) *M*(emory).]

rap•id•ly (rap′id lē) *adv.* with great speed: *They walked rapidly.*

read•y-made (red′ē mād′) *adj.* made in quantity and not to order: *ready-made dresses.*

re•al (rēl, rē′əl) *adj.* **1.** true; not imagined. **2.** genuine; not imitation or fake. —**re•al′i•ty,** *n.*

re•bel•lion (ri bel′yən) *n.* **1.** an armed uprising against a legal government. **2.** resistance or defiance against any control or authority.

re•call (*v.,* ri kôl′; *n.,* ri kôl′, rē′kôl′) —*v.t.* **1.** to call or bring back to mind; remember: *I don't recall your name.* **2.** to call back; to summon back: *The manufacturer recalled the cars because of defects.* —*n.* a remembering of someone or something.

re•ceipt (ri sēt′) *n.* **1.** a written statement acknowledging that something, such as money, goods, or mail, has been received. **2.** the act of receiving or the state of being received.

at, āpe, fär, câre; end, mē; it, īce, pîerce; hot, ōld, sông, fôrk, oil, out; up, ūse, rüle, pùll, tûrn; chin, sing, shop; thin, this; hw in white; zh in treasure. The symbol ə stands for the unstressed vowel sound in about, taken, pencil, lemon, and circus.

re•cent•ly (rē′sənt lē) *adv.* happening in a period of time before the present, or just before the present.

rec•i•pe (res′ə pē′) *n.* a set of directions for making something, especially a food dish.

re•cite (ri sīt′) *v.*, **re•cit•ed, re•cit•ing.** —*v.t.* to repeat from memory: *to recite a poem.*

re•con•struct (rē′kən strukt′) *v.t.* **1.** to construct again; rebuild. **2.** to recreate something that happened or existed in the mind from available evidence or information: *The detective tried to reconstruct the crime.*

reel[1] (rēl) *n.* a spool or similar device on which rope, tape, motion picture film, fishing line, or the like can be wound: *Each reel of film is in a separate box.*

reel[2] (rēl) *v.i.* to stagger or sway as if dizzy.

re•frain[1] (ri frān′) *v.i.* to hold oneself back: *Please refrain from laughing.*

re•frain[2] (ri frān′) *n.* a regularly repeated phrase or verse, especially at the end of each stanza of a poem or song: *The audience sang the refrain with enthusiasm.*

re•fresh•ment (ri fresh′mənt) *n.* **1.** something that refreshes. **2. refreshments.** food or drink: *Juice and sandwiches were served as refreshments at the meeting.*

refreshment

re•fuse[1] (ri fūz′) *v.*, **re•fused, re•fus•ing.** —*v.t.* to decline to accept: to reject. —*v.i.* to be unwilling to do something: *They can't refuse if you ask politely.*

ref•use[2] (ref′ ūs) *n.* anything thrown out as useless; trash; garbage.

re•gard (ri gärd′) *v.t.* to look upon or think of; consider: *to regard someone as a close friend.* —*n.* **1.** careful thought, notice, or attention; consideration. **2.** respect or affection. **3. regards.** best wishes: *Give my regards to your family.*

re•hearse (ri hûrs′) *v.*, **re•hearsed, re•hears•ing.** —*v.t.* to practice or train for a public performance: *to rehearse a play.* —*v.i.* to take part in a rehearsal.

rel•a•tiv•i•ty (rel′ə tiv′i tē) *n.* **1.** the quality, state, or fact of being relative. **2.** a theory, developed by Albert Einstein, that deals with the way in which measurements of physical quantities, such as space, time, and energy, differ when made by observers who are in motion relative to one another.

re•mark (ri märk′) *n.* a spoken or written statement or observation, especially a brief or casual comment. —*v.t.* to express as an opinion or observation. —*v.i.* to make remarks.

re•mind (ri mīnd′) *v.t.* to make (someone) think of something or someone; bring back to mind; cause to remember: *I reminded her to return her library book.*

re•pay (ri pā′) *v.t.*, **re•paid, re•pay•ing.** to pay or give back: *to repay a loan.* —**re•pay′a•ble**, *adj.* —**re•pay′ment**, *n.*

re•plen•ish (ri plen′ish) *v.t.* to bring back to a state of fullness or completeness, as by replacing what is lacking or has been used: *to replenish one's food supplies.*

rep•re•sent•a•tive (rep′ri zen′tə tiv) *n.* a person who is chosen or authorized to represent another or others; delegate; agent: *The company had a representative in Rome.* —*adj.* typifying a group, kind, or class; typical; characteristic.

Spelling Dictionary

re•quest (ri kwest′) *v.t.* to express a wish or desire for; ask for: *He requested permission to leave.* —*n.* the act or an instance of requesting.

re•quire (ri kwīr′) *v.t.,* **re•quired, re•quir•ing. 1.** to be in need of: *That cut will require a bandage.* **2.** to have as an obligation or condition: *Knitting requires much patience.* **3.** to order or compel (someone) to do something: *The law requires public buildings to have fire exits.*

re•search (ri sûrch′, rē′sûrch′) *n., pl.* **re•search•es.** study or investigation in a particular field, usually for the purpose of learning new facts and making new interpretations. —*v.t.* to do research on or for: *The students researched a paper for the history class.*

res•er•va•tion (rez ′ər vā′shən) *n.* **1.** an arrangement by which something, such as a theater seat or hotel room, is reserved. **2.** something that has been reserved. **3.** doubt; misgivings: *Do you have reservations about traveling alone?*

re•sign (ri zīn′) *v.i.* to give up voluntarily, as a job, position, or office. —*v.t.* **1.** to give up (a position or responsibility) voluntarily: *to resign a job with regret.* **2.** to make (oneself) accept without protest or complaint: *to resign oneself to a difficult situation.*

re•sist•ance (ri zis′təns) *n.* **1.** the act of resisting. **2.** the ability to resist something, especially disease. **3.** A force that opposes or hinders the motion of another: *Cars are streamlined to overcome wind resistance.*

re•spect (ri spekt′) *n.* **1.** high or special regard. **2.** reference: *Let me answer with respect to your wishes.*

res•tau•rant (res′tər ənt, res′tə ränt′) *n.* a public place to buy and eat a meal. [From French *restaurer*, meaning "to restore."]

re•turn (ri tûrn′) *v.i.* to come or go back, as to a former place or condition: *to return to consciousness, to return home.* —*v.t.* **1.** to take, bring, send, give, or put back. **2.** to give or pay back in the same way: *to return a visit.* —*n.* a coming or going back: *to make a return to one's home town.*

re•un•ion (rē ūn′yən) *n.* **1.** the act of reuniting or the state of being reunited. **2.** a social gathering of friends, classmates, or relatives after separation or absence: *My high school class is holding its tenth reunion.*

re•view (ri vū′) *v.t.* **1.** to study, go over, or examine again: *to review notes in preparing for an exam.* **2.** to write or give a critical summary or discussion of: *She was asked to review the play for the newspaper.* —*n.* **1.** a studying, going over, or examining again. **2.** a looking back: *a review of one's life.* **3.** a summary or evaluation.

rhu•barb (rü′bärb) *n.* a plant having edible leafstalks with a tart flavor.

risk (risk) *n.* **1.** danger; the possibility of injury or loss: *There is great risk involved with that plan.* **2.** the chance of loss or injury to a person or thing insured. —*v.t.* to expose to hazard or danger: *Each day the firefighter risks injury.*

roam (rōm) *v.t.* to wander from place to place with no special plan or aim.

ro•de•o (rō′dē ō′, rō dā′ō) *n., pl.* **ro•de•os.** a show or contest featuring cowhand skills such as roping and riding. [From the Spanish word *rodeo* meaning "roundup."]

at, āpe, fär, câre; end, mē; it, īce, pîerce; hot, ōld, sông, fôrk, oil, out; up, ūse, rüle, pull, tûrn; chin, sing, shop; thin, this; hw in white; zh in treasure. The symbol ə stands for the unstressed vowel sound in about, taken, pencil, lemon, and circus.

Spelling Dictionary

rot•ten (rot′ən) *adj.* **1.** unsound, spoiled. **2.** morally corrupt.

row•dy (rou′dē) *adj.* rough; coarse or quarrelsome in behavior.

RSVP *abbr.* please reply; often found on written invitations. [Short for the French phrase *r*(épondez) *s*('il) *v*(ous) *p*(laît) meaning "reply, if you please."]

rude (rüd) *adj.* **1.** crude; in a rough or unfinished state: *The cabin was furnished with rude furniture.* **2.** impolite. **3.** forceful, abrupt: *The siren gave us a rude awakening.* **—rude′ly,** *adv.* **—rude′ness,** *n.*

safe•ly (sāf′lē) *adv.* in a manner that is not dangerous: *Drive safely.*

sam•ple (sam′pəl) *n.* **1.** a part that shows what the whole is like. **2.** a part used as an example. *—v.t.,* **sam•pled, sam•pling.** test; to judge by taking or trying a part of: *Would you like to sample this soup?*

sar•dine (sär dēn′) *n.* a small food fish that is related to the herring.

sau•cer (sô′sər) *n.* a small, shallow dish, usually used to set a cup upon.

scald (skôld) *v.t.* **1.** to burn with extremely hot liquid or steam. **2.** to rinse with very hot water. **3.** to heat nearly to the boiling point.

scar•ci•ty (skâr′si tē) *n., pl.* **scar•ci•ties. 1.** an insufficient amount or supply. **2.** the state or quality of being scarce.

scarf (skärf) *n., pl.* **scarves or scarfs. 1.** a long piece of woven or knitted fabric worn around the neck for warmth. **2.** a square or rectangular piece of fabric worn around the head, neck, or shoulders.

scar•let (skär′lit) *n.* a bright red color. *—adj.* bright red.

scat•ter (skat′ər) *v.t.* **1.** to cause to go in different directions: *A strong wind will scatter the clouds.* **2.** to spread out in many places: *Don't scatter your belongings all over the house. —v.i.* to separate and go in many directions: *The crowd scattered.* **—scat′ter•er,** *n.*

scheme (skēm) *n.* **1.** plan: *Show me the scheme for the project.* **2.** plot: *We uncovered the scheme to close the park. —v.,* **schemed, schem•ing.** *—v.t.* to plot.

schol•ar (skol′ər) *n.* **1.** student; one who studies or goes to school. **2.** a wise or learned person. **—schol′ar•ly,** *adj.*

sci•ence fic•tion (sī′əns fik′shən) *n.* a made-up story that deals with the effects of actual or imagined science on society or individuals.

sci•en•tif•i•cal•ly (sī′ən tif′i kə lē, sī ən tif′i klē) *adv.* in a scientific manner.

scis•sors (siz′ərz) *n.* a cutting tool with two blades fastened together that form the cutting edge when they are closed over each other.

script (skript) *n.* **1.** writing in which the letters are joined together; cursive handwriting. **2.** a writing system or style: *Babylonian script, Gothic script.* **3.** a written text of a play, used by the performers to learn their lines. [From the Latin word *scribere* meaning "to write."]

scu•ba (skü′bə) *n.* equipment for allowing a diver to breathe while swimming underwater. [Short for *s*(elf) *c*(ontained) *u*(nderwater) *b*(reathing) *a*(pparatus).]

scuba

sea•son•al (sē′zə nəl) *adj.* relating to a particular time or season of year: *My town sees a seasonal rise in the number of tourists.*

sec•tion (sek′shən) *n.* **1.** a part cut off or separated: *She ate a section of the orange.* **2.** a part of a written work: *The first section of the book contains maps.* **3.** a part of a newspaper: *The score of the game will be in the sports section.* —*v.t.* to separate into parts.

sel•dom (sel′dəm) *adv.* not often: *We seldom go to the movies.*

self-dis•ci•pline (self′dis′ə plin) *n.* firm control or discipline of oneself, one's actions, or one's feelings.

sen•tence (sen′təns) *n.* **1.** a group of words containing a subject and a verb that expresses a complete thought. **2.** a judgment setting a punishment after a conviction, especially in a court case. —*v.t.,* **sen•tenced, sen•tenc•ing.** to condemn to a particular punishment.

sep•a•rate (*v.*, sep′ə rāt, *adj.*, sep′ər it, sep′rit) *v.*, **sep•a•rat•ed, sep•a•rat•ing.** —*v.t.* **1.** to keep apart; be a barrier between; divide: *A fence separates the garden from the sidewalk.* **2.** To set or place apart: *to separate black socks from white socks.*

—*v.i.* to come apart; withdraw; part. —*adj.* set apart or divided from others: *two separate rooms.* —**sep′a•rate•ly,** *adv.*

Sept. *abbr.* September.

se•quel (sē′kwəl) *n.* **1.** a literary work that is complete in itself but continues the story of a previous work. **2.** something that follows.

ser•geant (sär′jənt) *n.* **1.** a police officer ranking just below a captain or lieutenant. **2.** a noncommissioned officer in the army ranking just below a staff sergeant.

ser•vant (sûr′vənt) *n.* one who serves others, especially a person who is employed to do housework, cook, or look after someone.

se•vere (sə vîr′) *adj.,* **se•ver•er, se•ver•est. 1.** very strict or stern. **2.** serious or dangerous: *a severe illness.* **3.** plain: *The room was severe in appearance.* **4.** inflicting pain or hardship: *severe weather.* —**se•ver′i•ty,** *n.*

shade (shād) *n.* **1.** partial darkness. **2.** space sheltered from light or heat, especially from the sun. **3.** something that intercepts light or heat. **4.** the degree of lightness or darkness of a color. —*v.*, **shad•ed, shad•ing** —*v.t.* to shelter from heat or light.

shal•low (shal′ō) *adj.* **1.** not deep. **2.** lacking depth of thought: *Steve is a friendly but shallow person.*—**shal′low•ness,** *n.*

sham•poo (sham pü′) *n.* **1.** the act of shampooing: *I gave our dog a good shampoo.* **2.** a liquid or cream used in shampooing: *I bought some shampoo for*

at, āpe, fär, câre; end, mē; it, īce, pîerce; hot, ōld, sông, fôrk; oil, out; up, ūse, rüle, pu̇ll, tûrn; chin, sing, shop; thin, this; hw in white; zh in treasure. The symbol ə stands for the unstressed vowel sound in about, taken, pencil, lemon, and circus.

Spelling Dictionary

my hair. —*v.t.* to wash something, for example one's hair, with soap or with a special liquid or cream.

share•hold•er (shâr′hōl′dər) *n.* a stockholder; someone who owns one or more shares of stock in a business.

sheet (shēt) *n.* **1.** a wide piece of cloth, especially one used in bedding. **2.** a piece of paper, usually rectangular. **3.** the wide surface of something: *Today the sidewalk is a sheet of ice.*

shel•ter (shel′tər) *n.* a protected place. —*v.t.* to provide protection for: *The canopy sheltered us from the rain.* —*v.i.* to find or take shelter.

shine (shīn) *v.* **shone** or (*v.t.*) **shined, shin•ing.** —*v.i.* **1.** to send out light: *Move the light so it doesn't shine in your eyes.* **2.** to be bright by reflecting light: *These glasses really shine.* **3.** to show unusual abilities: *They all really shine in sports.* —*v.t.* to put a gloss or polish on: *I need to shine my shoes.*

shiv•er[1] (shiv′ər) *v.i.* to shake, as with a cold or fear; tremble. —*n.* a shivering sensation.

shiv•er[2] (shiv′ər) *v.t.* to cause to break into fragments or splinters; shatter.

shock•ing (shok′ing) *adj.* causing horror or surprise: *shocking news.*

short•en (shôr′tən) *v.t.* to make short or shorter: *to shorten a skirt.* —*v.i.* to become short or shorter.

shown (shōn) a past participle of **show.** **1.** placed in sight. **2.** revealed. **3.** pointed out or led: *The path was shown by blinking red lights.*

sig•nal (sig′nəl) *n.* **1.** an act, event, or word that starts some action: *The whistle was the signal to stop.* **2.** a sound or movement made to give a warning or command. **3.** an object placed to give a message or warning: *The traffic signal turned red.* **4.** a message or sound transmitted in electronic communication, as in radio or television. —*v.,* **sig•naled, sig•nal•ing.** *v.i.* to make a signal or signals.

si•lence (sī′ləns) *n.* **1.** the act or state of being silent. **2.** stillness; the state of being without noise. —*v.,* **si• lenced, si•lenc•ing.** to stop the noise or speech of.

si•lent (sī′lənt) *adj.* **1.** marked by the absence of sound; completely quiet: *the silent desert.* **2.** not uttered or expressed: *There was much silent opposition to the new rules.* —**si′lent•ly,** *adv.*

sim•i•lar (sim′ə lər) *adj.* having or bearing a marked resemblance; alike: *The designs of the two houses are similar.* —**sim′i•lar•ly,** *adv.*

sim•ply (sim′plē) *adv.* **1.** clearly: *The teacher gave the directions simply.* **2.** plainly: *Bob was simply dressed.* **3.** only, merely: *We stayed simply to talk to them.*

-sion (shən) *suffix.* see **-ion.**

skel•e•tal (skel′i təl) *adj.* of, relating to, forming, or like a skeleton.

sketch (skech) *n., pl.* **sketch•es. 1.** a rough, unfinished, or quick drawing: *The artist made several sketches of the model before starting the painting.* **2.** a short description or plan giving the main features of something; outline. —*v.* to make a sketch of: *The painter sketched the old barn.* [From a Dutch word meaning "a quick drawing."]

ski (skē) *n., pl.* **skis.** a long, narrow runner, usually of wood or metal, designed to be fastened to a boot for gliding over snow.

skill•ful (skil′fəl) *adj.* having or showing skill or ability: *a skillful chess player.* —**skill′ful•ly,** *adv.* —**skill′ful•ness,** *n.*

sky•scrap•er (skī′skrā′pər) *n.* a very tall building.

sleep•ing bag (slēp′ing bag) *n.* a bag warmly padded, used for sleeping, especially outdoors.

slip•per (slip′ər) *n., pl.* **slippers.** a light, soft-soled, low shoe with no laces, easily put on or taken off.

smell•ing salts, a preparation based on ammonia, inhaled to relieve headaches or faintness.

so•cial (so′shəl) *adj.* **1.** relating to companionship and friendliness: *Parties are social events.* **2.** friendly, conversational. **3.** living or growing in groups or communities: *Ants are social insects.*

sole[1] (sōl) *n.* **1.** the bottom surface of the foot. **2.** the bottom of a shoe or sock. —*v.t.,* **soled, sol•ing.** to put a sole on a shoe or boot.

sole[2] (sōl) *adj.* only: *the sole runner on the track.*

sole[3] (sōl) *n.* any of a group of ocean flatfish, such as the flounder.

sole•ly (sōl′lē) *adv.* **1.** without any other; by oneself or itself; alone: *The cat is solely to blame for the overturned milk bottle.* **2.** entirely; exclusively: *to work solely for the good of others.*

sol•emn (sol′əm) *adj.* **1.** serious and earnest; grave; sober: *a solemn judge, a solemn mood.* **2.** having much dignity or majesty: *a solemn occasion.* **sol′emn•ly,** *adv.*

so•lo (sō′lō) *n., pl.* **so•los.** *Music.* a musical composition for a single voice or instrument. —*v.i.* to perform a solo, especially to fly an airplane alone: *Lindsay will soon be ready to solo.* —*adj.* made or done by one person alone. [From Italian *solo* meaning "alone."] —**so′lo•ist,** *n.*

sor•row (sor′ō) *n.* grief; sadness due to loss. —*v.i.* grieve; to express sadness. —**sor′row•ful,** *adj.*—**sor′row•ful•ly,** *adv.*

spa•ghet•ti (spə get′ē) *n., pl.* a noodle-like food made of wheat that is in the shape of long, thin strands. [From the Italian word *spaghetti* meaning "little strings or cords," from the word *spago,* "cord."]

spar•row (spar′ō) *n.* any of several small, dull-colored singing birds related to finches.

sparrow

spe•cial (spesh′əl) *adj.* **1.** not ordinary: *She has always been a special friend.* **2.** For a particular occasion, person, thing, or purpose: *a special broadcast.* —**spe′cial•ist,** *n.* —**spe′cial•ize,** *v.*

spe•cies (spē′shēz) *n., pl.* **spe•cies.** **1.** *Biology.* **a.** a subdivision of genus in the classification of living things. **b.** an organism belonging to such a subdivision. **2.** a distinct type or kind; sort: *a strange species of humor.*

---

at, āpe, fär, câre; end, mē; it, īce, pîerce; hot, ōld, sông, fôrk, oil, out; up, ūse, rüle, pu̇ll, tûrn; chin, sing, shop; thin, this; hw in white; zh in treasure. The symbol ə stands for the unstressed vowel sound in **about, tak**e**n, penc**i**l, lem**o**n, and circ**u**s.**

Spelling Dictionary

spoon (spün) *n.* an eating or cooking utensil consisting of a small, shallow bowl at the end of a handle.—*v.t.* To take up and transfer in a spoon: *I spooned some soup into my bowl.*

sprang (sprang) a past tense of **spring.** *v.i.* moved forward or jumped up quickly; leapt.

squirt (skwûrt) *v.t* to send out in a sudden, rapid stream. —*n.* **1.** a quick, narrow stream of fluid: *Put a squirt of mustard on my hot dog.* **2.** the action of squirting.

squirt

St. *abbr.* **1.** Street. **2.** Strait. **3.** Saint.

sta•ble¹ (stā'bəl) *n.* a building in which horses or cattle are kept and fed.—*v.t.* **sta•bled, sta•bling.** to keep in a stable.

sta•ble² (stā'bəl) *adj.* **1.** not easily moved, shaken, or overthrown: *a stable platform, a stable government.* **2.** dependable, steady: *a stable personality.* **3.** continuing without much change: *to enjoy stable health.* —**sta'bly,** *adv.*

stake (stāk) *n.* a pointed piece (as of wood or metal) that can be driven into the ground as a marker or support. —*v.t.,* **staked, stak•ing. 1.** to mark the limits of with stakes: *We'll stake out the boundaries of the garden.* **2.** to fasten or support with stakes: *You need to stake your tomato plants.*

• **at stake** in question or danger: *The championship is at stake in this game.*

• **to pull up stakes** to move on or away: *We will pull up stakes and move to the country.*

starch (stärch) *n.* **1.** a complex carbohydrate found mainly in the seeds, fruits, tubers, and roots of plants such as corn, potatoes, and wheat. **2.** any of various substances used to stiffen fabrics.—*v.t.* to stiffen with starch. —**starch'y,** *adj.*

sta•tion•ery (stā'shə ner'ē) *n.* writing paper and envelopes.

stat•ue (stach'ü) *n.* a likeness of a person or animal carved, modeled, or cast in metal, stone, or another material; a sculpture. [From Latin *statua,* "statue," and *statuere,* meaning "to set" or "to place."]

steak (stāk) *n.* a cut of meat or fish that is usually broiled or fried.

steal (stēl) *v.,* **stole, sto•len, steal•ing.** —*v.t.* **1.** to come or go secretly or quietly: *You can steal out of the house after midnight.* **2.** rob; to carry away without right, and intending to keep, the property of another. —*v.i.* to commit or practice theft.

steam (stēm) *n.* **1.** water vapor resulting from heating water to the boiling point. **2.** water vapor kept under pressure to produce power. —*v.t.* to treat or expose to steam, as in cooking or cleaning. —*v.i.* **1.** to give off or appear to give off water vapor. **2.** to move or travel by steam power: *The ships steamed into the harbor.* —**steam'y,** *adj.*

steel (stēl) *n.* **1.** a hard, tough iron that contains carbon to make it more flexible. **2.** a quality like steel, such as toughness or strength: *She has nerves of steel. adj.* **1.** made of or resembling steel. **2.** relating to the production of steel.

steep (stēp) *adj.* **1.** with a very sharp or extreme slope: *The cliff is too steep to climb.* **2.** very high or great: *The prices are too steep for me to buy a painting.* —**steep'ly,** *adv.*

ster•e•o (ster′ē ō) *n., pl.* **ster•e•os.**
1. stereophonic reproduction. **2.** a
stereophonic sound system. —*adj.* having to
do with stereophonic reproduction or a
stereophonic sound system: *We bought a
new stereo cabinet.*

stern[1] (stûrn) *adj.* **1.** severe or strict.
2. showing displeasure; harsh: *to speak in a
stern voice.* **3.** firm, unwavering: *stern
determination to reach a goal.* —**stern′ly,**
adv. —**stern′ness,** *n.*

stern[2] (stûrn) *n.* the rear part of a boat or ship.

stitch (stich) *n., pl.* **stitch•es. 1.** one in-and-
out movement of a threaded needle in
sewing. **2.** a single loop of thread made by
taking a stitch: *Not a single stitch is visible
in that dress.* **3.** a sharp, sudden pain in the
side —*v.i.* to sew; to join with stitches.

• **in stitches** In a state of uncontrollable
laughter: *Emily was in stitches at the sight
of my muddy face.*

stock•ing (stok′ing) *n., pl.* **stock•ings.** a close-
fitting, knitted covering for the foot and leg.

stom•ach (stum′ək) *n.* **1.** a baglike organ of the
digestive system into which food passes to
begin being digested. **2.** the part of the body
containing the stomach; the abdomen; belly.

strength (strengkth, strength, strenth) *n.* **1.** The
state of being strong. **2.** the degree of
concentration or intensity. *The strength of
this medicine makes it very effective.*
—**strength′en,** *v.*

stress (stres) *n., pl.* **stress•es. 1.** emphasis:
*Ramona put stress on the facts of the
situation.* **2.** accent; emphasis given to a
word or syllable. **3.** something that causes
tension. —*v.t.* **1.** to emphasize: *Carol did
stress that we should drive carefully.* **2.** to
accent.

strict•ly (strikt′lē) *adv.* **1.** in a rigid, exact
manner: *to follow rules strictly.* **2.** in a stern
manner.

stu•dent (stü′dənt, stū′dənt) *n.* **1.** learner;
scholar. **2.** one who studies; a pupil.

suf•fix (suf′iks) *n., pl.* **suffixes.** one or more
syllables added at the end of a word to form
a new word. —*v.t.* to add at the end,
especially as a suffix.

suit•case (süt′kās′) *n.* a firm, flat, rectangular
traveling bag.

swal•low[1] (swol′ō) *v.t.* **1.** to cause something
such as food to pass from the mouth to the
stomach. **2.** to take in as if by swallowing:
The darkness swallowed them. **3.** to put up
with; accept without protest: *to swallow an
insult.*

swal•low[2] (swol′ō) *n.* any of a group of small
migratory birds.

sweep (swēp) *v.,* **swept, sweep•ing.** —*v.t.*
1. to clear or clean a surface with a broom,
brush, or the like. **2.** to drive or carry along
with great force: *The flood swept away cars
and homes.* —*n.* **1.** the act of sweeping or
clearing away. **2.** any swift, sweeping
movement: *a sweep of the hand.* **3.** *Sports.*
a victory in every game of a series.

syl•la•ble (sil′ə bəl) *n.* a word or part of a
word pronounced with a single
uninterrupted sounding of the voice: *The
words* bit *and* break *have one syllable.*

at, āpe, fär, câre; end, mē; it, īce, pîerce; hot,
ōld, sông, fôrk, oil, out; up, ūse, rüle, pùll, tûrn;
chin, sing, shop; thin, this; hw in white; zh in
treasure. The symbol ə stands for the unstressed
vowel sound in about, taken, pencil, lemon,
and circus.

Spelling Dictionary

sym•pa•thy (sim′pə thē) *n., pl.*
sym•pa•thies. 1. a sharing of feelings with
another person. **2.** the desire to share some
other person's thoughts and feelings. [From
Greek *sympatheia,* from *syn,* meaning
"with," and *pathos,* meaning "feelings."]

sym•pho•ny (sim′fə nē) *n., pl.*
sym•pho•nies. 1. a major composition for
an orchestra, usually having three or four
movements: *Beethoven's Fifth Symphony.*
2. a large orchestra.

tall (tôl) *adj.* **1.** high; great in height. **2.** of
specific height: *George is now five and a
half feet tall.*

tame (tām) *adj.,* **tam•er, tam•est. 1.** taken
by humans from a state of native wildness
and domesticated: *a tame elephant.* **2.** not
ferocious, fearful, or shy; gentle: *The deer
was tame enough to let us photograph it.*
—*v.t.* to subdue; to make or become gentle
or domesticated.—**tame′ly,** *adv.*

tar (tär) *n.* a dark, thick, sticky substance made
by distilling wood, coal, or peat. —*v.t.,*
tarred, tar•ring. to treat or smear with tar:
*We need to tar the garage roof to prevent
leaks.*

tax•a•tion (tak sā′shən) *adj.* **1.** the act or
system of imposing and collecting taxes.
2. an amount of money raised by taxes.

team•mate (tēm′māt) *n.* a member of the same
team.

tem•per•a•ture (tem′pər ə chər, tem′prə chər)
n. a degree of heat or coldness: *What is the
temperature at which roast chicken is
done?*

ter•rain (tə rān′, te rān′) *n.* a region or tract of
land, especially with regard to its natural
features: *hilly terrain, flat terrain, rocky
terrain.*

them•selves (thəm selvz′, them selvz′) *pl. pron.*
1. the form of **they** or **them** used to give
emphasis to the word it goes with: *They did
the job themselves.* **2.** their normal selves:
*They won't be themselves again until they
get over the shock.*

the•o•ry (thē′ə rē) *n., pl.* **the•o•ries. 1.** an
idea that explains a group of facts or an
event; assumption that has been proved to
be true: *the theory of relativity.* **2.** the rules,
facts, or methods of an art, science, or
profession rather than the actual practice or
application.

there•fore (thâr′fôr′) *adv.* for that reason; as a
result.

they're (thâr) *contr.* they are.

thief (thēf) *n., pl.* **thieves.** a person who steals.

thought•less (thôt′lis) *adj.* **1.** having or
showing little or no regard for others and
their feelings; inconsiderate. **2.** showing a
lack of thought; careless.

thou•sandth (thou′zəndth) *adj.* **1.** (the ordinal
of thousand) next after 999th. **2.** being one
of a thousand equal parts. —*n.* something
that is next after the 999th.

threat (thret) *n.* **1.** a statement of the intention
to do harm. **2.** a sign of something that
might bring danger: *There was the threat of
a tornado near our town.*

throttle (throt′əl) *n.* **1.** a valve that controls or
regulates the supply of steam in a steam
engine or turbine or the supply of fuel vapor
in an internal-combustion engine. **2.** a lever
or pedal that operates such a valve. —*v.t.,*

Spelling Dictionary

throt•tled, throt•tling. to reduce or shut off the flow of steam or fuel vapor in an engine.

thun•der (thun′dər) *n.* **1.** the loud noise that follows a flash of lightning and is caused by sudden air expansion in the path of the electrical discharge. **2.** bang, rumble; any loud noise: *The thunder of fireworks filled the air.* —*v.i.* to make a sound like thunder: *The train thundered.* —*v.t.* roar, shout: *Listen to the lieutenant thunder his orders.* —**thun′der•ous,** *adj.*

tick•et (tik′it) *n., pl.* **tickets. 1.** a card or piece of paper or token showing that a fare or admission fee has been paid. **2.** a card, tag, or other paper attached to something to show the price, who owns it, or the like. —*v.t.* **1.** to fasten a ticket to: *They ticketed our baggage at the airport.* **2.** to give a traffic ticket to: *The police ticket people for driving over the speed limit.*

tick•le (tik′əl) *v.,* **tick•led, tick•ling.** —*v.t.* **1.** to touch someone in such a way as to produce a tingling sensation, often causing laughter. **2.** to excite agreeably: *Chili always tickles my taste buds.*

tie (tī) *v.,* **tied, tying.** —*v.t.* **1.** to fasten with a rope, string, or similar material. **2.** to fasten with a knot or bow: *to tie one's shoes.* **3.** to draw together or join closely: *Common interests tie us together.* —*n.* **1.** anything that unites or joins together. **2.** an equal score in a game.

tool (tül) *n.* **1.** any of various devices held in the hand and used in doing work, such as a wrench or hammer. **2.** an instrument or object necessary to a task or job: *A word processor can be an important tool for a writer.*

tor•til•la (tôr tē′yə) *n.* a thin, flat, circular unleavened bread made from water and cornmeal or flour and baked on a griddle. [From the Spanish word *torta,* "cake."]

to•tal•i•tar•i•an (tō tal′i târ′ē ən) *adj.* of or relating to totalitarianism, a system of government in which one political party aims at total control over the lives of the people under it. —*n.* a person who supports totalitarianism.

tow•el (tou′əl) *n.* a cloth or a sheet of absorbent paper used for wiping or drying. —*v.t.,* **tow•eled, tow•el•ing.** to rub or dry with a towel.

tra•di•tion (trə dish′ən) *n.* beliefs, knowledge, customs, or the like handed down from one generation to another.

trail (trāl) *n.* **1.** a passage or path. **2.** a mark left by something that has passed or been drawn along. —*v.t.* **1.** to drag or draw along or behind: *Don't trail your tote bag on the ground.* **2.** to follow in the path of. —*v.i.* **1.** to let hang so as to drag on the ground: *Do you want your skirt to trail so much?* **2.** to lag behind. **3.** to fade; to decrease or lessen: *to trail off.*

trail

tramp (tramp) *n.* **1.** hike: *Let's take a tramp before breakfast.* **2.** The beating sound made

at, āpe, fär, câre; end, mē; it, īce, pîerce; hot, ōld, sông, fôrk, oil, out; up, ūse, rüle, pull, tûrn; chin, sing, shop; thin, <u>th</u>is; hw in white; zh in treasure. The symbol ə stands for the unstressed vowel sound in about, taken, pencil, lemon, and circus.

Spelling Dictionary

by marching feet. —*v.i.* **1.** to walk heavily. **2.** to wander through on foot: *I like to tramp through the woods.*

trap•e•zoid (trap′ə zoid′) *n.* a figure having four sides with only two sides parallel.

treat•ment (trēt′mənt) *n.* **1.** the act or manner of treating. **2.** a course of action or means used to treat or deal with something, especially an illness.

trem•ble (trem′bəl) *v.i.,* **trem•bled, trem•bling.** to shiver or shake, as with fear or cold. —**trem′bling•ly,** *adv.*

tri•al (trī′əl) *n.* **1.** a test; the act of being tried or tested. **2.** a formal examination before a judge or jury.

tri•umph (trī′umf) *n.* **1.** an outstanding success, achievement, or victory: *The discovery of penicillin is a medical triumph of the twentieth century.* **2.** great joy caused by victory or success. **3.** —*v.i.* to achieve a victory; be successful; win: *to triumph over the enemy.*

troop (trüp) *n.* **1.** a group of soldiers. **2.** a group of people or things: *A troop of students filed into the auditorium.* **3.** a unit of Boy Scouts or Girl Scouts under a leader. —*v.i.* to move in a group: *The players trooped onto the field.*

tro•phy (trō′fē) *n., pl.* **tro•phies. 1.** a prize awarded to a winner. **2.** anything that can serve as a reminder or proof of victory or achievement.

trou•sers (trou′zərz) *pl. n.* an outer garment that extends from the waist down to the ankles and covers each leg separately.

tru•ly (trü′lē) *adv.* **1.** in a true manner; sincerely; genuinely: *I am truly sorry that I hurt your feelings.* **2.** in fact; indeed; really: *You're truly the best friend I have.* **3.** accurately; correctly.

tu•lip (tü′lip, tū′lip) *n.* a plant, related to the lily, that grows from a bulb and produces a cup-shaped flower. [From the Turkish word *tulben* meaning "turban."]

tulip

tu•na (tü′nə) *n., pl.* **tu•na** or **tu•nas.** a large ocean fish caught for food.

tun•nel (tun′əl) *n.* an enclosed passage, especially one underground. —*v.i.,* **tun•neled, tun•nel•ing.** to make, use, or form a tunnel. —**tun′nel•er,** *n.*

tur•quoise (tûr′kwoiz, tûr′koiz) *n.* **1.** an opaque mineral, usually greenish blue, having a waxy luster and valued as a gem. **2.** a greenish blue color. —*adj.* having the color turquoise; greenish blue. [From French *turquoise,* meaning "Turkish," because long ago in Europe turquoise was called "the Turkish stone."]

twen•ty-five (twen′tē fīv′) *n.* the number following twenty-four; 25. —*adj.* one more than twenty-four.

twen•ty-one (twen′tē wun′) *n.* the number following twenty; 21. —*adj.* one more than twenty.

twirl (twûrl) *v.t.* **1.** whirl; to move or cause to move in a circle: *Can you twirl a baton?* **2.** to curl or twist: *Twirl the bow to make it look fancier.*

ty•ing (tī′ing) present participle of **tie.** See **tie** for more information.

ty•phoon (tī fün′) *n.* a tropical hurricane occuring in the western Pacific Ocean, usually from July to October.

ty•rant (tī′rənt) *n.* **1.** a person who uses power or authority in a cruel and unjust way. **2.** a ruler who has absolute power and governs in a cruel and unjust way.

ug•ly (ug′lē), *adj.* **ug•li•er, ug•li•est. 1.** very unattractive or unpleasant to the eye. **2.** bad-tempered: *an ugly mood.* **3.** morally offensive: *an ugly prejudice.*

um•brel•la (um brel′ə) *n.* a device used for protection from rain or sun, made of a round piece of material attached to narrow ribs radiating from a long central rod. [From Italian *ombrella,* meaning "parasol" or "umbrella."]

un- *prefix.* **1.** not. **2.** opposite of.

un•cer•tain (un sûr′tən) *adj.* **1.** not sure; not certain. **2.** not definitely known. —**un•cer′tain•ty,** *n.* —**un•cer′tain•ly,** *adv.*

un•dem•o•cra•tic (un′dem ə krat′ik) *adj.* not agreeing with or supporting the ideas or principles of democracy; not democratic.

un•e•ven (un ē′vən) *adj.* **1.** rough; not even: *Lynnie's handwriting was jagged and uneven.* **2.** not level: *The sidewalk was uneven and bumpy for bikes.* **3.** not equal: *The match was uneven at best.*

un•ion (ūn′yən) *n.* **1.** a joining together of two or more things, people, or groups. **2.** something formed by joining together: *There was a union of American nations.* **3.** a labor group formed to support or protect workers: *The union wants safer working conditions.*

un•less (un les′) *conj.* except on the condition that; if not: *Unless you return those books, you can't borrow any others.*

un•like (un līk′) *adj.* different: *The two children were unlike in many ways.* —*prep.* **1.** different from: *Unlike you, I enjoy dancing.* **2.** not typical of: *It was unlike Kerrie to be frightened.*

un•nec•es•sary (un nes′ə ser′ē) *adj.* not necessary; not required.

un•pop•u•lar (un pop′yə lər) *adj.* not generally liked or accepted; not popular: to hold unpopular opinions.

un•u•su•al (un ū′zhü əl) *adj.* not common; rare. —**un•u′su•al•ly,** *adv.*

ur•ban (ûr′bən) *adj.* having to do with a city or cities: *Urban streets are usually full of traffic.*

ur•gent (ûr′jənt) *adj.* **1.** pressing; needing immediate attention. **2.** communicating a sense of urgency: *The weather forecaster spoke in an urgent manner about the approaching storm.*

use•ful (ūs′fəl) *adj.* **1.** serving a good use or purpose; helpful: *A stapler is a useful tool.*

va•cant (vā′kənt) *adj.* **1.** empty. **2.** blank: *When he daydreams, he gets a vacant look on his face.* —**va′cant•ly,** *adv.*

at, āpe, fär, câre; end, mē; it, īce, pîerce; hot, ōld, sông, fôrk, oil, out; up, ūse, rüle, pùll, tûrn; chin, sing, shop; thin, this; hw in white; zh in treasure. The symbol ə stands for the unstressed vowel sound in about, taken, pencil, lemon, and circus.

Spelling Dictionary

vac•u•um (vak′ū əm, vak′ūm) *n., pl.* **vac•u•ums. 1.** a completely empty space. **2.** a space inside a closed container from which most of the air has been removed. **3.** a state of isolation from the reality or events of the outside world: *some people seem to live in a vacuum.* **4. vacuum cleaner.** a machine for cleaning carpets, floors, and the like, that operates by means of suction.—*v. t., v.i.* to clean with a vacuum cleaner.

vain (vān) *adj.* **1.** overly concerned with or proud of one's appearance or abilities: *Don't be so vain about your clothes.* **2.** worthless; useless: *We made a vain attempt to stop them.* **—vain′ly,** *adv.*

• **in vain** without success: *All attempts at rescue were in vain.*

val•ue (val′ū) *n.* **1.** the amount of worth, usefulness, or importance: *This chair has great historical value.* **2.** the amount of money something will bring. **3.** *Mathematics.* a numerical quantity: *Find the value of y if 6 + y = 10.* —*v.t.,* **val•ued, val•u•ing. 1.** to put a value on: *Art critics value the painting at a million dollars.* **2.** to think highly of: *to value someone's friendship.*

vane (vān) *n.* a device that shows the direction of the wind.

van•ish (van′ish) *v.i.* **1.** to pass from sight, especially suddenly or quickly; disappear: *The airplane vanished in the clouds.* **2.** to cease to exist: *All hope of winning the game vanished when our star player was injured.*

var•i•e•ty (və rī′ə tē) *n., pl.* **va•ri•e•ties. 1.** a number or collection of different things: *Sam had a variety of toys and games.* **2.** something different from others of the same kind: *Ruth grew a new variety of rose.*

var•y (vâr′ē) *v.,* **var•ied, var•y•ing.** —*v.t.,* **1.** to make a minor change in: *We may need to vary the rules a little.* **2.** to give variety to.* —*v.i.,* to show or undergo change: *This restaurant's menu varies with the season.*

vault¹ (vôlt) *n.* **1.** an arched ceiling of stone, brick, or concrete. **2.** a well-protected room or compartment, as in a bank, used for safekeeping of money or valuables.

vault² (vôlt) *v.t.* to jump over, especially using the hands or a pole: *to vault the fence.* —*v.i.* to jump; spring: *to vault over a wall.* —*n.* the act of vaulting; a jump or leap. **—vault′er,** *n.*

veg•e•ta•ble (vej′tə bəl, vej′ i tə bəl) *n., pl* **veg•e•ta•bles.** edible part of a plant eaten as a side dish or as the main part of a meal.

veg•e•ta•tion (vej′i tā′shən) *n.* plant life: *a region of lush vegetation.*

ve•loc•i•ty (və los′i tē) *n., pl.* **ve•loc•i•ties. 1.** rapidity of motion; speed. **2.** *Physics.* the rate of motion in a particular direction in relation to time.

venture (ven′chər) *n.* **1.** a risky or dangerous undertaking. —*v.,* **ven•tured, ven•tur•ing.** —*v.t.* to offer at the risk of argument or criticism: *I'd like to venture my opinion on the budget cuts.* —*v.i.* to do something despite risk or danger: *Jeremy decided not to venture out into the storm.*

ver•ti•cal (vûr′ti kəl) *adj.* at a right angle to the plane of the horizon; upright; perpendicular: *a vertical climb up the face of a cliff.* —*n.* something vertical, such as a line or plane.**—ver′ti•cal•ly,** *adv.*

vi•brate (vī′ brāt) *v.,* **vi•brat•ed, vi•brat•ing.** —*v.i.* **1.** to move back and forth or up and down rapidly: *A guitar's strings vibrate when plucked.* **2.** to produce an echoing sound: *The shouts vibrated through the tunnel.* —*v.t.* to cause to move back and forth or up and down rapidly.

vice pres•i•dent (vīs′prez′i dənt) *n.* an officer ranking second to a president and acting in the president's place when necessary.

vid•e•o (vid′ē ō′) *n, pl.* **vid•e•os. 1.** the visual part of televison. **2.** a program or performance, as of a popular song, recorded on videotape.

vid•e•o•tape (vid′ē ō tāp′) *n.* The magnetic tape used to make a visual and audio recording of something.—*v.t.,* **vid•e•o•taped, vid•e•o•tap•ing.** to make a visual and audio recording of something on magnetic tape.

view (vū) *n.* **1.** an inspection; the act of seeing or examining. **2.** a scene. **3.** the range of vision: *The airplane passed out of view.* —*v.t.* **1.** to see. **2.** to look at carefully.

vine (vīn) *n.* a plant whose stem requires support and climbs or creeps along the ground.

vi•sion (vizh′ən) *n.* **1.** the ability to see: *Marty has very good vision when he is wearing his glasses.* **2.** something seen in the imagination.

void (void) *n.* an empty space: *Much of outer space is a void.* —*v.t.* to cancel: *I wish to void my order for ten thousand pink widgets.* —*adj.* empty: *The garbage can was void of contents.*

vol•ca•no (vol kā′nō) *n., pl.* **vol•ca•noes** or **vol•ca•nos.** an opening in the surface of the earth through which molten rock, gases, and rock fragments are forced out.

volcano

vow•el (vou′əl) *n.* **1.** a speech sound formed with the mouth held open. **2.** a letter representing a vowel (*a, e, i, o, u,* and sometimes *y*).

waist (wāst) *n.* the part of the human body below the bottom of the ribs.

wall•pa•per (wôl′pā′pər) *n.* decorated paper used to cover the walls of a room.

wal•rus (wôl′rəs, wol′rəs) *n., pl.* **wal•rus** or **wal•rus•es.** a large sea animal related to the seal.

waltz (wôlts) *n., pl.* **waltz•es.** a dance in three-quarter time with a strong accent on the first beat. —*v.i.* to dance a waltz. —*v.t.* to lead in a waltz.

waste (wāst) *n.* **1.** something thrown away as worthless after it is used. **2.** empty land with few or no living things. **3.** the act of wasting. —*v.,* **wast•ed, wast•ing.** *v.t.* **1.** to wear away a little at a time. **2.** to spend carelessly. —*v.i.* to lose energy, strength, health, or the like.

we'd (wēd) *contr.* **1.** we had. **2.** we should. **3.** we would.

wharf (hwôrf, wôrf) *n., pl.* **wharves** or **wharfs.** a structure built along a shore to be used as a landing place for boats; a dock. [From the Old English word *hwearf,* meaning "embankment."]

at, āpe, fär, câre; end, mē; it, īce, pîerce; hot, ōld, sông, fôrk, oil, out; up, ūse, rüle, pu̇ll, tûrn; chin, sing, shop; thin, this; hw in white; zh in treasure. The symbol ə stands for the unstressed vowel sound in about, taken, pencil, lemon, and circus.

wher•ev•er (hwâr ev′ər, wâr ev′ər) *adv.* where in the world: *Wherever did you get that dress? —conj.* at, in, or to whatever place: *He makes friends wherever he goes.*

wind•mill (wind′mil′) *n.* a machine or pump worked by the wind to produce energy.

windmill

wit•ness (wit′nis) *n., pl.* **wit•ness•es.** someone who has personally seen or heard something and can therefore give a firsthand account of it. —*v.t.* to be present to see or hear: *to witness an argument.*

won (wun) *v.* past tense and past participle of **win. 1.** gained victory, as in a game, contest, or battle **2.** got something by effort.

work•out (wûrk′out′) *n.* a period of practice or exercise to test or improve one's fitness, especially in athletics.

wor•thy (wûr′the͞) *adj.* **wor•thi•er, wor•thi•est. 1.** having worth or value. **2.** honorable.—**wor′thi•ness**, *n.*

-y¹ (ē) *suffix.* **1.** characterized by: *rainy, funny.* **2.** containing; full of: *juicy.* **3.** resembling; like: *flowery.*

-y² (ē) *suffix.* little; dear: *kitty, daddy.*

-y³ (ē) *suffix.* **1.** state or act of: *honesty.*

you'll (ūl) *contr.* **1.** you will. **2.** you shall.

youth (ūth) *n.* **1.** the time of life marked by growth and development, especially the time between childhood and maturity. **2.** a young person or persons. **3.** youthfulness.

Spelling Dictionary

Handwriting Models

A B C D E F G H I
J K L M N O P Q R
S T U V W X Y Z

a b c d e f g h i j
k l m n o p q r s
t u v w x y z

PHOTO CREDITS

3, Jin Cummins/FPG International; **7**, Laurance B. Aiuppy/FPG International; **9**, Stephen Ogilvy; **11**, Mark Reinstein/FPG International; **15**, David Pollack/The Stock Market; **17**, Joe Bator/The Stock Market; **19**, Farrell Grehan/FPG International; **29**, Antony/Edwards/The Image Bank; **33**, John Feingersch/The Stock Market; **35**, Corbis-Bettmann; **37**, Anderson/Monkmeyer; **41**, David W. Hamilton/The Image Bank; **45**, Michael P. Gadomski/Photo Researchers, Inc.; **55**, Photofest; **59**, Ben Van Hook/Duomo Photography; **63**, Culver Pictures; **67**, Tom Saunders/The Stock Market; **71**, Richard Bernholtz/The Stock Market; **81**, Michael Krasowitz/FPG International; **85**, Sovfoto/Eastfoto; **89**, Rafael Macia/Photo Researchers, Inc. ; **91**, Dennis M. Gottlieb/The Stock Market; **93**, Phillip Waltick/The Stock Market; **97**, John Terence Turner/FPG International; **99**, Richard Pasley/Gamma Liaison; **107**, Donna McLaughlin/The Stock Market; **109**, Mel DiGiacomo/The Image Bank; **111**, Tim Davis/Photo Researchers, Inc.; **115**, Peter Gridley/FPG International; **119**, David Woods/The Stock Market; **121**, Steve Dunwell/The Image Bank; **123**, Michael Melford/The Image Bank; **133**, Mark M. Laurence/The Stock Market; **137**, Photofest; **141**, Gary Buss/FPG International; **145**, Dann Coffey/The Image Bank; **149**, Gilbert S. Grant/Photo Researchers, Inc.; **219**, Will & Deni McIntyre/Photo Researchers; **221**, Susan Van Etten/PhotoEdit; **224**, Steve Maslowski/Photo Researchers, Inc.; **228**, Pete Saloutos/The Stock Market; **230**, Tom McHugh/Photo Researchers, Inc.; **236**, Murray & Associates/The Stock Market; **240**, Zeffa/The Stock Market; **244**, Alan & Linda Detrick/Photo Researchers, Inc.; **246**, Runk/Schoenberger/Grant Heilman Photography; **252**, David Pollack/The Stock Market; **255**, Sonya Jacobs/The Stock Market; **259**, Francois Gohier/Photo Researchers, Inc.; **260**, Tom Tracy/The Stock Market; **267**, Gregory K. Scott/Photo Researchers, Inc.; **271**, Ron Thomas/FPG International; **275**, Franco Salmoiraghi/The Stock Market.

COVER PHOTO
Ron Kimball

ART CREDITS
Andy Levine, Susan Darwin Ordahl, Dan Potash, Laura Shatz, Debrah Welling